# The Hidden Tombs
## of Memphis

NEW ASPECTS OF ANTIQUITY

General Editor: COLIN RENFREW

Consulting Editor for the Americas: JEREMY A. SABLOFF

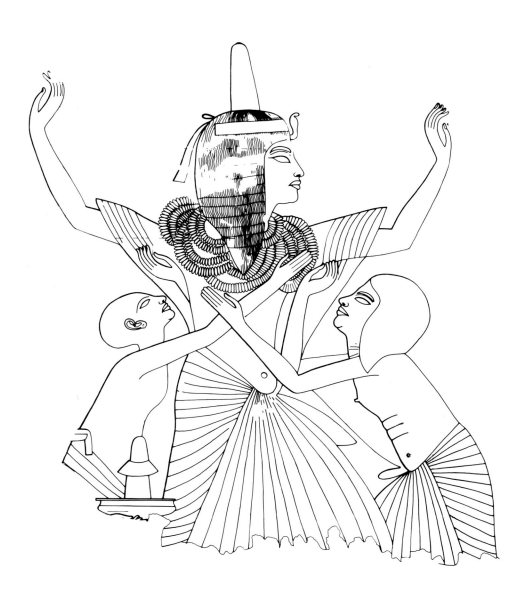

GEOFFREY T. MARTIN

# The Hidden Tombs of Memphis

## New Discoveries from the Time of Tutankhamun and Ramesses the Great

*with 140 illustrations, 11 in color*

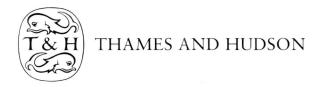

THAMES AND HUDSON

*To Jean-Philippe Lauer*

*Frontispiece*: Horemheb at the royal court, his neck loaded with gold collars. Detail of illustration 46.

© 1991 Thames and Hudson Ltd, London

First published in hardback in the United States of America in 1991 by Thames and Hudson Inc., 500 Fifth Avenue,
New York, New York 10110
First paperback edition 1992
Reprinted 1993

Library of Congress Catalog Card Number 89-51642

Printed and bound in Singapore

# CONTENTS

## Part III: Epilogue

# GENERAL EDITOR'S FOREWORD

'My God, it's Maya' came the cry, as the inscription in the richly painted chamber showed that the tomb of the great nobleman had at last been located. In this book Geoffrey Martin tells the tale of the quest for Maya and of the remarkable insights which this work at Memphis, the great capital of ancient Egypt, and in its vast cemeteries at Saqqara have brought.

Several things are special to the practice of archaeology in Egypt. One, of course, is the excitement of the unexpected – the long-lost tomb of some high official at pharaoh's court. Another is the sheer romance associated with the greatest Egyptian sites, whether Thebes, Karnak and the Valley of the Kings in Upper Egypt, or Giza and the pyramids, or indeed Memphis with its great necropolis – for once the term 'city of the dead' is no exaggeration – at Saqqara, in the midst of which lies one of the earliest of Egypt's mighty monuments, the Step Pyramid of King Zoser. But perhaps most fascinating of all is the ability of Egyptology to bring forward not just lost cities and wonderful works of art, but to introduce us to named individuals. We come face to face with real people forgotten for nearly 4,000 years, but brought to light again through careful research and systematic excavation.

Professor Martin tells us not only of the search for Maya's tomb, noted in the nineteenth century by the pioneer German Egyptologist Karl Richard Lepsius, but then lost again beneath the sands of the desert at Saqqara. He brings to life the court of the boy king Tutankhamun, successor of that strange and still enigmatic figure the pharaoh Akhenaten, who died in about 1334 BC. Tutankhamun ascended the throne of Egypt at the age of nine, and died at eighteen, to be buried like so many Egyptian pharaohs in the Valley of the Kings at Thebes. In his court were several remarkable men, whose names Egyptology has revealed to us. One of these was Maya, the overseer of the pharaoh's treasury, and the man probably responsible for much of the rebuilding of the temples and other public buildings that followed the death of Akhenaten.

The expedition recounted in this book started with the search for Maya's tomb, but it brought about unexpected surprises. In 1975, due to a slight inaccuracy in Lepsius' map which the excavation team was using as a guide, another long-lost tomb was found: that of one of the most famous men of Egypt, the general (later pharaoh) Horemheb. The site of this tomb had been lost and its location was a major event. Like nearly all the tombs found today, it had been plundered centuries ago. But much of its superstructure has been preserved. Professor Martin guides the reader around the finely detailed reliefs of the courts and chapels, and then below ground, through the labyrinth of chambers intended to hold the burial of the general and his family.

In fact, Horemheb was never buried there. For Tutankhamun, last of the royal line of the Eighteenth Dynasty, was succeeded first by the ageing courtier Ay, and then by the great general himself. So, like most of the pharaohs of the Eighteenth and Nineteenth Dynasties, Horemheb was buried in the Valley of the Kings in Thebes.

It is finds such as these that allow the history of Egypt to be pieced together. The names of the great nobles occur upon inscriptions, in some cases at Amarna, the capital city of the 'heretic' Akhenaten. Others are found at Thebes and Memphis. So it is that Professor Martin is able to rehearse some of the titles of Horemheb who helped to govern – and subsequently ruled – Egypt some 3,300 years ago:

*Hereditary Prince; Sole Companion; Fanbearer on the Right of the King; Master of the Secrets of the Palace; Generalissimo; Scribe of Recruits; Overseer of all Overseers of Scribes of the King; Sealbearer of the King of Upper and Lower Egypt; Mouth Who Appeases the Entire Land; Overseer of Works in the Hill of Gritstone; Chief of the Entire Land*

It is through discoveries such as these that the strange hieratic, bureaucratic world of ancient Egypt comes increasingly to light. And they have the happy consequence of revealing many major works of art; the relief scenes of the period are among the finest from Egypt, and give a splendidly graphic picture of the daily life of one of the greatest nobles at the royal court.

Through his researches at Memphis and Saqqara, Professor Martin is able to illuminate, with his detailed treatment of the tombs of Maya and Horemheb and the others which he has unearthed, many aspects of society and life that lay at the heart of the New Kingdom, when ancient Egypt was at the height of its power.

*Colin Renfrew*

# PREFACE

Saqqara is the name of part of the most extensive city of the dead of the ancient world, a cemetery beginning at Abu Roash just to the north of the Giza pyramid plateau and stretching practically as far as the eye can see to the pyramid of Meidum in the south, not far from the entrance to the Faiyum oasis. From the summit of the Great Pyramid of Cheops, on a crystal clear day, the viewer can enjoy an unrivalled panorama of the entire necropolis, as well as extensive stretches of the deserts to east and west. In the distance the stepped outline of the pyramid of Zoser is to be seen. The inhabitants of the ancient capital Memphis were buried in the Saqqara cemeteries, and as a result tombs of most periods of Egyptian history can be seen there, though the majority date from the Archaic Period and Pyramid Age (c. 3150–2181 BC). Strangely, for the New Kingdom (c. 1570–1070 BC), the height of Egyptian power and influence, there was hardly anything to be viewed until recently. Yet there were many indications from inscribed and documentary sources that Memphis was extremely important in the Eighteenth, Nineteenth and Twentieth Dynasties (the New Kingdom). The probability was, therefore, that many of the high-ranking officials of the government of that period, as well as royal courtiers and others, had tombs in the Memphite necropolis, Saqqara. The problem was: where were those monuments?

Numerous relief blocks and other material of New Kingdom date, clearly from Saqqara, entered the Cairo Museum and European collections in the nineteenth century, especially in the 1820s and 1830s. Hardly any of it was precisely provenanced or properly recorded. It was this material which spurred on the present writer to locate the tombs from which it all derived.

This book describes the principal aims of the author, and how the work was initiated. It will be concerned mainly with the results of thirteen seasons of excavating carried out by a joint expedition of the Egypt Exploration Society (London) and the National Museum of Antiquities (Leiden, The Netherlands) which the author has been directing since its inception in 1975. Three large tombs and a number of smaller tomb-chapels are described in some detail. Account is also taken of the material, particularly the tomb reliefs, in museum

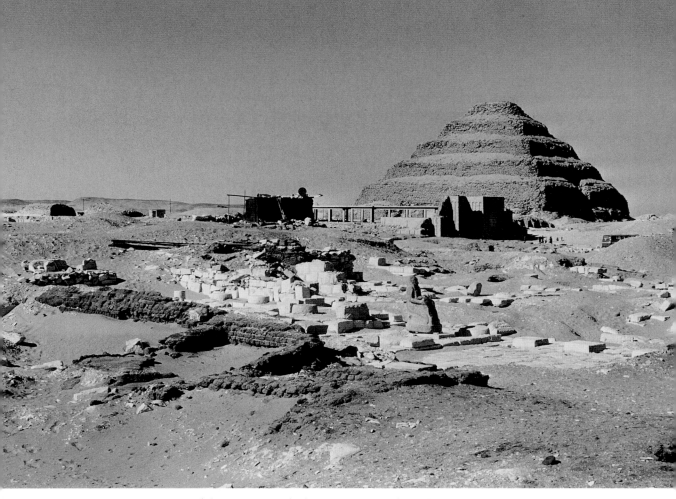

*1 View of the Step Pyramid of King Zoser seen from the New Kingdom necropolis at Saqqara.*

collections. These provide a most important source of information about the people who lived and worked in Memphis in the New Kingdom – the period with which we are concerned. Indeed, the emphasis throughout our work has been on what the monuments have to tell about the daily life, administrative responsibilities and religious beliefs of the inhabitants of one particular part of the Nile Valley, the area of the capital. The enormous potential of the site we are excavating will be stressed.

This is unashamedly a detective story, a search for clues to unravel the lost history of Memphis in the time of Tutankhamun and his five immediate successors.

# INTRODUCTION

I am often asked if there is anything left to discover in the Land of Egypt. My answer is always an unequivocal *yes*, though it depends of course what you are looking for. There are areas that have hardly been touched, archaeologically speaking, in modern times at least. Take the great cemetery at Saqqara for instance, with which we shall be concerned in this volume. All of it was plundered and raked over in antiquity – pyramids and temples, as well as private tombs – but vast tracts remain to be systematically uncovered and recorded by archaeologists. Royal tombs, and the lure of intact burials, beset the Egyptologist, or at least in the popular imagination such monuments are thought to be the only things worth seeking. The chances of finding an unrobbed royal tomb or even an undisturbed private tomb of any consequence are remote, though the possibility cannot be altogether discounted.

Most expeditions working in Egypt have specific scientific tasks to carry out or problems to attempt to resolve, whether they be historical, architectural, epigraphic, or anthropological. Herein lies the perennial fascination of Egyptology. The subject is not cut and dried, even after a century and a half of scholarly activity. Numerous questions need still to be asked, and many things, especially relating to daily life and economic and social history, await clarification or solution. The various phases of the ancient language too present problems to the philologist. Most texts can be read with relative ease, especially those dating from the period covered by this book, but those surviving from the beginning of recorded Egyptian history (the First and Second Dynasties) and documents written in the highly cursive script known as demotic, surviving in great quantities from the late Pharaonic period, are a major challenge. Because of the variety and vast number of its surviving sources, and its relatively firmly fixed chronology, Egyptology impinges on all other branches of ancient Near Eastern studies and indeed on the Aegean and Classical world.

Field archaeologists – not only those working in the Nile Valley – are sometimes urged to call a halt to excavation in order to assimilate the mass of material already excavated from innumerable sites and to catch up with the interpretation of a considerable backlog of published and unpublished work. While sympathizing with this view, my belief is that the injection of new knowledge is vital to any scholarly discipline. Mulling over known material is often very rewarding, but if nothing new is forthcoming a subject risks becoming moribund. Human nature being what it is there is no guarantee, even if excavation ceased, that the backlog of unpublished work would be tackled thoroughly and systematically.

Ancient sites and monuments, not least those still under the ground, are greatly at risk in many parts of the world. Sometimes it is a question of salvaging what is left after commercial and other exploitation, cupidity, and ignorance, ancient and modern, have taken their toll. In Egypt some of the monuments which were in pristine condition in the early nineteenth century, to judge from the accounts of early travellers, are now shattered wrecks. These vandalized structures still, however, preserve important evidence on the lives and beliefs of the ancient Egyptians, and the detailed recording of such monuments has to go hand in hand with new excavation.

In some ways archaeology in the Nile Valley has a strange 'press'. In the popular imagination Egyptologists employ a cast of hundreds and work is conducted on an epic scale. This view contrasts with the actuality of most current fieldwork in Egypt where the emphasis is on meticulous recording and careful interpretation, particularly on the settlement sites now being worked. We ourselves rarely employ more than fifty labourers drawn from Saqqara and Abusir villages near our site, and most of these are needed to shift the daunting accumulations of windblown sand and other debris that cover the unexcavated monuments in the desert cemeteries. This done, the work is taken over by a smaller band of skilled workmen, who generally show remarkable sensitivity in the use of seemingly clumsy excavating tools – the metal hoes known as *turriahs* which have been employed in Egyptian agriculture and other work since time immemorial.

I have explained that there are still large areas of Egypt which, from a scientific point of view, are relatively unexplored. This is certainly the case in the deserts, where the ancient cemeteries were for the most part located. The fertile plain was too valuable to waste on graves, even in antiquity when the population was much smaller. This meant that people dying in the towns and villages in the midst of the cultivation must sometimes have been carried some distance overland – or in boats during the annual inundation of the Nile – to the ancestral burial grounds. Until recently hardly any archaeological excavation had been carried out in the settlement sites in the valley proper. There most of the inhabitants lived in villages and hamlets, the ancient remains of which, if they survive at all, lie totally or partially underneath the modern settlements. We, in the following account, will be concerned mainly with the tombs of officials who lived and worked in Memphis, the principal Egyptian city from its foundation at the beginning of recorded history (*c.* 3150 BC) down to the end of dynastic times. These administrators and their families were ultimately buried

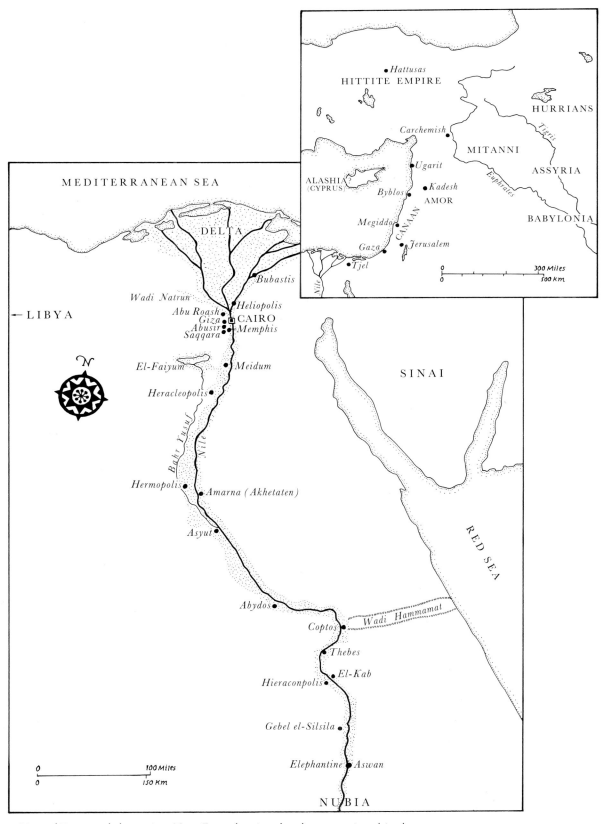

MEDITERRANEAN SEA

DELTA

HITTITE EMPIRE

*Hattusas*

HURRIANS

*Carchemish*

MITANNI

*Ugarit*

ASSYRIA

ALASHIA? (CYPRUS)

*Byblos*

*Kadesh*

AMOR

*Megiddo*

CANAAN

BABYLONIA

*Gaza*

*Jerusalem*

*Tjel*

*Nile*

*Tigris*

*Euphrates*

300 Miles

300 km

*Bubastis*

*Wadi Natrun*

*Heliopolis*

LIBYA

*Abu Roash*
*Giza* CAIRO
*Abusir* *Memphis*
*Saqqara*

N

*El-Faiyum*

*Meidum*

*Heracleopolis*

SINAI

*Bahr Yusuf*

*Nile*

*Hermopolis*

*Amarna (Akhetaten)*

*Asyut*

RED SEA

*Abydos*

*Coptos*

Wadi Hammamat

*Thebes*

*El-Kab*

*Hieraconpolis*

*Gebel el-Silsila*

*Elephantine* *Aswan*

100 Miles

150 Km

NUBIA

2 Map of Egypt and the ancient Near East, showing the places mentioned in the text.

in the neighbouring cemeteries, which we know collectively as Saqqara.

Important discoveries are rarely a matter of chance, though luck does of course play a part. More often they are the result of foresight and planning. The supreme example of this was Howard Carter's discovery of the tomb of Tutankhamun, which was not simply a matter of incredible good fortune but was the outcome of years of painstaking and sometimes unproductive investigation in the Valley of the Kings. Careful detective work, checking the results of earlier excavations published and unpublished, and looking for clues on the ground, rarely fail to yield results, as it is hoped to demonstrate in the following pages.

The primary objective of our own expedition has been to uncover new information on the history of the Memphite area in the New Kingdom, especially the period (c. 1334–1212 BC) covered by the reigns of Tutankhamun, Ay, Horemheb, Ramesses I, Sety I, and Ramesses II. Egypt during this time was the major power in the Near East, immensely wealthy, and militarily and culturally dominant in the area. To all intents and purposes self-supporting, especially in agricultural produce, Egypt needed to control Syria-Palestine and the area south of the First Cataract at Aswan not only for strategic reasons but in order to have access to the few products that were not available in the Nile Valley and its adjacent deserts. Imports such as large timbers, minerals like silver, iron and lapis lazuli, and precious unguents and oils, were brought into Egypt in the New Kingdom, but never, at least in respect of the metals, in great quantities. Gold, which Egypt obtained in considerable amounts from its eastern desert and from the south, was the most highly-prized export of the period, and featured in diplomatic exchanges of gifts which the Egyptian pharaoh and government maintained in the New Kingdom with the great powers of the Near East and the Aegean, and with a network of small city-states in the Levant. Choice objects of Egyptian manufacture were much sought after abroad, and even small objects like scarabs and amulets were instrumental in diffusing Egyptian culture over a wide area.

I like to imagine the impression an envoy from one of the small vassal states of the time, such as Byblos, would have received as he travelled to Memphis (shall we say in the reign of Tutankhamun) through the Delta and then upstream to Thebes. Such an ambassador cannot fail to have been awed by the size and superabundant fertility of the country or to have marvelled at the stupendous monuments – palaces, temples, pyramids and tombs – that met his eye on every side, many of them ancient even in his own day. It is strange therefore that the story of Memphis, the capital during the reign of Tutankhamun and his successors, is to us in most respects a closed book. The religious capital Thebes, in the south, is by contrast well documented for most of its history, at least as regards its temples and royal and private cemeteries. Not much is known about its settlements other than Deir el-Medina, the village of the royal necropolis workmen, and the great palace complex known as Malkata in Western Thebes. This latter was occupied for a brief period at the

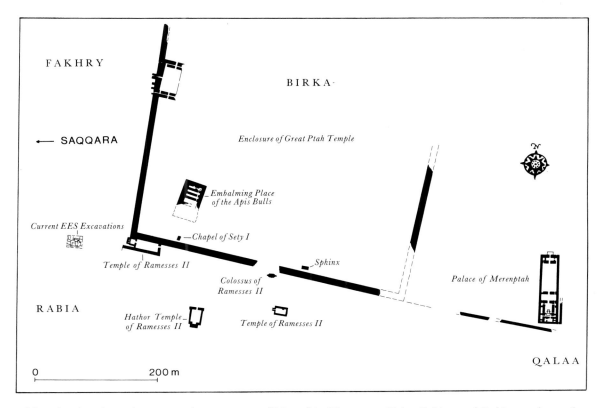

FAKHRY

BIRKA·

SAQQARA

*Enclosure of Great Ptah Temple*

*Embalming Place
of the Apis Bulls*

*Current EES Excavations*

*Chapel of Sety I*

*Temple of Ramesses II*

*Colossus of
Ramesses II*

*Sphinx*

*Palace of Merenptah*

RABIA

*Hathor Temple
of Ramesses II*

*Temple of Ramesses II*

QALAA

0          200 m

*3 Map showing the main excavated monuments of Memphis. The names Birka, Fakhry and Rabia are those of
modern settlements in the ancient ruinfield.*

end of the Eighteenth Dynasty. Most of the surviving information on the New
Kingdom derives from Thebes, Upper Egypt, and Nubia, as well as from the
short-lived capital of Akhenaten and Nefertiti – immediate predecessors of
Tutankhamun – at Amarna in Middle Egypt. Comparatively little comes from
the Delta or from Memphis, situated at the apex or junction of Upper and
Lower Egypt, a little to the south of the modern capital Cairo. Thus there is a
marked disparity in the quantity of source material for studying a crucial
period of Egyptian history, especially when it is borne in mind that Memphis
was the main administrative and cultural focus in the New Kingdom.

The numerous and spectacular standing monuments of Thebes, often well
preserved, have been studied in detail since the pioneer days of Egyptology in
the early decades of the last century. Memphis, on the other hand, rapidly lost
its identity and importance after the foundation of the city of Cairo in AD 969.
Its monuments, undoubtedly vying in number and size with those of Thebes,
were dismantled for building material. In due course the site became a
ruinfield. Today there is little to see in Memphis, save some fragments of stone
temples peeping out in romantic fashion from the ponds, swamps and palm

plantations. Here and there fragments of mud-brick walls, sometimes of enormous girth, provide clues to the location of important public buildings. The discerning visitor will, however, with the aid of a sketch map, be able to visualize the great city as it was in its heyday, particularly in the Eighteenth and Nineteenth Dynasties.

The size of the ancient settlement is daunting. This has not deterred an expedition organized by the Egypt Exploration Society of London from making a detailed survey of the site. For the first time scholars have at their disposal a comprehensive plan of the remains of a major Egyptian city. An important element of the work has been the systematic recording of all inscribed and decorated stone fragments littered over the site. Many of these are quite unprepossessing, but they give valuable chronological clues when they bear royal names, and help to locate monuments which, although known from literary and other sources, have virtually disappeared. Selective excavation by the Society, with financial and other assistance from Memphis State University, USA, is now under way. The work has begun in the south-west quadrant of the city in an industrial and domestic area, not far from the great temple of Ptah, one of the great creator gods of Egypt, and near the embalming place of the Apis bulls, the manifestation or 'living soul' of Ptah. The area proves to have been occupied in the Ramesside period. By a happy coincidence the joint expedition directed by the present writer is currently uncovering tombs of this very epoch, and of a slightly earlier period, in the Memphite cemeteries at Saqqara. These funerary monuments were built by officials and others who worked in the royal palaces, temples, administrative offices and government workshops, arsenals, and dockyards in the capital.

# PART I The Search

## CHAPTER ONE

# THE EXPEDITION IS FORMED

I became interested in the desert area stretching southwards from the causeway of the pyramid of Unas at Saqqara as long ago as the mid-1960s. I was then one of the members of the late Professor W.B. Emery's excavation team working further north in the Sacred Animal Necropolis, where multitudes of ibises, falcons, baboons, and even the cow-mothers of the Apis bulls were interred. There was not much leisure time in those days: finds were coming up in great quantities almost every day and we were kept hard at work recording, drawing, and copying. But I did manage to explore the desert areas to the south, between the Monastery of Apa Jeremias and the pyramid complex of the Third Dynasty King Sekhemkhet. Not that there was very much to see except scatterings of potsherds of the Christian period, clearly emanating from the Monastery. Fragments of uninscribed limestone blocks, greatly weatherworn from their long exposure on the surface of the desert, and worked pieces of other stones such as granite and quartzite, could be observed here and there. I looked in vain for any remains of a standing structure. One thing, however, immediately struck me about the area I was exploring: that was the presence of large depressions in the sand, roughly rectangular in some cases. The depressions immediately suggested the presence of open courtyards of tombs of New Kingdom type – rather like miniature temples – buried deep in the sand. Such tombs had been excavated earlier this century in the necropolis at Abydos in Upper Egypt.

Reference to the standard bibliography of Egyptian sites showed that the great Prussian scholar Karl Richard Lepsius had visited the area south of the Unas causeway in 1843 during his campaign to record the standing monuments of Egypt and Nubia. At Saqqara he recorded parts of several New Kingdom tombs which were still at that time mostly buried under the sand. Among the New Kingdom monuments he saw in the Unas area were those of a general named Iurokhy, an overseer of the royal apartments of the harim at Memphis called Raia, and an official with the same title called Hormin. All these functionaries lived in the Nineteenth Dynasty. Dating from a somewhat earlier period Lepsius was also able to record reliefs of superlative quality then in

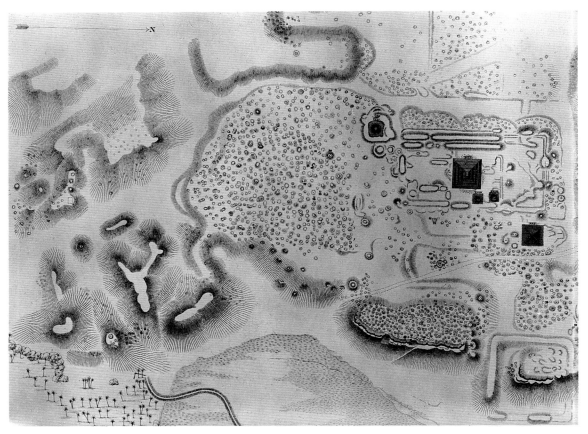

4 *Lepsius' map of the necropolis south of the causeway of the pyramid of Unas. Maya's tomb is No. 27 (centre of picture).*

position in a courtyard of the tomb of Maya, overseer of the treasury, and one of the most influential men in the government of Tutankhamun. Such an official controlled the vast wealth in agricultural produce, minerals, and other goods that flowed into the state treasury, from where it was disbursed to the vast hierarchy of officials who administered the realm, and to the priesthood and others who staffed the temples.

Lepsius marked the position of these tombs on a map of the area which was drawn by his surveyor. The mystery for me was: did these tombs still exist? There was no trace of them to be seen in the stretch of desert south of the causeway. Some of the blocks Lepsius recorded subsequently found their way into museum collections, yet astonishingly no one had tried to relocate the lost tombs in which the reliefs were last seen more than a hundred years ago. It seemed to me that a unique chance was possible of greatly extending, even conceivably revolutionizing, our knowledge of Egypt in the New Kingdom, by resurrecting the funerary monuments of the citizens of Memphis, buried in the city of the dead that must assuredly lie under the desert sand at Saqqara. We must remember too that Lepsius saw only *parts* of the monuments he recorded. Even in his day most of the superstructures of the monuments were still sanded up. It occurred to me that there must be streets of such tombs awaiting excavation, not just the few tombs seen in the last century. Of course these tombs would not be intact; most would have been partly dismantled in antiquity (the ancient Egyptians had scant respect for their forbears' tombs) and even in more recent times. The fact that dozens of loose blocks, clearly from Memphite tombs of the New Kingdom, were in museum collections was an indication of this. Such reliefs were found by local people in the nineteenth century, well before the foundation of the Egyptian Antiquities Organization which now supervises and controls the ancient sites. In 1975, when my responsibilities as Site Director of the Animal Necropolis excavations came to an end, a joint expedition of the Egypt Exploration Society and the Leiden Museum was formed to work in what I now confidently termed the New Kingdom Necropolis at Saqqara.

The question was: how should we proceed? Just about anywhere in the chosen area would have yielded results, but the obvious approach was to establish a fixed point in the necropolis by relocating one of the monuments seen by Lepsius. With the generous permission of the Egyptian Antiquities authorities I decided to pinpoint, excavate, and record the tomb of Maya, Tutankhamun's treasurer, which could not fail to be of great interest from many points of view. The only clue to its position was the map of Lepsius, the accuracy of which had never been tested. Our surveyor was able, with the assistance of this map, to place the location of the tomb within a very limited triangular area of the desert. We in fact 'missed' the monument by a matter of metres in 1975 – as we now know – and instead found ourselves in another tomb, the existence of which had been speculated about since the early days of Egyptology. This was the long-lost funerary monument of a colleague of Maya's, the general Horemheb, regent of Tutankhamun. This splendid tomb will be dealt with in some detail below, but to set the scene we must first outline the history of the Saqqara necropolis and describe the nature of the terrain.

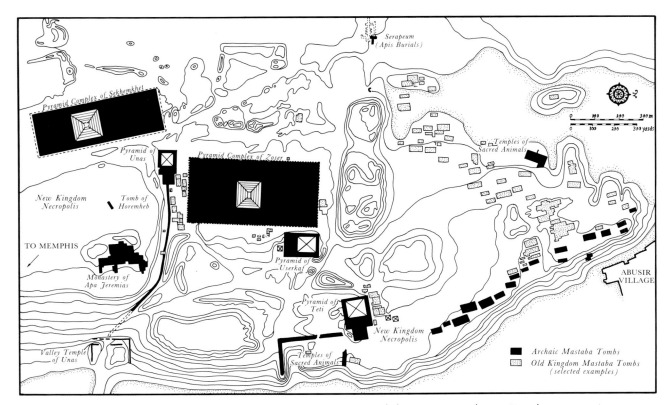

Serapeum
(Apis Burials)

Pyramid Complex of Sekhemkhet

Temples of
Sacred Animals

Pyramid of
Unas

Pyramid Complex of Zoser

New Kingdom
Necropolis

Tomb of
Horemheb

TO MEMPHIS

Pyramid of
Userkaf

ABUSIR
VILLAGE

Monastery of
Apa Jeremias

Pyramid of
Teti

New Kingdom
Necropolis

Valley Temple
of Unas

Temples of
Sacred Animals

■ Archaic Mastaba Tombs
▨ Old Kingdom Mastaba Tombs
  (selected examples)

5 Plan of Saqqara, showing the major excavated monuments and the two principal New Kingdom cemeteries.

## CHAPTER TWO

# MEMPHIS AND ITS NECROPOLIS SAQQARA

Menes, the first king of Egypt, is credited in Egyptian tradition with the foundation of the capital city Memphis. This event took place around the year 3150 BC. No traces of the city of Menes and his immediate successors of the First Dynasty have yet been found, though there must be remains buried many metres deep in the alluvium that now covers the ancient settlement. Most of the surviving buildings in Memphis date from the New Kingdom and later, and lie at a considerable distance westwards of the Nile as it runs in its present course. Until the recent survey of the ruinfield of Memphis this fact was something of a puzzle; logically one would expect the capital city to be located on the banks of the Nile. We now know, however, that the Nile has been gradually shifting its bed eastwards since antiquity, and one must imagine that Menes laid out his settlement on the river bank when the Nile was flowing much further to the west than at present. I visualize the primitive city being somewhere in the area of the present ruins of the great temple of Ptah, assuming that the New Kingdom temple would have been constructed over the site of the original cult building, which would have been the focal point of the early settlement. At this stage the 'city' was doubtless no more than a small village. Tradition has it that Menes surrounded it with a white wall, no doubt a whitewashed mud-brick structure also enclosing the temple and royal palace. In later times 'White Wall' or 'The Walls' were two of a number of names of Memphis which we find in inscriptions and documents. The toponym 'Memphis' itself is Greek, but is thought to derive from the ancient Egyptian 'Mennefer', the name of the pyramid complex of Pepi I, a king of the Sixth Dynasty. This pyramid stands opposite the city on the edge of the desert in South Saqqara. Why this name should have been singled out by the Greeks – Pepi I is not known to have been one of the greatest of Egyptian rulers – is something of a conundrum.

Tombs dating from the time of the foundation of the city are still to be seen in the neighbouring Saqqara cemeteries. The Egyptian archaeologist Rizkallah Macramallah excavated a group of shaft tombs of simple type in the neighbourhood of the later burial place of the Apis bulls, the Serapeum. Other Egyptologists such as J.E. Quibell, C.M. Firth, and W.B. Emery cleared a

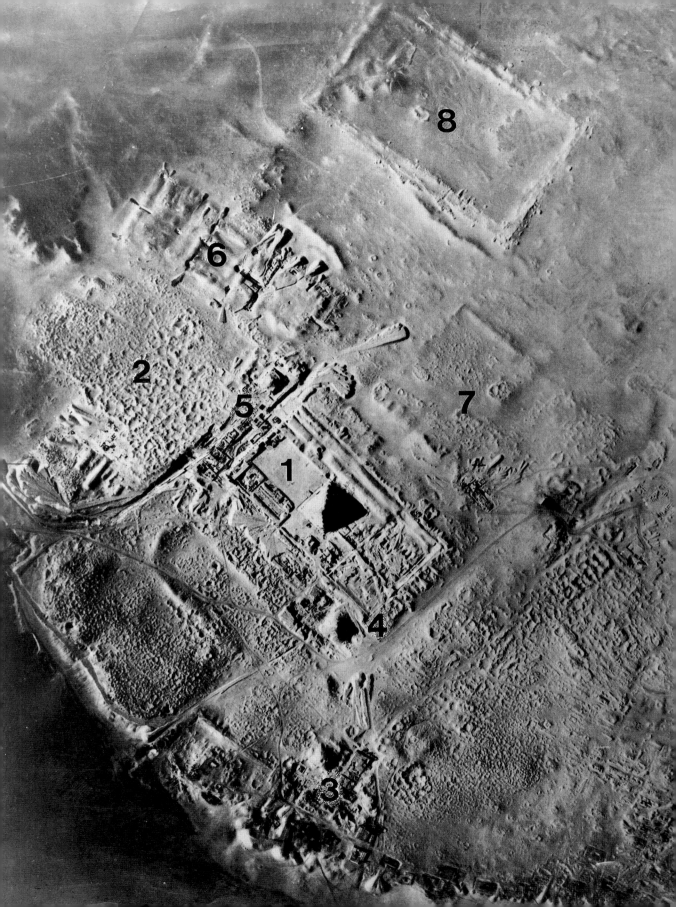

number of massive tombs of members of the royal family and their entourages on the edge of the escarpment of the necropolis, with a spectacular view eastwards to the newly founded capital. Controversy rages as to whether some of these great tombs are those of the kings of the First Dynasty or whether they should be classified as funerary monuments of private people. Few would deny that in any case some of them are 'royal' in concept, and it is not improbable that in this early period of Egyptian history the governing class was drawn from the male members of the king's immediate family.

From this time onwards Saqqara was the principal cemetery of the citizens of Memphis. In the Old Kingdom or Pyramid Age, embracing the Third to Sixth Dynasties (c. 2686–2181 BC) Saqqara and the Giza plateau were the favoured sites for the elaborate burial places of the kings. Around the pyramids grew up extensive cemeteries of 'mastaba' or bench-like tombs of members of the royal family, nobility, and administrators, in attendance on the divine monarch in death just as they had been in life. In antiquity the Third Dynasty funerary complex of King Zoser dominated the Saqqara skyline, just as it does to this day. On a huge stretch of open desert, some way west of the escarpment, the monarch erected the first true pyramid in the history of Egypt, though its four sides were not smooth but were in the form of gigantic steps, six in number. Zoser's architect Imhotep was one of the most innovative men of the ancient world; half a century of patient and selective restoration in the Step Pyramid complex, by the scholar to whom the present volume is dedicated, now enables visitors to appreciate the genius of a man who even in his own time must have been regarded as a phenomenon. Later he was accorded semi-divine status by the priesthood.

The Step Pyramid is set in the middle of a huge rectangular enclosure, the walls of which are made of limestone of the finest quality from quarries on the east side of the desert opposite Memphis. The enclosure incorporates, in addition to the pyramid proper – the burial place of Zoser and other members of his family – many other architectural features. For instance, there is a ceremonial columned entrance hall, a great open courtyard with altars, a so-called *hebsed* court wherein were a series of dummy chapels symbolizing the archaic shrines of Upper and Lower Egypt. In the *hebsed* area the king ritualistically received a renewal of power and physical strength after reigning thirty or more years. In actuality the ceremony was probably carried out in Memphis, whereas the simulacrum at Saqqara was for the king's use in perpetuity in the next world. On the north side of the pyramid is a large mortuary temple with a *serdab* or enclosed chamber attached, the latter containing a statue of Zoser, the focal point of an offering cult. Extensive

6 (Opposite) *Aerial view of Saqqara, showing the Step Pyramid enclosure (1) with the main New Kingdom cemetery (2) to the south. The pyramids of Teti (3), Userkaf (4) and Unas (5) can also be seen, as well as the Sekhemkhet pyramid complex (6) and two other anonymous Third Dynasty enclosures (7,8).*

storage magazines for food, drink, and equipment, and a large open-air altar carved out of the living rock complete the architectural arrangements on the north side of the complex. Incorporated in the south wall of the enclosure is a second 'tomb' of Zoser, usually called the Southern Tomb from its location. Its purpose is not quite clear, but it may have symbolized the interment of Zoser as King of Upper Egypt.

The Step Pyramid enclosure at Saqqara is the first great monumental building in the history of mankind: the whole complex is an astonishing evocation in stone of primitive reed and mud structures. Because so few inscriptions were found in it a number of problems of interpretation remain, including the extent to which the buildings in the enclosure duplicate those in the royal palace of the Third Dynasty in the nearby capital, Memphis. Certain parts of the complex have yet to be excavated fully, and doubtless still have secrets to reveal.

At least three other great Third Dynasty enclosures for pyramids were built or partially laid out at Saqqara. The most complete is that of Sekhemkhet, partly excavated and published by the Egyptian archaeologist, Zakaria Ghoneim. It has a number of elements which we have already seen in the Zoser enclosure, including the beginnings of a stepped pyramid, a 'Southern Tomb', and a recessed enclosure wall. On the west side of the Zoser compound is another complex, faintly visible on aerial photographs, but so far not investigated. Further out in the desert is a fourth enclosure, much greater in extent than any of those already mentioned and likewise unexplored for the most part.

None of the other pyramid enclosures of the Old Kingdom at North Saqqara – those of Unas, Teti, and Userkaf – is as well preserved as the Zoser complex, but they have all furnished valuable information on the development of royal tombs in the Fifth and Sixth Dynasties and on the ramifications of the royal mortuary cult. In particular the pyramid of Unas, which is open to the public, is one of the best surviving examples of a developed pyramid complex of the Old Kingdom, exhibiting all the architectural, symbolic, and ritualistic elements necessary for the king's survival in the next world. These may be summarized, moving east to west, as follows: a valley temple at the edge of the cultivation, a covered causeway leading from there up to the high desert and thus to the pyramid enclosure. The latter contains the main pyramid (where the ruler was interred), and a mortuary temple where his cult was maintained, in theory in perpetuity. The mortuary temple contains in addition a complex of rooms and magazines for the storage of vessels, service books, vestments, and offerings used in the daily cult, the building culminating in a stela set against the east face of the pyramid. This was the focus of the mortuary cult of the king buried inside the pyramid proper. The entry to this is by way of a sloping passage leading down from the north face. Within the enclosure is a mock pyramid perhaps symbolizing the monarch's southern 'burial', and in similar complexes we find satellite pyramids for members of the royal family.

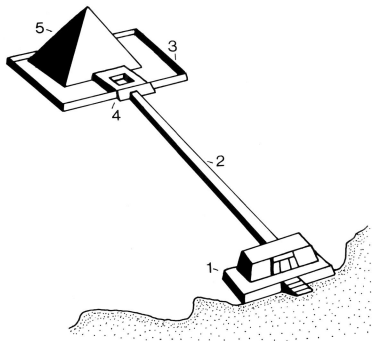

*7 A developed pyramid complex of the Old Kingdom, showing the main architectural components of such a structure. (1) Valley temple and quay at the edge of the cultivation. It is usually assumed that a canal linked the temple with Memphis and the Nile. (2) Covered and decorated causeway leading over the high desert to the pyramid temple. (3) Boundary wall surrounding the most important parts of the complex. (4) Mortuary or pyramid temple, the focus of the cult for the deceased ruler interred in the pyramid behind. (5) The pyramid.*

The Unas monument is famous for the first known version of the so-called Pyramid Texts, carved on the walls of the burial chamber and antechamber inside the pyramid. The texts hark back to remote antiquity, and form the earliest corpus of religious literature in the history of the world. They have thrown a flood of light on the religious beliefs prevalent in a remote epoch, though many of the texts are not easy to understand. To the east of the pyramid is a cemetery of the great officials who served Unas and subsequent kings. Some members of the royal house also had their tombs there. Royalty and administrators were for the most part interred in large stone-built mastaba tombs, many of which are decorated and inscribed. Such mastabas, both here and elsewhere at Saqqara, as well as in Abusir, Giza, and the contemporary rock-cut tombs in the provincial districts, have furnished us with most of what we know about the military, economic, and social history of the Old Kingdom, and the scenes carved in them are of fundamental importance from many points of view, not least that of the history of art. Some of the most famous tombs of the Old Kingdom are those of Ptahhotep, Ty, Mereruka, Kagemni, and Ankhmahor. All are at Saqqara and open to visitors, and there is a host of others. The reliefs in them portray vividly many aspects of the duties and daily life of great officials and nobles, and they shed much light, available from no other source, on the life of the times.

In the Middle Kingdom (Twelfth and Thirteenth Dynasties, *c.* 2040–1782 BC) the focus of attention swung away from Saqqara to regions further south in

Dahshur, Lisht, and the Faiyum, where the kings built their pyramids and where the great court officials had their mastaba tombs and funerary cults. At Saqqara, by contrast, only isolated burials of the Middle Kingdom occur, and the tomb owners are mainly connected with the revived cult of the Old Kingdom rulers, whose pyramid temples, supported by legally constituted endowments, had before the Twelfth Dynasty fallen into neglect or disrepair. The cult of Unas was, for instance, resuscitated in this dynasty, as was the cult of Teti. The kings of the Middle Kingdom ruled from a new capital called It-towe. This settlement is known from a number of documents but has yet to be located on the ground; it may have been a suburb of Memphis itself.

Passing now to the New Kingdom (*c.* 1570–1070 BC) we are confronted with a curious anomaly. Memphis continued to be of prime importance throughout the Eighteenth Dynasty when Egypt was at the height of its power and influence, even though our knowledge of the layout of that city and details about its inhabitants during that period are meagre in the extreme. Most of our information about Egypt in the New Kingdom comes from Thebes, which was the religious capital, the principal seat of the cult of Amun, the new state deity, and the site of the royal tombs and mortuary temples. It can be demonstrated, however, that comparatively few of the great officials during this epoch were actually buried in the so-called but misnamed nobles' tombs at Thebes, familiar to all visitors to Egypt. Rather, the officials interred there were those primarily concerned with the administration of the southern part of Egypt and of Nubia, the land beginning south of Aswan, or were those concerned with the all-important cult of Amun and his domains. These latter officials were priests, stewards, administrators, and craftsmen. By contrast, in the Memphite necropolis at Saqqara, there are no known important tombs of New Kingdom officials until the time of Amenophis III, and more particularly of Akhenaten and Tutankhamun, in the late Eighteenth Dynasty. Earlier New Kingdom tombs of high-ranking Memphite officials assuredly existed, and it may be that they await discovery in an area of the necropolis that is now being excavated by the writer for the Egypt Exploration Society of London and the National Museum of Antiquities at Leiden. The excavations are taking place in a part of the open desert south of the causeway of the pyramid of Unas. The tombs there were plundered in antiquity not only for the valuable contents of the burial chambers but also for building material: stone and mud bricks. In the nineteenth century the region was a happy hunting ground for collectors, antiquities agents, and others. No scientific work was carried out until the mission directed by the author began excavating there in 1975.

Though population statistics for Memphis in the early and middle parts of the Eighteenth Dynasty are totally lacking there is no reason to doubt that the city was large, and one would expect to see many tombs of this era in the nearby Saqqara cemeteries. Yet, as I have just pointed out, the earliest known tomb of the New Kingdom on the high desert dates from the reign of Amenophis III. Here is a strange state of affairs. The answer may be that the tombs of officials and other Memphite residents of the early and mid-Eighteenth Dynasty were hewn in the rock escarpment of the necropolis, rather than built on the high desert. Almost all this part of the desert is completely obscured by deep drifts of windblown sand. Here and there, where the rock face is exposed by a freak of nature or for other reasons, rock tombs are to be seen, which indicates that the escarpment was used for funerary monuments. I am sure many rewarding discoveries await explorers there in the future. The outlook is promising; recent work by a French archaeologist in a limited area of the terrain to the north of our excavations has disclosed rock tombs, one of which was prepared for no less a person than Aperia, vizier or chief minister of Akhenaten in the northern part of Egypt, and there are other decorated and inscribed rock tombs nearby.

## Egypt in the New Kingdom

In order to provide a setting for the description of the tombs and Memphite personalities that follow I shall give a brief synopsis of the history of Egypt in the New Kingdom.

The somewhat obscure era that preceded the Eighteenth Dynasty has been dubbed the Second Intermediate Period (*c.* 1782–1570 BC). During this time Egypt had the traumatic experience of being invaded by foreigners from Western Asia. We know them as the 'Hyksos'; the term seems to derive from the ancient Egyptian *heka-khasut* (ruler(s) of foreign countries). There seems to be no evidence that a horde invasion was involved, but it was a period when Egypt was militarily and psychologically at a low ebb, and the foreigners were able to take over the chief organs of government with relative ease, particularly in the north. For the Egyptians it was a unique and profoundly disturbing experience. Egypt had been weak before (in the so-called First Intermediate Period *c.* 2181–2040 BC): the country then had fractured internally, the various administrative areas or nomes becoming largely independent of whatever relics of the old state structure still lingered on in Memphis. Nevertheless, despite these problems Egypt continued to be governed by Egyptians. In the Hyksos Period, by contrast, many of the rulers had foreign names (Khamudy, Apopi, Khayan, for instance), which looked, and no doubt sounded, outlandish to the sophisticated Egyptians.

The foreigners did not signal their presence in the Nile Valley by any lasting cultural influence. On the military side they are credited with introducing the horse-drawn chariot into the military repertoire of Egypt. No doubt their own expertise with these swift-moving vehicles played a decisive role in their conquest and control of the Egyptians, who soon, however, turned their newly-acquired knowledge of chariot warfare to their own advantage. From the point of view of technology the Hyksos also left a reminder of their presence in the form of the *shaduf*, the rather primitive equipment which enables a fieldworker to lift water from the Nile or a canal to a higher level for the purposes of irrigation. (The *shaduf* consists of a pole balanced on a frame or pillar, often made of hard mud and stones. A container is fixed at one end of the pole and is dipped by the labourer into the water. He then uses the weight tied to the other end of the pole to lift up the container, full of the life-giving water.) The implement is a permanent reminder of the 'Rulers of Foreign Countries' in the Land of Egypt, because it can still be seen in use on the banks of the Nile. One feels, though, that after four millennia it is soon, with the advance of technology, doomed to extinction.

The ancient Egyptians did their best to obliterate the memory of the hated Hyksos. The native Theban rulers of the Seventeenth Dynasty (*c.* 1663–1570 BC) inaugurated a programme of resistance and conflict, particularly under Sekenenre and Kamose, which culminated, in the reign of the latter's brother Ahmose I (founder of the Eighteenth Dynasty) in the total expulsion of the remnants of the Hyksos.

These foreigners, originating as we have said somewhere in Western Asia, no doubt had close links with the people of that area before, during, and after their domination of Egypt. In the reigns of Ahmose's successors the central government, now firmly based once again in Memphis, made continual forays into Palestine-Syria, largely to assert their influence over the area for strategic reasons and to prevent any recurrence of an 'Hyksos' invasion, but also partly to maintain control over the sources of supply of certain commodities, such as large timbers, silver, and other minerals mostly not available within the confines of the Nile Valley. From their point of view they succeeded admirably, if we are to trust the long and unusually informative historical sources – mainly inscriptions set up in the temples – which admittedly must to some extent be biased. Memphis, aside from being the administrative capital, took on a new role as a military, and to some degree a naval, base, whence the expeditions to Western Asia set out; likewise to Nubia, control over which vast land was also needful for strategic and economic reasons.

It is not surprising therefore that funerary monuments of high-ranking military officers as well as powerful state administrators should have been present in the Saqqara necropolis, the burial ground of the capital city. The tomb of the generalissimo Horemheb, which we shall examine shortly, is the prime example. It, and the much smaller tomb-chapel of Ramose, also described later on, are the only completely excavated examples of such soldiers' monuments, but judging from tomb reliefs now in the museum collections, belonging to military men and certainly from Saqqara, it is certain that others await discovery in the necropolis.

The Egyptians had always been in contact with their neighbours in the Levant: the distances involved are not great. Egyptian culture undoubtedly influenced the diverse peoples of that part of the ancient Near East. Egypt in turn derived artistic and perhaps religious influences from the city-states of Western Asia. Perhaps this was mainly the result of the influx into Egypt during the New Kingdom of quite large numbers of foreigners, particularly in the

Eighteenth Dynasty. Many of them were captives; we have some statistics from the historical texts, if they can be believed. The foreign peoples brought their gods with them. Deities such as Reshep, Baal, Astarte, Qadesh and others became entrenched by the later part of the Dynasty, and cult-temples, or more likely perhaps rather smallish shrines, were erected for them, particularly in the Memphite area. It has been suggested, but without proof, that the foreign cults influenced the royal court, particularly when, for diplomatic reasons, the pharaohs began to take foreign wives. It would be natural if their wives' deities had some influence on their husbands, but all the surviving documentary and iconographical evidence makes it clear that the state cults, particularly those of Amun, Ptah, and Re-Harakhty, continued to be pre-eminent, and that the Pharaoh functioned as high-priest of all the Egyptian deities. Whether he was also chief-priest of the 'imported' foreign gods is a moot point.

In the reign of Amenhotep III (c. 1386–1349 BC), or even slightly earlier under Tuthmosis IV, there are hints of the emergence of a new deity, Aten. Aten had always featured in the Egyptian pantheon as a solar god, but almost without warning, under Amenhotep's son Akhenaten (previously Amenhotep IV), who ruled from c. 1350–1334 BC, Aten, the Disk of the Sun, is elevated to the paramount position in the pantheon, to the virtual exclusion of most of the ancient gods of the Nile Valley. From about the ninth year of Akhenaten's reign monotheism, to all intents and purposes, emerges, since Aten is the *only* god, at least to the royal family, the court, and the government.

This is not the place to describe in detail why and how this religious 'revolution' happened. Indeed, if we are honest we have to admit that most of what is written about the momentous events in the history of the Amarna Period in our secondary sources is speculation. The events affect our story in that Akhenaten decided to abandon the old administrative capital Memphis, and the religious capital Thebes, to found a new city in Middle Egypt on the east bank of the Nile, a virgin site untainted by any association with polytheism. This is the settlement called by Akhenaten 'The Horizon of the Aten' (Akhetaten), and by Petrie and other explorers Tell el-Amarna. On Akhenaten's orders, subsequently immortalized on a series of large inscribed stelae cut into the hills bordering Akhetaten to east and west, there was swiftly laid out a city, immense by ancient standards, with temples to the Aten, palaces, administrative offices, workshops, and villas for the officials who accompanied the king to the new capital. The puzzling thing is that although we have a good idea who these men were (from their well-preserved tomb-chapels cut into the cliffs due east of the town) none of them seems to have had administrative careers in Memphis or elsewhere prior to the move. Perhaps it is not so surprising after all: Akhenaten probably wanted to make a clean 'sweep' of the old guard, and duly surrounded himself with new men, whom some historians have labelled parvenus, at least at Amarna itself. Actually we know nothing of their antecedents. Among them were almost certainly Maya, whom we shall meet later, and just possibly Horemheb, the latter functioning at

Amarna under another name, Paatenemheb. It would be fascinating to know what happened to the old bureaucracy based in Memphis, Thebes, and other major centres. These places obviously continued to function, and there is even evidence that Aten temples were erected in those towns. Many of the lesser functionaries at least, one imagines, must have been left in place. Future excavations in the Memphite necropolis will undoubtedly reveal tombs of officials who worked in Memphis under Akhenaten (there are isolated blocks from such tombs in the museum collections), and it will be of the greatest interest to see if the reliefs and inscriptions from those monuments will throw light on the religious cataclysm and artistic innovations of the controversial Amarna Period. Most of the evidence for the reign of Akhenaten not unnaturally stems from Amarna, the capital he established. It cannot fail to be intriguing to know what was happening in the established administrative centre of Memphis in the north and the provincial areas.

Observant travellers to Egypt today with a knowledge of the hieroglyphic script will notice that very often the name of Amun has been cut out of the inscriptions in the temples and tombs. Sometimes the name was recarved after Akhenaten's death, not seldom maladroitly. The excision of the name of Amun must have been carried out on the orders of Akhenaten to obliterate the memory of the most potent of all the old gods, though we do not have any written evidence or tradition to prove this hypothesis. Akhenaten's iconoclasts were very thorough – but who were they? We can imagine the consternation there must have been in the countryside among the ordinary people when the Pharaoh's agents arrived to carry out their task; even more when these unwelcome visitors received orders to smash or melt down the cult images, to close the temples, and to divert their incomes to the Aten. I feel sure that Akhenaten must have had the backing of the military in this extraordinary enterprise which, one imagines, cannot have been carried through without *some* opposition. It is not unlikely that Akhenaten organized his programme from the royal palace at Memphis, the city where his army officers were based. It is curious that his militia was not brought into play to crush more effectively the foreign rebellions and intrigues we read about in a cuneiform archive found at Amarna. Clearly Akhenaten made no determined attempt to emulate his warlike ancestors Tuthmosis III and Amenophis II.

After Akhenaten's death (*c.* 1334 BC) the return to religious orthodoxy was not instantaneous. His successor was a nine-year-old boy, Tutankhaten, who may have been his son, to judge from an inscription found at Hermopolis, within the confines of Amarna. Political, economic, military, and doubtless also religious policy inevitably fell into the hands of government officials, chief of whom was Horemheb. Akhetaten was, within a few years, dismantled and abandoned, and the Aten temples levelled to their foundations. The archive of cuneiform tablets just mentioned was left behind in the records office at Akhetaten. They were resurrected, illicitly, in the 1880s and, although some of the tablets were no doubt lost or broken on that occasion, close study of the remnant opened up a whole new world of intrigue, perfidy, and diplomatic activity at the end of the Eighteenth Dynasty.

By about the third year of the reign of the young king, now styled Tutankhamun (c. 1334–1325 BC), the centre of government reverted to Memphis, and the ancient temples were reopened and refurbished, mainly a responsibility, it seems, of the treasurer Maya, whose Memphite tomb we shall examine later. Thebes resumed its prestigious role as a religious centre, the site of the cult of Amun and of the royal cemetery and mortuary temples. Egypt was once again on course for several centuries of prosperity and influence.

With the death of Tutankhamun the male line of the royal house was extinct: a succession of private citizens – Ay, Horemheb, Paramessu – was installed as pharaohs. Paramessu (Ramesses I) inaugurated the Nineteenth Dynasty, a period which, for building activity, was almost unprecedented in the history of Egypt. In the royal necropolis in Western Thebes the pharaohs' tombs became ever more lavish and grandiose, and the tombs of some of their queens did not lag far behind. Ancient cult temples were demolished and rebuilt, or their existing structures added to, sometimes with results that are not always artistically harmonious, at least from our point of view; for example, the additions made by Ramesses II to the work of Amenophis III and Tutankhamun at the Luxor temple. Memphis, the capital, flourished in the Ramesside Period, and it too received its complement of new religious buildings, now almost totally destroyed.

Throughout the Nineteenth, and into the Twentieth Dynasty, Egypt undertook military campaigns, particularly in Western Asia, where the power of the Hittite empire was now the principal threat to Egypt's hegemony. Under Merenptah, and later, in the reign of Ramesses III, there was a real possibility that history would repeat itself: the country was once more threatened with invasion, this time by hordes of foreigners, many of whom seem to have originated in Europe. The Libyans, long settled on Egypt's western flank, were also involved. This mass movement of 'Sea Peoples', as they were known, was repelled by both rulers, but particularly under Ramesses III the effort must have taken its toll. Historians have traced a progressive decline in Egypt's fortunes from this time to the end of the New Kingdom. There is evidence, in the Twentieth Dynasty, of economic stress and, for the first time in recorded history, of strikes, in the latter case of workmen whose task it was to hew and decorate the royal tombs in the Valley of the Kings. We need not, however, read too much into the fact that the Twentieth Dynasty pharaohs after Ramesses III did hardly any large-scale temple building. Previous kings, particularly Ramesses II, had provided what was necessary.

## Maya's tomb: the search for a lost monument

I have mentioned more than once already the treasurer Maya. Three statues of Maya and his wife Meryt, chantress or songstress of the god Amun, had as early as the 1820s entered the collections of the Leiden Museum in The Netherlands. Originally they were positioned in a room or courtyard of the owners' funerary monument in the Saqqara necropolis. These statues rank high on the list of acknowledged masterpieces of Egyptian art of the New Kingdom, and miraculously are virtually undamaged.

Once the Egypt Exploration Society and Leiden decided to join forces I immediately planned, as I have indicated, to relocate, excavate, and record Maya's tomb, which could not fail to be of enormous interest from many points of view. Using Lepsius' map of the Saqqara plateau our surveyor endeavoured in 1975 to pinpoint the tomb (marked on the map). The map must be very slightly inaccurate, enough to throw us somewhat off beam. We 'missed' the tomb of Maya and came down instead on the superstructure of the tomb of the generalissimo Horemheb, commander of the armies of Tutankhamun (and himself later Pharaoh), a monument of paramount importance for the history of the short reign of Tutankhamun and the even shorter rule of his successor Ay. The tomb is decorated with reliefs of singular quality. We did not, however, in our excitement forget the tomb of Maya, which we were certain was close by.

Having established a fixed point in the necropolis, in subsequent excavating seasons we had the task of investigating areas adjacent to Horemheb's tomb, which in some ways even in antiquity must have been considered the most important funerary monument of its period in the necropolis. Our aim was to see if it formed the nucleus of a group of tombs of officials of similar rank or occupation, or to find out if other patterns of 'settlement' emerged. The amount of information that has rapidly accrued on all aspects of the Memphite area and its inhabitants has astonished even us. In 1980 we cleared the tomb-chapels of Paser, chief of builders under Ramesses II, and Raia, chief of singers in the temple of Ptah-lord-of-Truth in Memphis (Ptah was the chief deity of the ancient city and one of the creator gods of the Nile Valley). In 1982, the centenary year of the Egypt Exploration Society, we excavated the great funerary monument of Tia, sister of Ramesses II, and of her like-named husband, Tia. He was a high-ranking official in the administration, concerned mainly with the treasury of the mortuary temple of his brother-in-law the king. In 1985 we cleared the shaft and tomb-chambers of Iurudef, an official in the entourage of Tia and Tia. His tomb, containing the skeletal remains of members of his family, and numerous items of funerary equipment, was found to have been re-used for later interments at a subsequent period, approaching one hundred in number. This find yielded unprecedented amounts of material from the anthropological point of view, enabling experts to study in detail the actual physical remains of a group of inhabitants of ancient Memphis. Many of the burials were in coffins, and here again we have an unparalleled series for study, at least as regards Memphis and Saqqara. They are all the more interesting in some ways because they were made for ordinary people who lived in the Memphite region at the beginning of the first millennium BC rather than for high officials. In 1986 we uncovered three more tombs, those of Khay, goldwasher of the Lord of the Two Lands (the Pharaoh), his son Pabes, who was a tradesman, and that of a high-ranking military officer called Ramose. All are close to the major tombs already mentioned. In the same year we achieved our original aim when we entered the substructure of the tomb of Maya, overseer of the treasury of Tutankhamun, by way of one of the tomb shafts located in Ramose's courtyard.

Even so, after thirteen years of work, our expedition has opened up only a small segment of the necropolis. Egyptian colleagues, notably Professor Sayed Tawfik, directing work for the University of Cairo, have also recently been excavating along the eastern edge of the necropolis, adjacent to the great Coptic monastery of Apa Jeremias. They have uncovered rows of tombs of considerable importance, some dating from the late Eighteenth Dynasty, others from the time of Ramesses II, including that of Neferronpet, one of the viziers or prime ministers of that Pharaoh.

All these tombs provide information, not only about the tomb owners but also about their immediate families, relations, colleagues in the administration and servants, who are depicted or named on the walls of the monuments or on objects found in the burial chambers. Thus a detailed picture of the people of ancient Memphis is emerging as we proceed with our work. As one of several additional bonuses we are also providing a context for the numerous loose relief blocks and myriads of objects and documents which were removed from the Saqqara cemeteries in the early years of the last century by local people, who passed on their finds to agents acting for the recently created national museums of antiquities in a number of European countries.

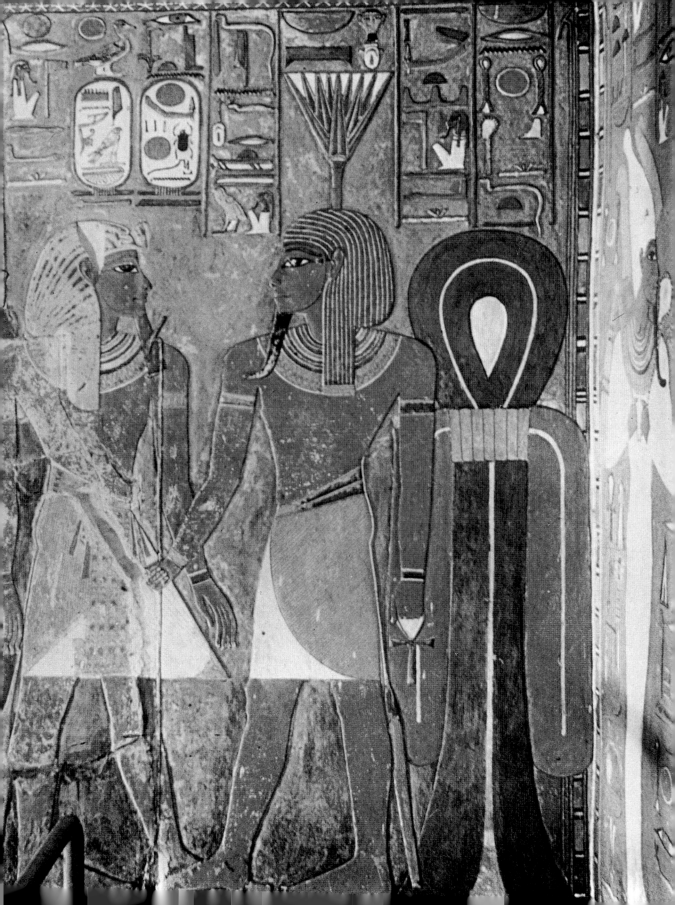

# Part II  The Discoveries

## CHAPTER THREE

# THE TOMB OF HOREMHEB, REGENT OF TUTANKHAMUN

Before our campaign opened in 1975 scholars had speculated on the whereabouts of the tomb of Horemheb. Most had assumed that the monument was totally destroyed so that there would be virtually nothing to excavate. In any case the Memphite tomb of Horemheb was not our primary concern when, full of enthusiasm at the beginning of a new venture, our small team set out for Egypt early in January 1975. I had been given permission by the Egyptian authorities to relocate the tomb of Maya, overseer of the treasury of Tutankhamun. At the back of my mind, however, there lurked the thought that since Maya was a contemporary of Horemheb the tombs of these great officials might be near one another in the Saqqara necropolis. Only a few days after we opened the work, a column bearing the representation and name of the army commander Horemheb began to emerge from the sand as our band of workmen began their systematic sweep across the terrain, removing the debris from the limited area we had chosen for the opening campaign. We were then convinced that, by a miracle, we had found the long-lost tomb of one of the most famous men of Egypt, the general (later Pharaoh) Horemheb, whose deeds were well known to scholars from many surviving monuments and other sources. In fact, at the outset of our work, we had unwittingly positioned our *zir*, or large pottery water-jar from which our workmen quenched their thirst during the heat and burden of the day, on top of what quickly proved to be the south wall of the outer court of the tomb. Our project had clearly got off to an auspicious start.

Before describing the tomb, which took four seasons of concentrated effort to unearth, we should look briefly at Egyptian history during Horemheb's time, and his own career.

## Egypt after Tutankhamun

The history of the period following the death of Tutankhamun in 1325 BC may be briefly summarized. He was only eighteen years old, and with him the male line of the royal family became extinct. His wife Ankhesenamun, third

*8 (Opposite) From Horemheb's tomb in the Valley of the Kings: the pharaoh in the presence of the god Nefertem. Behind the god is a* tyet *amulet.*

daughter of Akhenaten and Nefertiti, seems to have been the only surviving member of the royal house founded by Ahmose I in 1570 BC. As such the young queen may well have had a legitimate claim to the throne as a female pharaoh. Whether in fact she made such a claim cannot be proved. A fascinating document sent from Egypt and found in modern times in the archives of the royal palace at Hattusas, the Hittite capital in Asia Minor, at least hints at the possibility. Most scholars are agreed that Ankhesenamun rather than Nefertiti, widow of Akhenaten, is referred to, though the writer is unnamed. The text reads: 'My husband has died and I have no son. They say concerning you that you have many sons. You might give me one of your sons and he might become my husband. I would not want to take one of my servants. I am loath to make him my husband.' The letter was addressed to the King of the Hittites, Shuppiluliumash, who was clearly a little suspicious of the motives behind it. An envoy was sent to the Egyptian court to investigate. Some time later he returned with another message from the Egyptian queen (who again is not named), complaining about the Great King's hesitancy: 'I have not written to any other country, I have written only to you . . . He will be my husband and King in the Land of Egypt.' Eventually a young prince, Zannanzash, was sent to Egypt as a willing or unwilling consort and to cement a diplomatic alliance. He was murdered on the way. The perpetrators of the deed are unknown, but probably they were members of a faction in Egypt unwilling to tolerate a foreigner on the throne of the Pharaohs, a position which Zannanzash would certainly have occupied had he married Ankhesenamun. With Tutankhamun dead and the Hittite prince eliminated, the Egyptian government was faced with a pressing problem: the selection of a new Pharaoh, the divine monarch whose presence in Egypt was absolutely essential for the efficient functioning of the state. Egypt's northern neighbours too, especially the Hittites, had become a potential threat, since the assassination of prince Zannanzash gave them an excuse, if they needed one, to prepare for an attack on Egypt and on Egypt's vassals, the city-states of North Syria. Not unnaturally, therefore, the Egyptian government in Memphis turned to the military, and promoted an army commander named Ay to the pharaonic office. Curiously, he was not the chief citizen of the realm prior to his election, nor even the senior army officer. He was outranked by the generalissimo Horemheb. Ay must have come to some kind of arrangement with Horemheb about the eventual succession. King Ay died without an heir after four years, and again the country turned to a military man: the famed Horemheb.

## General and Pharaoh

Nothing is known for sure about the career of Horemheb before the reign of Tutankhamun, but he can hardly have sprung into prominence overnight as the chief army commander and regent of the boy king. Some writers think he is the same person as Paatenemheb, a military man and one of the close adherents of

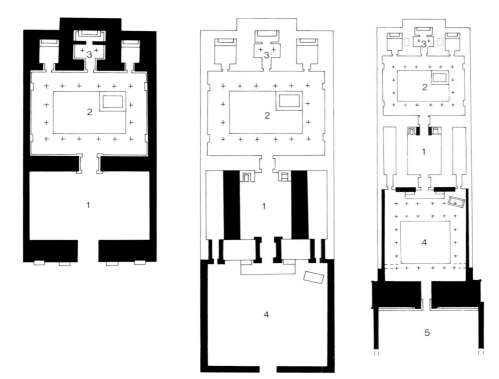

9 *The three main building stages of the tomb of Horemheb, probably reflecting his increasing prestige in the administration. In the initial stage the monument comprised: (1) an enclosed forecourt; (2) an interior colonnaded court; (3) a cult room flanked by chapels. The intermediate stage saw the original forecourt (1) converted into a statue room and side rooms by the addition of cross walls and doorways. A large new forecourt (4) was added on the east side. In the final stage the latter was transformed into an outer colonnaded court fronted by a massive pylon gateway. A new forecourt (5) was constructed beyond. The result bears a marked resemblance to a small 'purpose-built' temple.*

Akhenaten, Tutankhamun's predecessor, but there is no certainty in the matter. The alleged identification rests on the similarity of Horemheb's titles with those inscribed in Paatenemheb's tomb at Amarna, and the possibility that the name Paatenemheb ('[the god] Aten is in festival') could have been transmogrified into Horemheb ('[the god] Horus is in festival') after the Amarna Period. Akhenaten had proscribed most of the ancient gods, including presumably Horus, thereby incurring censure from the priesthood, particularly the clergy of Amun, after his death. By and large the royal heretic's views were repudiated under Tutankhamun.

Horemheb himself is reticent about his forbears. Like many people who have attained high rank and influence in Egypt even today he may have sprung from *fellahin* or peasant-farmer stock. His family came from Herakleopolis, an ancient city near the entrance to the Faiyum. His home town was the seat of the cult of Herishef or Arsaphes, a ram-headed deity, but there is no evidence to suggest that his family was prominent enough to be involved in the cult. Curiously, no monument survives from Herakleopolis naming the great commander, though one would have expected him to have honoured his local deity once he himself became famous and even more when, as we shall see, he became pharaoh. Nor is there any suggestion that he instituted a funerary cult for his parents or ancestors in his native town. He may have done so of course, but no surviving text or relief suggests it.

In his Memphite (that is, Saqqara) tomb we shall see Horemheb at the height of his power, though there is no hint that when it was being built, on the accession of Tutankhamun, the tomb-owner would eventually accede to the divine kingship. A close study of the architecture has shown that the tomb has three distinct building stages (*ill. 9*), culminating in the monument visible today. Probably these stages coincide with Horemheb's increasing power and influence resulting from his military successes abroad on behalf of the government, campaigning in Syria–Palestine and Nubia, and just possibly in Libya. The objective was to re-establish Egyptian domination of these areas after disaffection and reversals in the reign of Akhenaten. The final building activity in the Memphite tomb was just before the unexpected death of Tutankhamun or possibly in the four-year rule of his successor, Ay. This seems evident from the fact that the wall decoration of the last part of the tomb to be built (the east end of the outer courtyard) was mostly in painted outline, faded now almost to the point of invisibility. Hardly any of it was sculpted, unlike the other walls of the monument.

### The Memphite necropolis in Horemheb's day

Horemheb was not the first great official of state to build his tomb-chapel in the necropolis south of the causeway of Unas. From the evidence of blocks seen or found in the area in the last century some favoured administrators had preceded him there by a few years, for instance Amenhotep called Huy, great steward of Memphis, who lived under Amenhotep III. There can be no doubt though that Horemheb's tomb was the most important in the period covered by the late Eighteenth Dynasty. The area chosen by him was not an untouched one, because many hundreds of years earlier courtiers and officials in the reign of Unas and doubtless later kings built their mastaba tombs there. We ourselves found blocks from Old Kingdom mastabas re-used in the superstructure of the tomb of Horemheb, and it seems likely that the New Kingdom architects simply dismantled the stone mastabas where this had not already taken place and re-used the stone in their own work. They also saved themselves a lot of trouble because they were able to re-employ the deep shafts and burial chambers associated with the earlier tombs, altering them where necessary and adding further rooms if required. Even royal monuments were not immune from stone plundering. Quite a lot of stonework in Horemheb's monument comes from the nearby Step Pyramid enclosure of Zoser. We found in Horemheb's tomb pieces of the boundary wall and fragments from the entrance colonnade, the stone drums from the latter being used as blocking material in the doorways of certain burial chambers in Shaft i, situated in the first court of Horemheb's tomb. The fact that Zoser's monument was being used as a quarry as early as the end of the Eighteenth Dynasty is interesting from the point of view of the history of the Step Pyramid. It was quite a thrill for us to return the colonnade fragments to the Zoser enclosure, especially as M. Jean-Philippe Lauer, the great authority on the Step Pyramid, was able to put some of them back in place three thousand years and more after they had been taken down by Horemheb's architect.

When Horemheb walked (or was more likely carried in a palanquin) over the desert to choose the site of his 'house of eternity', the terrain must have looked much as it did before our expedition started work in 1975. The Old Kingdom mastaba tombs were very probably covered with windblown sand and debris, and thus totally neglected, the funerary cults of their owners long since abandoned. Curiously, Horemheb did not choose what we would regard as the prime site on the edge of the escarpment, with a fine view to the east over the lush cultivation and the city of Memphis. Instead he picked a spot much further westwards in the desert. The reason for this is that, with plenty of ground to spare, he preferred to select an area that was private; he did not want his tomb to be hemmed in by other funerary monuments. Religious reasons may also have been a factor, since the tomb was nearer the 'goodly West', the abode of the ancestors or the 'blessed dead'. The mastaba builders of the time of Zoser and slightly later did the same in the vast area stretching northwards from the Step Pyramid enclosure, positioning their tombs not in fairly neat rows or streets (as was the case with the First and Second Dynasty monuments) but far and wide over the terrain, almost as if they were private estates.

Most visitors to Egypt will be familiar with the Valley of the Kings and the rock-cut tombs of the Theban officials, in the hills of the great necropolis opposite the modern town of Luxor. The rock escarpment at Saqqara is relatively low, and by the late Eighteenth Dynasty its potential for rock tombs had been probably virtually exhausted. A group of rock-cut sepulchres now being investigated by a French archaeological mission at Saqqara predates, as we have noted, the tombs we ourselves are excavating. Although it is too early to be certain in the matter it may well be that the Memphite citizenry from the beginning of the Eighteenth Dynasty (c. 1570 BC) down to about the reign of Akhenaten (c. 1350–1334 BC) continued the tradition of having rock tombs, perhaps in some cases even re-using earlier examples dating from the Old Kingdom. Future work will no doubt throw more light on this problem. In the meantime, from the evidence of our own work, and from clues provided by blocks found in the necropolis in the last century, it seems evident that around the reign of Tutankhamun or a little before a new type of funerary monument came into being: the 'temple-tomb', as I prefer to call it for want of a better or

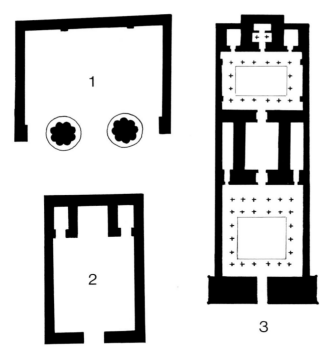

10 *The three main tomb types excavated so far in the necropolis south of the Unas causeway at Saqqara. (1) Simple one-room chapel (Raia). (2) Archetypal Memphite New Kingdom tomb, showing a cult room flanked by chapels, and an open courtyard (Paser). (3) Developed 'temple' tomb reserved for high officials (Horemheb).*

already established term. A typical 'temple-tomb' has a forecourt, an impressive pylon (tower-shaped) entrance gateway, open courts, storage rooms (sometimes called magazines), and chapels. Such funerary monuments resemble in a striking way not only the small 'purpose-built' temples of the New Kingdom (such as the small temple of Ramesses II in Memphis, recently recorded by an epigraphic mission of the Egypt Exploration Society), but also the mortuary temples of the pharaohs of that epoch. It is perhaps not too much to suggest that the 'temple-tombs' of the New Kingdom at Saqqara functioned as miniature mortuary temples of their owners. Probably such monuments as those of Horemheb and the Tias were reserved for the highest in the land (such tombs having all the architectural elements just described), the lesser officials (like Paser, Raia, Khay, Pabes and Ramose) being provided with simplified versions of the type. All these tombs are examined in this volume.

The 'temple-tombs' were erected on the desert surface, the courtyards being positioned in such a way as to enable the earlier tomb shafts mentioned above to be re-employed. This means that the builders must have undertaken a great deal of excavation, not only to locate the rims of the shafts but also to reach bedrock, on which they founded the new tombs under construction. Because so few tombs have been fully excavated we should not be too categorical, but it seems that three tomb types (*ill. 10*) prevailed. The simple or archetypal variety consisted of an open courtyard (or courtyards) with one or more shafts, an antechapel, and a cult chapel with side rooms. Such monuments are basically of mud brick, with embellishments in stone, confined apparently to the main chapel, doorjambs, stelae, and the like. An even smaller type of tomb, built of limestone, consists simply of a cult room or rooms preceded by a tiny forecourt in which the shaft is sunk. The third type comprises the elaborate miniature 'temples', built of mud brick in the late Eighteenth Dynasty and of stone in later times, of which the tomb of Horemheb is the prime example.

No doubt personal preference played a part in the type of funerary monument an official would commission, but rank in the administrative and military hierarchy was undoubtedly the main factor, the great officials forming the latter groups having the wealth and influence necessary to employ masons, expert outline draughtsmen, sculptors and painters. Horemheb, being the regent, chief army commander, and overseer of all works of the king, was in the happy position of having the greatest artists in Egypt at his disposal to prepare his 'monument of eternity'. If we are fortunate, one day we shall find at Saqqara evidence about the no doubt large gangs of workmen and others who prepared the great Memphite funerary monuments in the New Kingdom. Some of the workers probably lived down below in the cultivation or in the city and suburbs of Memphis itself, but there must have been a place on the high desert that functioned as their headquarters and from whence they drew their tools and supplies. From the evidence of recently published papyrus documents this atelier could have been in or near the Step Pyramid enclosure, which was conveniently sited both for the great New Kingdom necropolis south of the Unas causeway, where we are now working, and also for the lesser but still important cemetery to the north in the area of the pyramid of Teti.

To gain an impression of the necropolis let us imagine we are standing on a high sand hill not too far to the east of Horemheb's tomb, a position which affords a kind of bird's-eye view of the area. There are plenty of such sand hillocks (covering up other tombs) in the desert at present. In antiquity the alleyways and streets in the City of the Dead (Saqqara), leading to individual funerary chapels, must have been kept clear of windblown sand, otherwise the relatives of the deceased and the mortuary priests would not have been able to get to the tombs to perform the vital offering rituals, consisting basically of the presentation of food, drink and incense at certain specified intervals. We can picture also a steady stream of relations and visitors (there is ancient evidence too for what we today call 'tourism') making their way up onto the high desert on feast days and holidays to be with their deceased ancestors. No doubt these activities were a welcome break then as now from the daily routine in the capital and the surrounding villages.

We must picture the developed Memphite necropolis as being somewhat different from what we see on the desert at present. In the fourteenth and thirteenth centuries BC many of the great monuments we visit today at Saqqara as ruins were in almost pristine state, or at least were still functioning. In the New Kingdom there was a revival of interest in the monuments of the past, such as the pyramid complexes. The funerary cults of potent kings of the third millennium (especially those of the Old and Middle Kingdoms) were revived and their funerary monuments repaired, mortuary priests re-appointed and services inaugurated. Not only that, but there must have been constant building activity on the high desert: mud bricks (when they were not manufactured on the spot), blocks of limestone, wooden beams and builders' paraphernalia all had to be manhandled from Memphis onto the desert plateau for the erection of tombs, much as we do ourselves today when attempting to rebuild or restore the monuments we find in a plundered or dilapidated state. Picture too not only the gangs of necropolis workmen (masons, builders, plasterers, carpenters) but the cadres of outline draughtsmen, sculptors, and painters who must have flocked to the desert on most days of the year. Add to this the weeping and wailing of paid mourners in the funerary processions, which must have been constant given the relatively low life expectancy of the inhabitants of the Nile Valley (forty years was considered a good age). Thus in its heyday the Saqqara necropolis must have been a hive of activity, the noise of the masons' mallets shattering the profound peace and serenity of the desert landscape often remarked upon by present-day visitors. Several funerals a day (the population of Memphis must have been considerable, though there are no reliable statistics), the burial of an Apis bull in the Serapeum north-west of our site (the earliest Apis interment known to us dates from the Eighteenth Dynasty) with its attendant cortège, and the braying of donkeys, would have added to the clamour.

Today at Saqqara all is calm, at least in our area of the desert. The wonderful stillness is broken only by the distant call of *muezzin* from the minarets of the mosques in nearby villages (alas, the call to prayer is usually tape-recorded in today's mechanized age), or the sound of aircraft occasionally passing overhead on their way to or from Cairo airport. Such things barely intrude on the peace and stillness of this part of the Saqqara cemeteries. The cries of tourist guides, shepherding their flocks through the Step Pyramid enclosure, are just a little too far away to reach us.

With these things in mind we can now turn to the great monument of Horemheb excavated by our expedition at Saqqara.

## The architecture of the tomb

In order to grasp the architectural details, which may now be regarded as archetypal for large tombs at Saqqara dating from the end of the Eighteenth Dynasty, we need to look at the individual elements, beginning our 'tour' logically at the pylon entrance on the east side.

The approach to the tomb entrance is by way of a paved forecourt. As will be seen from a glance at the plan the tomb is situated not on the edge of the escarpment, which we have suggested might have been the prime site overlooking Memphis, but some distance westwards. Only future excavation will show whether there was a ceremonial approach from the cultivation to the tomb itself. This is not unlikely in theory for such a prestigious monument, but

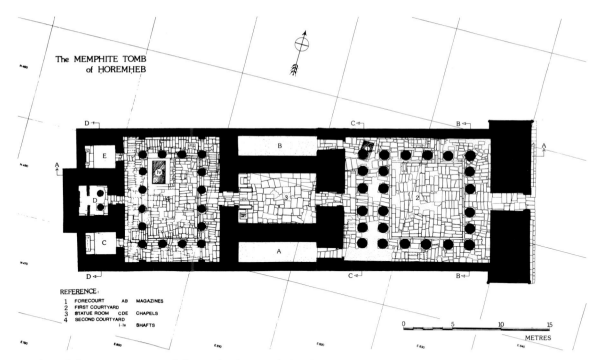

*11 Plan of the superstructure of the tomb of Horemheb. The monument in its final stage of development, shown here, resembles an Egyptian cult or mortuary temple.*

even if it existed it may have been dismantled or built over by later tomb architects. As already suggested, the tomb proper looks very much like a smaller version of a 'purpose-built' cult temple, with a ceremonial entrance gateway and open courtyards leading, by way of a statue room, to the offering chapel – the equivalent of a holy-of-holies in a temple – at the western end.

The pylon or ceremonial gateway was a massive structure, originally at least 7 metres high, emphasizing the tomb's overall resemblance to a temple. In effect the pylon consisted of two towers, each with a 'battered' or sloping front. In a temple it symbolized a bastion protecting the building, and was usually decorated with scenes showing the Pharaoh smashing the skulls of Egypt's traditional enemies with a stone mace, a theme appropriate to a royal monument but not to a private tomb. Thus Horemheb's pylon was undecorated.

Sun-dried mud brick was used in the construction of the tomb. This was the traditional and inexpensive building material, used even for royal palaces. We ourselves, in restoring the walls of the tomb, manufacture the bricks on site, using mud and water brought from the cultivation. It is possible that Horemheb's architect did the same, thus minimizing the number of broken bricks, which would probably have been numerous had they been brought in panniers on donkey back all the way from the brickyards of Memphis.

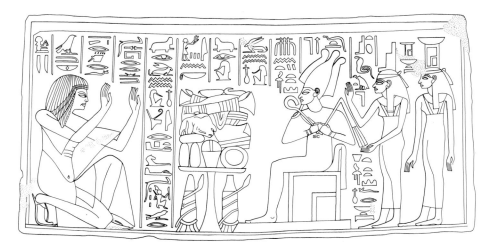

12 *Horemheb adores Osiris-Onnophris, Isis and Nephthys. In front of the deities there is an altar loaded with offerings. This is one of the few instances in Horemheb's Memphite tomb, prepared for him as a state official, in which the uraeus was not added to his brow on his accession to the throne.*

The exterior of the pylon was cased with blocks of limestone, dressed to form a smooth surface. The internal courts and chapels were lined with carefully fitted slabs of good quality limestone, hewn no doubt from the quarries at Tura on the east side of the Nile, opposite Memphis. The smoothed surfaces were carved with scenes and hieroglyphic inscriptions, all of which were painted in bright colours, extensive remains of which survive to this day.

Passing through the pylon, which in its complete state would have been surmounted by a cornice as in temple architecture, we find ourselves in a large courtyard open to the sky for the most part. Columns round the sides supported the roof of a colonnade, which provided shade for the visitor and protected the reliefs carved on the walls beneath from the elements. The floor of the court is slightly lower than that of the surrounding colonnade, and provision was made by the architect for the draining of water, rain occurring from time to time in the northern part of Egypt in winter, which we ourselves have experienced during the excavations. The columns stood some 3 metres high and each was carved with a rectangular panel. These bore texts and scenes showing Horemheb worshipping various deities, of whom Re-Harakhty would have been one. The panels were orientated inwards towards the main east–west axis of the tomb, so that the tomb owner appears to be perpetually adoring the sun-god Re as the deity makes his way in that direction across the heavens. An attempt has been made by us and the Organization of Egyptian Antiquities to restore this courtyard and the inner court and chapels to something like their pristine appearance. When we found them in 1975 and 1976 much had been dismantled, many pieces of the stone revetment having been prised off the walls in antiquity and to a certain extent in the early nineteenth century. Even the mud bricks themselves had in some instances been loosened and carted off millennia ago to build other structures. It is a remarkable fact that mud bricks from ancient monuments in the Nile Valley have often survived the centuries so well that they are better than anything produced locally today, and indeed make fine building material. I myself have picked up mud bricks moulded in the time of Menes that are still in perfect condition.

In the north-west corner of the courtyard a deep shaft (Shaft i) gives access to burial chambers on two levels, one at 9 metres, the other at just over 17 metres. The lower belonged to the original owner of the mastaba tomb demolished to make way for the tomb of Horemheb. He was a judge named Khuywer, who lived in the late Fifth to Sixth Dynasties (*c.* 2375–2345 BC). His granite sarcophagus bearing his name and titles is still in position on the south side of the chamber. It had been completely robbed in antiquity. We shall return to the subterranean parts of Shaft i later.

## Horemheb and his tomb

Before examining the reliefs in the courtyard and penetrating further into the tomb let us pause for a moment to digress. I like to think that the great general visited the tomb site himself while the building work was in progress, though

*13 Restoration work in progress in the tomb of Horemheb. Workmen from Saqqara repair the west wall of the inner court of the monument with mud bricks and mortar prepared on the site, employing the techniques used since antiquity throughout the Nile Valley.*

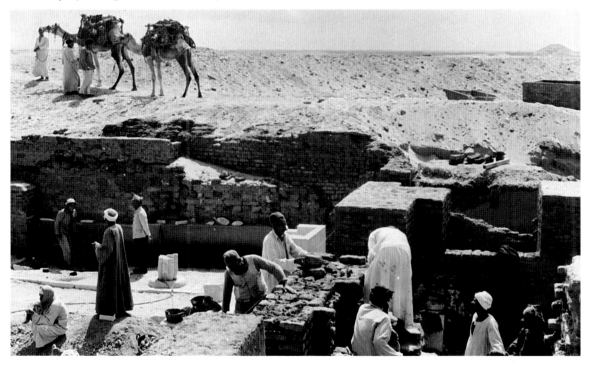

there is no written or pictorial evidence to prove it; it is hard to imagine that he neglected to do so. As far as we can see he was a completely self-made man who forged his way to the top by means of his position in the army. We cannot however trace the individual steps in his *cursus honorum*. He held a number of important administrative titles, and his duties included responsibility for overseeing all the building works of the king. Since coined money did not exist in ancient Egypt the salaries of administrators were paid mainly in agricultural produce. In addition, one of the prized perquisites of office was the provision of a tomb at the expense of the state. No individual had the wherewithal to mount private expeditions to the mines to extract stones for funerary monuments. Nor could a government official afford to commission skilled artisans and craftsmen to build and decorate his 'house of eternity'. With the consent of the Pharaoh such men were sent from government workshops to hew (or in the case of Memphite private tombs of the New Kingdom to erect) a great official's tomb and to decorate and furnish it with the requisite necessaries for the Afterlife.

Horemheb as a 'man of the people' is likely to have paid particular attention to the work in progress on his prestigious tomb in the Saqqara necropolis, and to have watched closely the activities of the craftsmen. There are so many individual touches and unique features in the scheme of decoration that I feel that they could only have been put in hand at his insistence. The scenes must have been selected with care, given the exigencies of space in even a large tomb, to highlight what Horemheb regarded as the pinnacle of his achievements. Some will be pointed out shortly as we examine the reliefs on the walls of the courtyards, where episodes in his public life in Egypt and military career in Western Asia, Libya and Nubia were so realistically carved. Such scenes were obviously not drawn from the standard repertoire of themes which are so familiar from the private tombs of the New Kingdom in Thebes.

When he eventually succeeded to the throne of Egypt after the death of his former army colleague King Ay it must have been difficult for Horemheb to relinquish or abandon entirely his private tomb in the Memphite necropolis, which would have been almost complete at the time of his assumption of regality. As king it was necessary to begin a completely new tomb on a far grander scale, comprising all the requisite corridors, chambers, religious texts, and iconographical detail, furnished with the equipment unique to a god-king. Such a tomb was duly hewn and equipped for him in the Valley of the Kings at Thebes. He never lived to see it completely decorated, though he was eventually buried in his royal tomb. The outline drawings on the walls, with corrections by a master hand, never carved by the sculptor, make it one of the most interesting and informative in the Valley.

Horemheb's first wife, whose name seems to have been Amenia, had died and was already buried in the Saqqara tomb of her husband. Contrary to custom, Horemheb's second and royal wife Queen Mutnodjmet was also later interred there; at least that is what certain inscribed objects such as a statuette and a funerary vase seem to indicate. Both were found in the tomb. One can hardly imagine a more splendid resting-place than the Memphite tomb of Horemheb in its completed state, even for a queen of Egypt. It is a curious fact that kings' consorts in the New Kingdom were not accorded 'royal' tombs until the Nineteenth Dynasty. This seems clear from the evidence of the Queens' Valley at Thebes, where no decorated tombs date from the preceding dynasty. In the earlier part of the New Kingdom the wives of kings, and lesser members of the royal house, male and female, had to be content with comparatively simple rock-cut tombs, usually ordinary shaft graves, undecorated and unmarked on the surface. Of course, their equipment, though not extensive, was probably sumptuous as befitted their rank. One can judge how sumptuous from the Theban burial of three minor wives of the great warrior Pharaoh Tuthmosis III, plundered only in modern times.

Why the mastaba tomb-type was abandoned at Saqqara and elsewhere in Egypt by the New Kingdom is something of a mystery. Tombs with open courts, such as Horemheb's, were clearly less easy to protect and were more vulnerable to the effects of the weather, whereas the mastaba was a solid structure of mud brick or masonry. In no time at all the courtyards of tombs such as the one we are examining would have been filled with windblown sand, and to obviate this problem constant clearing and maintenance would have been necessary. Perhaps this was a chore of the paid mortuary priests, or more likely of their subordinates. This would not have been a difficulty while the funerary cults were maintained and visitors came regularly. Human nature being what it is, however, hardly anyone would have bothered to maintain the cults of great-grandparents and even more remote ancestors (how many of us can even *name* our great-grandparents or great-great-grandparents on both sides of the family?). It is not clear how the funds set aside for the mortuary cults were diverted to other uses, but diverted they must have been. Once the cult had fallen completely into disuse and the tombs started to sand up, the despoilers and people looking for stone blocks to re-use as building material would soon move in. Having taken note of these things we can now return to the First Courtyard of Horemheb's tomb to examine what is left there after the hand of man, ancient and modern, had taken its toll.

## The First Courtyard

The Expedition did not find many of the original reliefs in position in the courtyard, but what survives is of great interest, especially when combined with blocks found loose in the debris of the court and reliefs now in museum collections which can be assigned to the scheme of decoration. Apart from the panels on the columns, already mentioned, almost all the surviving scenes are concerned with Horemheb's public career and with the bringing of provisions for the funerary cult in anticipation of his eventual demise. We shall begin with the south wall of the court, in the area abutting the pylon.

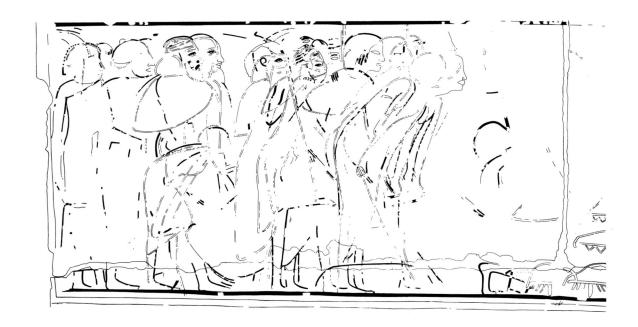

### South wall (*ills. 14–16*)

At first glimpse this wall seems to be completely blank, but this misleading impression was dissipated when, by the judicious application of moisture, a scene was revealed showing a group of foreigners, perhaps a delegation at the Egyptian court. From their characteristic dress and hairstyles we can discern men from Libya, Western Asia, Nubia, and the Aegean area. We shall see elsewhere in the tomb superbly preserved reliefs depicting the first three groups, but it is of considerable importance to discover here the presence of a man from the Greek mainland or from the isles of the Aegean Sea. The text, which was no doubt meant to accompany and to describe the event, has disappeared. The scene may well be a commemoration of a visit to Egypt – and very probably specifically to the capital Memphis – by ambassadors and others on the accession of King Ay or during other events of national importance. There are traces, though, which could be interpreted to indicate that the people depicted were captives, and thus were not there of their own free will. This wall was the last to be built before Horemheb himself became king. Chariots and horses are associated with the scene, in which the tomb owner must have been the principal commoner present. Later on we shall examine, in the Second Courtyard, wonderfully preserved reliefs which commemorate military successes, with foreigners exhibited as trophies at court during the reign of Tutankhamun. In the present scene attention should be drawn to the head of one of the spans of horses sketched in outline on the dado, a masterly example of the draughtsman's art. A most puzzling feature is the group of objects with humped outlines and curious appendages beneath. They seem to be unique in Egyptian iconography, and for want of a better explanation I interpret them as tents. Very probably some of the foreigners, such as the Libyans, seen on the left of the wall, lived in such shelters.

14 (Left) *A delegation of Egyptians and foreigners, including representatives from the Aegean and Western Asia, make obeisance. This is one of the last scenes to be depicted, in outline only, in the tomb of Horemheb. It was drawn in black pigment by a draughtsman, but there was no time for the sculptor to complete the work before the tomb owner became pharaoh.*

15 (Right) *Chariotry depicted in outline on an unfinished wall in the tomb of Horemheb. The finely rendered outlines of a span of horses on the scene below was drawn on the dado of the wall. The identification of the three objects to the left in the upper register is problematical.*

16 (Below) *The 'Window of Appearances', probably in the royal palace at Memphis. It was the custom for the pharaoh to distribute rewards to faithful servants, especially generals and administrators, from this window. Part of the cushion on which he leaned during the ceremony can be observed on the ledge at the top of the scene.*

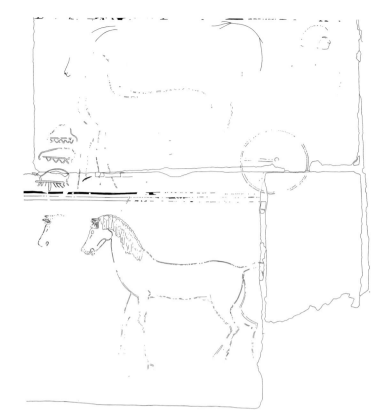

The only other relief worth signalling on the south wall is one showing part of the so-called Window of Appearances in the royal palace, in this case probably in Memphis. In the finished scene the king would have been shown distributing rewards to Horemheb who was standing in the courtyard below. This relief is no doubt connected with the episode just described, and the great commander may well have been introducing the foreigners during the

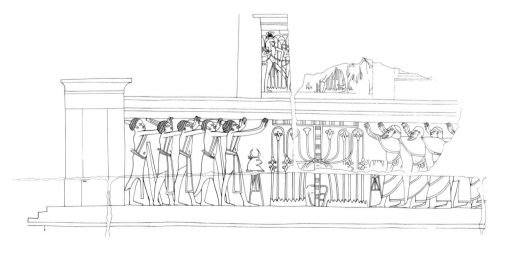

ceremony of his investiture with the gold 'collars of honour'. The decoration of the front part of the window will be noted. It shows the symbolic union of the Two Lands of Upper and Lower Egypt, and peoples of the south and north adore the Pharaoh who was standing on the balcony above. A small fragment of the relief was identified recently in the Oriental Institute Museum in Chicago, and has been incorporated in the illustration.

For lack of space we shall only draw attention to reliefs or fragments in the following descriptions that have important information to yield, though of course even tiny shattered pieces provide clues to the content of scenes now destroyed.

**West wall** (*ill. 17*)

Moving round to the west wall of the court we see a large intact stela adjacent to the door leading to the Statue Room. The original was acquired by the British Museum in 1835, and we have recently erected a cast. It bears the longest surviving hieroglyphic text in the tomb. In the lunette or upper part of the stela Horemheb is seen worshipping the sun-god Re-Harakhty, Thoth the god of wisdom, and Maat, goddess of Truth. Under Tutankhamun's predecessor, Akhenaten, the worship of most of the ancient deities other than those associated with the sun was prohibited. The main body of the inscription is a hymn, and it is worth translating a part to give an impression of the kind of religious text great officials at the court of Tutankhamun caused to be inscribed in their tombs, just after the end of the iconoclastic period during which Akhenaten reigned.

Hail to you who are beneficial and effective, Atum-Harakhty. When you have appeared in the horizon of the sky praises to you are in the mouths of everyone, for you are beautiful and rejuvenated as the Disk in the embrace of your mother Hathor. Appear everywhere, your heart being glad forever! . . . Adoration to you Thoth, lord of Hermopolis, who brought himself into being, who was not born, unique god, leader of the Netherworld . . . may you cause the royal scribe Horemheb to stand firmly by the side of the sovereign as you were at the side of the lord of the universe, as you fostered him when he came forth from the womb! . . . Adoration to you Maat, lady of the north wind . . . may you cause the hereditary prince Horemheb to breathe the winds that are brought forth by the sky . . .

Apart from its great importance from the religious point of view, this and other inscriptions in the monument provide quite detailed lists of Horemheb's official titles and epithets, a valuable source for studying his military and administrative career. Probably most of the extant titles were conferred by Tutankhamun, and there is no reason to think that Horemheb was obliged to relinquish any of them during the reign of Ay, except perhaps that of 'regent'. This title, literally 'King's deputy', would not have been appropriate in the reign of Ay, who came to the throne as a mature man. It could however have been retained on the understanding that since Ay had no heir Horemheb was to take over the reins of government and the divine kingship in due course.

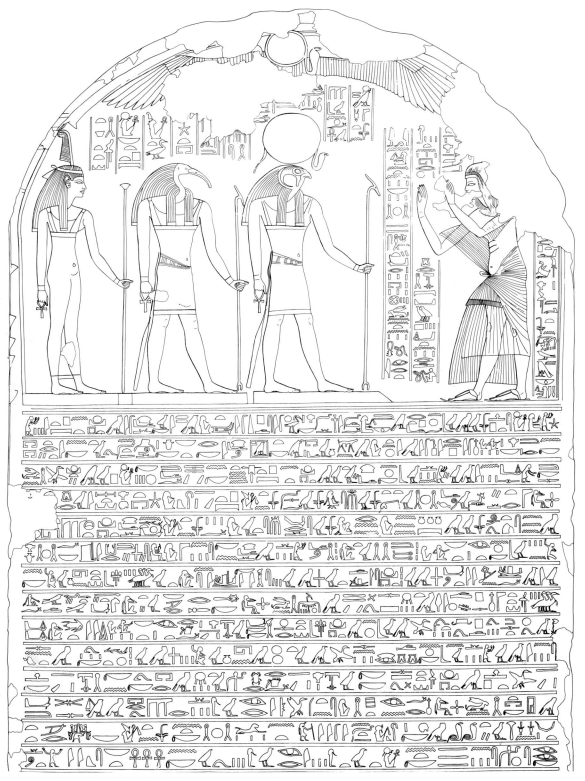

17 Horemheb adores Harakhty, Thoth and Maat. Below, part of a 25-line hymn to the sun god, the longest and best-preserved text in Horemheb's tomb. Originally the stela was positioned as one of a pair against the west wall of the outer courtyard.

This is a useful place to list the main official titles and descriptive epithets held during the lifetime of Horemheb but before he acceded to the throne. They are garnered from the various inscriptions in his Memphite tomb, and give a clear indication of his standing in the various branches of the pharaonic government. At a glance one can see that he held many important (and no doubt lucrative) offices.

**Vis-à-vis the Pharaoh and central government**

Hereditary prince (of Upper and Lower Egypt)
  and Count
Sole companion
Deputy (Regent) of the King in the entire land
Foremost of the King's courtiers
Fanbearer on the right of the King
Master of the secrets of the Palace
Overseer of (all) offices of the King
One elected by the King above the Two Lands
  to carry out the government of the Two
  Banks [Egypt]

**Military**

Overseer of the generals of the Lord of the
  Two Lands
Generalissimo
King's envoy
Scribe of recruits
Overseer of recruits of the Lord of the Two
  Lands

**General administration**

Chief of the entire land
Sealbearer of the King of Upper and Lower
  Egypt
High steward
Mouth who appeases in the entire land

**Scribal**

True royal scribe
Overseer of all overseers of scribes of the King
One who has authority over the library

**Public works**

Overseer of all works of the King in every place
Overseer of works in the hill of gritstone

**Religious**

Overseer of all divine offices
Overseer of priests of Horus, lord of Seby

*These are only a selection from an extensive list of titles and epithets which Horemheb received from Tutankhamun, and which are inscribed in his Memphite tomb. Some of the titles were executive, i.e. they represented real posts in the organs of government, some were purely honorific and were conferred for prestige purposes or as special marks of royal favour. Horemheb clearly bestrode the administration and military affairs during his long career as an official. Once he relinquished his titles on becoming Pharaoh there was no doubt much jockeying for position by his erstwhile colleagues for the posts he had held, since all major offices guaranteed access to the sovereign and were important sources of patronage, influence and income.*

The counterpart of the British Museum stela stood on the opposite or north side of the Statue Room doorway. It has a curious history. A large part of it must have been in position when a hand-copy of the text was made by a distinguished French Egyptologist, Emmanuel Vicomte de Rougé, in the earlier part of the nineteenth century. We ourselves found in 1975 only a tiny fragment still *in situ* when we excavated the courtyard. Enough remained to identify it as part of the inscription published earlier by de Rougé. Presumably some time after his visit, but at a date undetermined, the stela was shattered by vandals.

The present writer found most of the smashed fragments reassembled into one block in a storeroom in the Cairo Museum. On recopying all the pieces, the work of de Rougé was found to be remarkably accurate, despite some earlier modern opinions to the contrary. This fact is a timely reminder that students today, with all the resources and works of reference at their disposal, are still often standing on the shoulders of giants, the great scholars who founded the discipline of Egyptology in the last century.

The text on the stela comprises an important hymn to the sun-god to compare and contrast with numerous other hymns in the private tombs of the New Kingdom at Thebes. The following extract will give an idea of the content of the hymn:

The hereditary prince Horemheb, he says: I have come to you that I may praise your beauty, that I may honour your majesty at both daytimes [i.e. at morning and evening]. May you place the royal scribe Horemheb with you in heaven . . . may his name be among the great crew who drag Re to the West . . . you will seize the prow-rope of the night-barque when Re sets in his going to the Netherworld, the Westerners [the deceased ones] saying: 'Welcome, welcome!' When he penetrates the Netherworld he dispels darkness, the sleepers [the dead] jump to their feet when he reaches them.

The story is not over yet, however. Since the early nineteenth century a round-topped stela showing Horemheb worshipping Atum, god of Heliopolis, Osiris-Onnophris, King of the Underworld, and the Memphite deity Ptah-Sokar, has been in the collection of the Hermitage Museum, Leningrad. There is no longer any doubt that this is the 'missing' top of the de Rougé stela, which now lacks only a short section from the beginning of the main text, filling yet another gap in our knowledge of the decoration of the Memphite tomb of Horemheb.

Flanking both stelae were scenes showing processions of offering-bringers moving inwards towards the Statue Room and thus ultimately in the direction of the main cult chamber at the west end of the monument. Such scenes were *de rigueur* in Egyptian tombs. They served as magical substitutes for actual offerings of food, drink, and other commodities when the funerary cult of the deceased fell into abeyance, as we have seen it was bound to do.

### North wall (ills. 18–20)

From the fragmentary remains on the north side of the court it looks as though one of the principal themes represented there was feasting. Scenes in a military encampment too were also carved on the walls. A small fragment *in situ* showing loaves of bread gives a clue to the probable location of blocks we ourselves found loose in the debris of the court, as well as of a series of other magnificent reliefs now in Bologna and East Berlin. These must have been found nearby in the early decades of the last century. The museum blocks – and these we found for that matter – are major works of art of the late Eighteenth

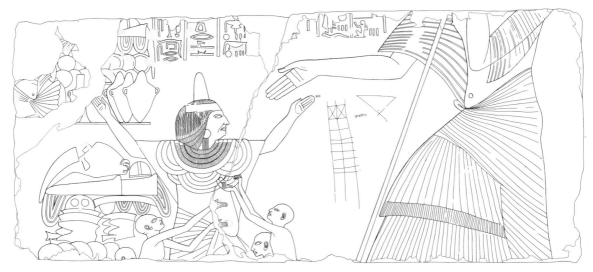

18 *Horemheb (on the right) receives a recently honoured colleague in the administration. The identification of the realistically rendered official is uncertain, but he may have been the future Ramesses I. His gold collars are being adjusted by his attendants.*

Dynasty, and are worth examining in some detail, though for the most part the illustrations speak for themselves.

First let us glance at the reliefs we ourselves found. Had the decorated walls of the court not been dismantled and dispersed in antiquity they would have been a major historical source. Even in their fragmentary state they have a story to tell.

Iconographically and historically one of the most important loose blocks is part of a scene, the remainder of which is lost. It shows Horemheb (on the right) deputizing as regent for the youthful Tutankhamun. A senior colleague of the tomb owner has just been decorated with gold 'collars of honour' for his services to the state. The identification of the recipient cannot be absolutely certain. He would undoubtedly have been named elsewhere on the scene; the fragmentary text surviving on the present block has to do with the ceremony itself. Hitherto the conduct of such ceremonials had been the prerogative of Pharaoh, and to see the regent Horemheb officiating emphasizes his supreme position in the realm at this stage in his career, perhaps early in the reign of Tutankhamun. The king might have been considered too young to take part. The head of the anonymous colleague of Horemheb is one of the finest surviving examples of Egyptian realistic portraiture. It shows a man well past the first flush of youth, with a jowly face and pronounced belly. His aquiline profile is emphasized, reminding us of some of the royal portraits of the Ramesside period, particularly of Ramesses II, whose mummy has a markedly hooked nose. Can the unnamed official be Paramessu, who became Pharaoh as Ramesses I, founding the Nineteenth Dynasty and succeeding Horemheb on the throne of Egypt? I consider it highly probable. Certainly Paramessu was a military colleague of Horemheb in the government of Tutankhamun. Perhaps

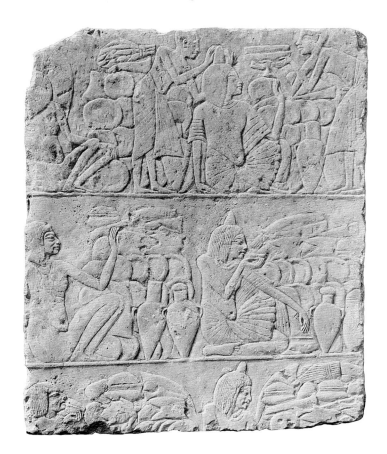

19,20 *Scenes of feasting. Honoured guests are plentifully supplied with food and drink at a celebration to commemorate Horemheb's victorious campaigns on behalf of Tutankhamun, or perhaps to mark his promotion. (Above) Horemheb's entourage enjoys the feast. (Below) The guests are individually provided with food and drink, indicating that a real celebration is being depicted rather than a symbolic funerary repast.*

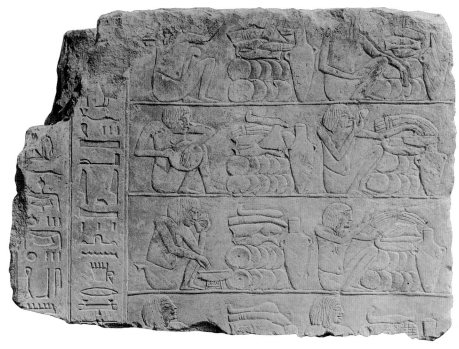

we shall be fortunate enough in future excavations to find a joining block that will answer the question once and for all.

Two other reliefs found by us, which may well be related to the preceding although there is no physical join, depict in a realistic way a scene of feasting. It would not be surprising if a great *fantasia* took place at an important reward ceremony; a great man's dependants would thereby reap some of the advantage. It will be noted that the guests are individually provided with food. Such a detail is not, strange to say, commonly found in tomb decoration. It doubtless emphasizes that the representation depicts an actual event rather than a symbolic banqueting scene in the Afterlife, a commonplace motif in Egyptian tombs.

**Military scenes** (*ills. 21–23*)

One of the most badly abraded reliefs found in the courtyard proves, after repeated examination in different kinds of light, to be part of a scene in a military encampment. Soldiers have already put up one tent, and nearby a meal is being prepared. Balls of food, perhaps dough for bread, are being rolled out. One man is chewing an onion and another is about to help himself to food that has already been prepared. Other soldiers are filling water-skins from nearby streams or canals; others are shinning up a pole, perhaps as a preliminary to erecting a tent. All this and more has been rescued from a block that on first glimpse looked as if it were going to be useless from the scientific point of view. On it we see the rough soldiery in their tented encampment, whether near a battlefield or somewhere in Egypt itself is not clear. Related blocks, some of the finest works of art of the New Kingdom, were removed from the tomb in the last century, and are now in Bologna and Berlin. We may now look at these in some detail.

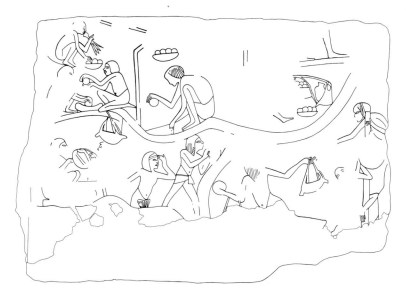

21 A much damaged relief preserving interesting details of life in a military encampment. Soldiers are preparing a meal and filling their water-skins. The undulating lines are streams or pathways winding through their bivouac.

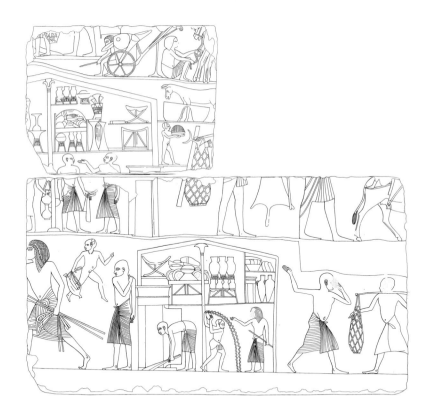

22 *The camp of the commander-in-chief, with soldiers and others receiving instructions and going about their daily tasks. These include the transport of water and the cleaning and provisioning of Horemheb's tent.*

The focal points of the scene we shall examine (the block is in Bologna) are the roofed structures which one authority has described as a sectional view of two 'sheds roofed over with a gable upon a central row of columns and accessible through a side door'. I prefer to identify them as tents. In the bottom register an officer moves towards the left at a smart pace, apparently having just left his tent. Probably he has just received an order from the commander-in-chief Horemheb to attend a meeting. The officer's batman stands in a respectful attitude at the door of the tent, while towards it runs a small naked boy, whose job is to fill up the water jars seen inside the tent. Now that the officer has left, his other servants set about cleaning the tent and replenishing its supplies. One throws down water to settle the dust, while his companion sweeps the floor with brushes made of twigs, thereby creating no doubt more dust. To one side we see a table loaded with food and drink. The main item of furniture is a folding stool, the seat of authority of the officer who has just left. In a military context the folding stool is especially appropriate: it could be packed and carried with ease. We also note another attendant gesticulating to a heavily burdened water-carrier, who lugs two jars suspended in nets from a yoke round his neck. All these activities, and more, would have been everyday occurrences in a military camp, and our representation is perhaps the most vivid example surviving from the art of the ancient Near East.

If we move now to the middle register of the scene we again observe an officer's tent, larger than those in the register below and perhaps therefore that

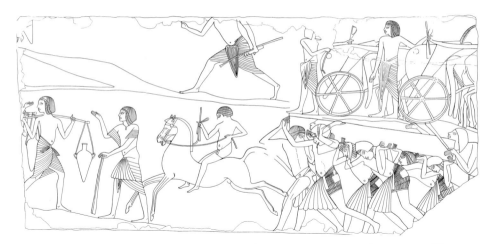

*23 Charioteers, a water-carrier, a rider and soldiers in an Egyptian military camp. The group in the lower register are manhandling a large object, which may be the rolled-up tent of the commandant.*

of the commander-in-chief himself. Servants, supervised by the inevitable overseer, are busy at work. In the background supplies of food and drink, a bouquet of flowers, and items of furniture are to be seen. The folding stool has a footstool this time, and a rigid stool is also provided for Horemheb's comfort. Outside the tent an officer, followed by his servant, walks to the right. The attendant carries sundry belongings of his master, which included an animal's hide perhaps used as a groundsheet or coverlet, and the very necessary water skin. Walking ahead of the officer is a pack animal with cloths hanging over its flanks. Evidently a small child (most of whose figure is missing) was riding on the mare, and the artist has also shown another naked boy, this time carrying a basket with provisions. These small children are no doubt the offspring of the camp followers who were responsible for the commissariat and the cleaning activities in the camp.

In the topmost register of the block are more attendants. Alongside, a span of horses has been unharnessed from a chariot, its pole now resting on a support with a splayed foot.

Another large relief in Bologna is certainly related to the one we have just examined, although there is no direct join. It too depicts activities in a military camp, where there is plenty going on. The great sculptor who carved this block rivets the eye on a scene showing a group of soldiers, urged on by an overseer, manhandling a long rectangular object which I believe to be the rolled-up tent of the commander-in-chief. Such a tent-cloth, probably of leather, would be heavy and difficult to manœuvre, and would need a 'fatigue' party to move it from one place to another. Like so much else shown on the walls of Horemheb's tomb it is a scene unique in Egyptian iconography. The soldiers wear openwork loincloths made of leather with a square patch at the rear. Such garments were made by cutting rows of tiny slits which break joint with one another. Actual examples have been found in New Kingdom tombs at Thebes.

Before quitting the outer courtyard of the tomb let us note another fine block, likewise in Bologna, which certainly was once positioned on the north wall, where it was connected with a scene already described, to judge from the quantities of food and drink represented. The theme is the preparation of a great feast, one which took place in actuality rather than in the Netherworld. Can it be a celebratory banquet prepared in honour of Horemheb, either to welcome him back to Memphis after a great victory or on the occasion when he was awarded the gold collars of honour by the Pharaoh? At any event, no expense was spared to make this a memorable *fantasia*; all that seems to be lacking is a group of singers and musicians who would have entertained the guests. These could well have been depicted on an adjacent block stripped off the wall in antiquity and now lost.

The middle register of the present relief depicts more action in the military encampment. Two runners approach briskly from the left, while a squatting scribe, palette and papyrus in hand, is jotting down instructions, perhaps from the tomb-owner himself. The obviously important figure wearing sandals just to the right is doubtless Horemheb. On the far left an official faces towards the general in an attitude of respect, left hand clasping his right arm, hand on shoulder. Behind the commander-in-chief a scribe takes down instructions, perhaps concerning the forthcoming feast.

All these reliefs, as well as fragments of others we found in the debris of the courtyard, give an unparalleled insight into the day-to-day activities of the greatest man in Egypt of his time. It is easy to imagine what a wealth of detail was recorded in this part of the tomb when the scheme of decoration was complete. Hardly any – perhaps none – of the scenes were drawn from the standard 'ritualistic' repertory which are met with in so many tombs, Memphite as well as Theban. These unique glimpses into the daily life of Horemheb must have been selected for commemoration by Horemheb himself.

Having examined the First Courtyard we may now leave it by the west door to enter the vestibule leading to the Statue Room.

## The Statue Room

The long rooms flanking the Statue Room were designed originally as chapels. At a later stage they may have been used for the storage of foodstuffs and liquids in pottery containers. In the last phase of their existence monks from the nearby Monastery of Apa Jeremias converted them into anchoritic cells, where members of the community could live from time to time, isolated to a certain extent from their brethren.

On the south wall of the small vestibule east of the Statue Room is a large relief in the best style of the late Eighteenth Dynasty, and practically complete. On it we see depicted a seated statue of Horemheb, with a priest to the left making an offering of incense. He is engaged in the ritual known as the 'Opening of the Mouth' of the statue so that it could function as a recipient of future offerings. The actual statues were positioned in niches against the west wall of the adjacent chamber. The text accompanying the scene gives a vivid insight into a ritual that was carried out not only on statues in temples and tombs but also on the mummies of deceased persons: 'How well-provided with teeth (?) is your mouth! Your mouth has been adjusted to your bones, your mouth has been opened, your mouth has been disclosed with the adze of Anubis, the *mesketyu*-adze of iron with which the mouth of the gods has been opened.' The adze was only one of a number of instruments held up to the mouth of the statue (or the mummy) during the ceremony.

The priest who carries out the ritual is not named. Horemheb had no children, or at least none who survived him. Consequently he had to rely on others to maintain his funerary cult. (In the event it was not required at Saqqara because he became king and was buried ultimately in the royal valley at Thebes.) From the evidence of the relief under discussion, and from two other representations in the Memphite tomb, Horemheb seems to have had a special affinity for Sementawy, his army scribe, who is depicted behind him on the present relief. Perhaps the relationship amounted to a kind of adoption. At some stage, Sementawy died or was replaced, and another name, Ramose, was carved over his (*ill.* 24). At the same time Sementawy's title was altered to 'documents scribe' or 'private secretary' of the great army commander. It

24 *Horemheb's private secretary Sementawy. This official's name was later overcut by that of Ramose, indicating that he may have died or have been superseded in Horemheb's regard. His arms are held in a characteristic gesture of respect.*

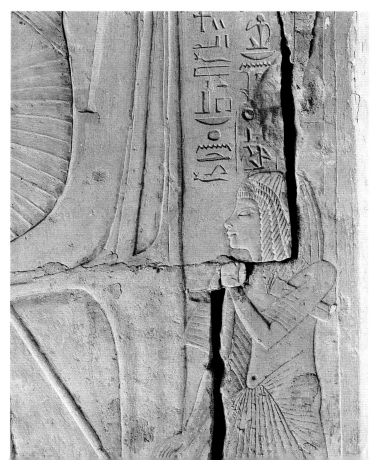

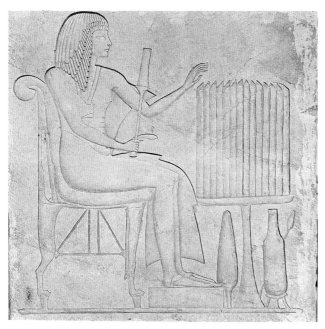

25 *Horemheb seated before a table loaded with stylized loaves of bread. A uraeus, the serpent symbol of Egyptian kingship, has been added to his brow to signify that he had become pharaoh.*

would be pleasant to think that Ramose, seen in Horemheb's tomb at presumably an early stage in his (Ramose's) military career, was none other than the Paramessu, the high-ranking officer who eventually succeeded him as pharaoh; but the vital evidence is lacking.

The register beneath the Opening-of-the Mouth representation continues the frieze of offering-bearers carved on the west wall of the outer courtyard. During the time of Ramesses II, however, a personal name and title, 'the lector-priest Pehefnefer' was carved in front of one of the figures. We shall encounter him again shortly.

Moving into the Statue Room itself we see it as a large rectangular chamber, originally with a vaulted ceiling in mud brick. No reliefs were apparently placed on the walls; instead, the walls were finished with a coating of mud plaster with a lime wash. It is not improbable that they would have been painted with mythological or other scenes like the chapels in the private tombs at Thebes. The roof having collapsed in antiquity the weather has completely destroyed the decoration, but we did notice one or two minute traces of paint here and there on the walls when we excavated them in 1975.

Several architectural features of great interest survive in the Statue Room. The inscribed door jambs in the interior give valuable historical information and personal details about the tomb-owner. The pair on the east side of the room have a section at the bottom showing Horemheb seated before an offering table. These representations are quite different in style although they are, of course, exactly contemporary, and only one (the northern) has a uraeus added to the tomb-owner's brow to signify that he had become Pharaoh. The renowned Egyptologist Auguste Mariette made copies of these texts and representations about the middle of the last century, but unwittingly misled scholars since that time because he seems to have regarded the south jamb as a duplicate of the northern. In reality they are different, not only in style but also in content.

The inscriptions on the jambs are quite informative, especially in regard to Horemheb's supreme position in the state. On the north jamb we read that he was 'greater than the great ones, mightier than the mighty ones, great chieftain of the subjects . . . who follows the king on his journeys in the southern and northern foreign land . . . chief of the most important courtiers, who listens to the confidences of the unique ones . . . master of the secrets of the Palace.' On the other jamb Horemheb's military supremacy is stressed: He was 'messenger of the king at the head of his expedition to the southern and northern foreign land . . . elected by the king above the Two Lands to carry out the government of the Two Shores [the Two Lands and Two Shores signify Egypt], overseer of generals of the Lord of the Two Lands . . . the unique one who counts the troops . . . one who was in attendance on his lord [the Pharaoh] on the battlefield on this day of smiting the Asiatics.' The hints at military conflict are fascinating, and doubtless refer to actual events in which Horemheb, as generalissimo, was responsible for reasserting Egypt's domination over the city states of Western Asia and the tribes of Nubia sometime after the accession of Tutankhamun. There is a clear implication too in the second of the texts that the young Pharaoh was present on the battlefield, a welcome clue to the date of the military activity. Presumably this was rather late in the reign (when Tutankhamun was in his late teens) rather than when he was barely an adolescent. The other inscribed doorposts in the Statue Room also add to our knowledge about Horemheb's military career, but we need not linger here.

### The cult of the deified Horemheb

It has been mentioned more than once that Horemheb ultimately succeeded to the throne of Egypt. He was not the first private citizen to achieve this eminence, but aside from the ephemeral kinglets of the two Intermediate Periods of Egyptian history the number of instances is not many. Much of Horemheb's wealth, when he was Tutankhamun's commander-in-chief, must have been lavished on his Memphite tomb, and no doubt the finest craftsmen and artists of the time had a hand in the decoration of it. Even though it was never used by the great general it must have had a special place in his affections (there is no evidence that the Egyptians ever feared their ultimate resting-place). The Memphite tomb was also special to the family of Horemheb's successor as Pharaoh, Ramesses I (Paramessu). Clearly Horemheb, having no heir himself, chose him as the next ruler. It is not surprising therefore to find that Ramesses II, grandson of the founder of the new dynasty, instituted a cult for his putative ancestor Horemheb.

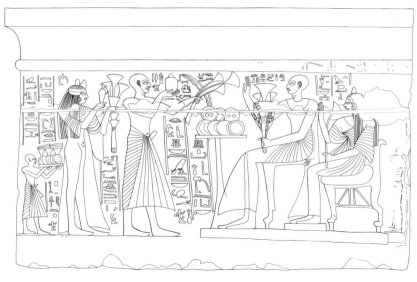

26 *A family of lector priests of the deified King Horemheb. The priest Pehefnefer and his wife are seated on the right, and are being purified with water and presented with bouquets by members of their family. The plinth on which this scene was cut originally supported a large figure of a recumbent jackal, the god Anubis, guarding the innermost parts of the tomb of Horemheb.*

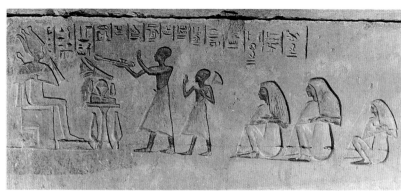

27 *A priestly family adores a seated figure of Osiris, god of the Underworld. The worshipping official was responsible for servicing the cult of the deified Pharaoh Horemheb in the Ramesside Period, many years after his death. The relief is carved on the side of a plinth, one of a pair on which were positioned figures of the jackal god Anubis.*

In the Statue Room of Horemheb's tomb two plinths supporting recumbent statues of the jackal-god Anubis were erected during the reign of Ramesses II on either side of the west doorway, their heads facing eastwards towards the tomb entrance. They were meant to act as guardians of the most westerly or intimate part of the monument. The reliefs and inscriptions on the fronts and sides of the plinths give us some fascinating details about the family of mortuary priests who were employed to carry out the cult of the dead and deified King Horemheb. Their responsibilities would have involved the presentation of foodstuffs and drink on the altars in the tomb on high days and festivals, as well as the general upkeep of the fabric of the tomb. One of them was Pehefnefer, whom we saw named in the relief in the vestibule. Horemheb's name would thus be remembered and venerated, in theory for ever. We do not know how long the cult actually lasted in this place, but it would not be surprising if it did so right down to the end of the Ramesside Period.

The west door of the Statue Room leads into the Second Court of the tomb. On the wall to the left as we leave the Statue Room is a relief and a hymn of considerable importance from the point of view of Egyptian religion.

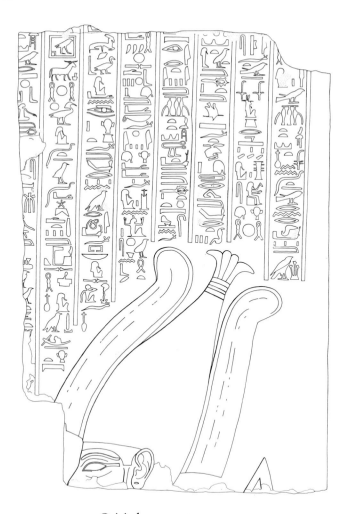

*28 Osiris and a hymn lauding him, recorded in a line drawing to show the details of the fragmentary but important hieroglyphic inscription accompanying his figure.*

## Osiris hymn

Only fragments of the scene survive, showing Horemheb adoring Osiris, god of the Underworld. There is nothing new in this of course, but the accompanying text, so far unique, immediately lifts it out of the ordinary. It is, in fact, a hymn to Osiris as the nocturnal manifestation of the sun-god Re. Originally there would have been twenty-seven columns of inscription, of which about a third survive. No exact parallel text of the hymn seems to be known, and it differs from all other hymns to Osiris known from the period before the Nineteenth Dynasty. The theme itself is not new, since it is already present in the Coffin Texts of the Middle Kingdom and the Book of the Dead documents of the New Kingdom: the sun-god Re dies every evening and enters the Underworld via the western horizon, where he is said to 'embrace' the body of Osiris resting there. In this way Osiris becomes Re and illuminates the darkness of the Underworld as nocturnal sun god. When morning comes Re arises from the arms of Osiris and is reborn as Re-Horus-of-the-Horizon (Re-Harakhty).

It is interesting that this charming and understandable myth is not included in the corpus of 'hymns' until the time of Tutankhamun. This fact has been explained as a reaction against the monotheism of Tutankhamun's predecessor, Akhenaten:

Akhenaten had replaced the plurality of gods of the traditional religion by the sole god Aten, who was in the first place a god of light, upon whose life-giving power everyone and everything upon earth depended. Darkness and night were interpreted only in a negative way: during the night the Aten is absent and the whole world falls back into a state of non-existence. In Amarna religion there was no place for Osiris, who therefore shared the fate of Amun and the other traditional gods. However, this being so Akhenaten was unable to deal with one of the most essential aspects of Egyptian religion, that is, death and life after death. In the period after the Amarna interlude the traditional religion was re-interpreted in reaction to Akhenaten's doctrines. The problem of unity and plurality was solved by the concept of a universal god from whom all other gods emanate, and who manifests himself in his creation, which includes the present world and the Hereafter. The cult of Osiris became much more important than before the Amarna Period, and in the tombs of private persons Osiris and Re have a role of equal weight. (J. van Dijk)

Horemheb's hymn reflects just this state of affairs, and as such it is a most welcome addition to the documentation of Egyptian religion in the crucial period following the demise of Akhenaten and the almost total repudiation of his monotheistic ideas.

## The Second Courtyard

Moving westwards out of the Statue Room we find ourselves in a smaller version of the outer courtyard of the tomb. The columns are just over 2 metres in height, and the reliefs are much better preserved. Indeed, it is not too much to say that the scenes we are about to examine are among the most vivid and important to have survived from any period of Egyptian history, and they are particularly interesting since they illustrate graphically the military policy of Tutankhamun and his advisers.

A number of blocks are still in position on the walls, having miraculously escaped the attentions of ancient and modern despoilers. We ourselves found others in the debris of the courtyard and elsewhere in the vicinity, which we were able to put back on the walls. Not only that, but some celebrated reliefs removed from the tomb in the early decades of the last century and now in the Leiden Museum and other major collections in Europe, including the British Museum, can now be repositioned with certainty (we have recently placed casts on the walls).

The south side of the east wall, and the south and west walls of the court are decorated with sculpted scenes showing selected episodes in Horemheb's career. Officials liked to show some of their day-to-day activities on the walls of their tombs, but it is rare to find, as in Horemheb's case, so many representations. Though we have only a fairly small proportion of the reliefs that once decorated the walls enough is preserved to show that most of those in the Second Courtyard were military in content. The various episodes – the submission of prisoners and their exhibition at court – were telescoped by the ancient artists for effect and because of reasons of space. Some funerary scenes are also preserved on two of the walls, and we are afforded a glimpse into what is probably Horemheb's private estate on other reliefs.

Parts of the hieroglyphic texts, which ran along the upper part of the walls and explained the events depicted, are extant. All in all the material is a prime source of information about the history of Egypt in the reign of Tutankhamun. The reliefs, carved by the chisels of anonymous craftsmen, are some of the most accomplished to survive from ancient Egypt, and form a major source for the historian of art. They also deserve the attention of physical anthropologists,

*29 The superstructure of the tomb of Horemheb after excavation. A view looking east towards Memphis and the cultivation of the Nile Valley before the restoration of the monument. In the foreground is the cult room, flanked by chapels.*

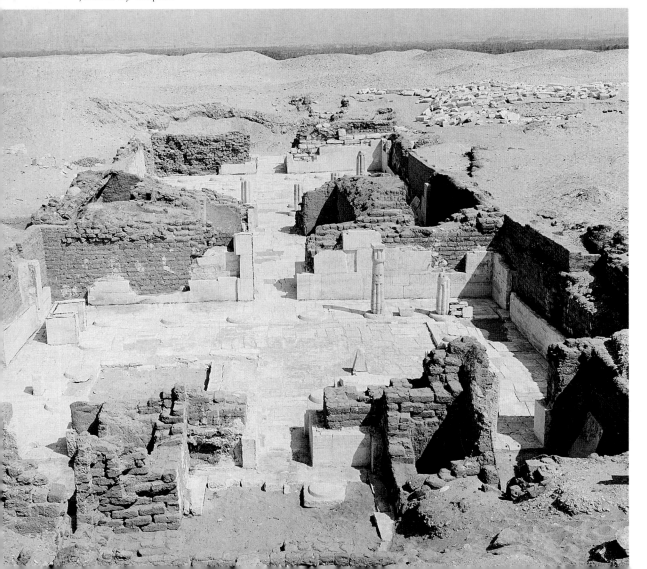

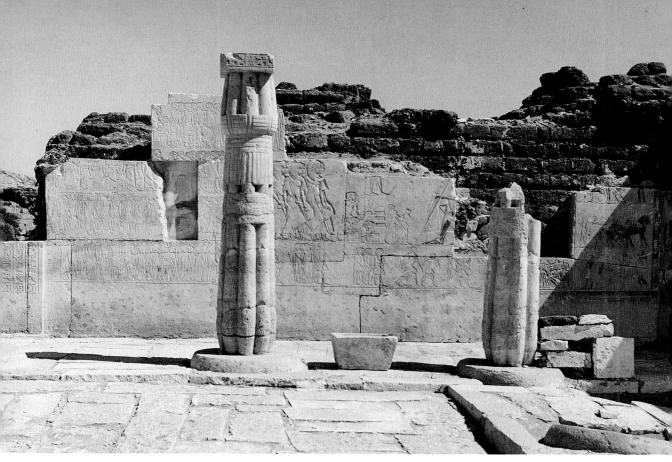

30 *The southeast corner of the inner courtyard of Horemheb's tomb, showing the best-preserved wall in the monument. The decoration of the wall shows episodes in Horemheb's military career in expeditions against Libya, Western Asia and Nubia.*

because of the vivid and realistic way in which the human figures, and in particular the foreign captives, are rendered.

### East wall, south side: military scenes

The focus of the relief on this wall is naturally the commander-in-chief himself, who is standing towards the right of the scene. A Nubian chieftain is about to be toppled over by an Egyptian soldier to make him submit by 'kissing the ground' (to use an Egyptian expression) in front of Horemheb's feet. Six army colleagues, their figures carved by a master sculptor, as well as lesser officials, are taking part in the event. To the left long files of captives from Libya, the Western Asiatic city states and Nubia, representing the totality of the captured, are seen being guarded by Egyptian soldiers. These are carved on a smaller scale, a device to show either that they were young recruits or that the prisoners were larger and more burly than their captors. His list of titles shows that one of Horemheb's many functions was concerned with recruits for the army. No surviving historical inscription hints at a major military conflict in the reign of

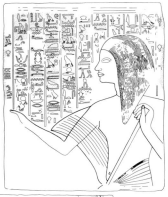

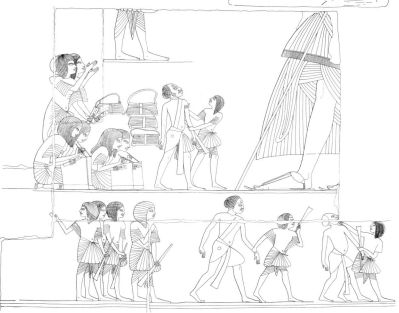

31 Part of a relief depicting Horemheb receiving the submission of Egypt's foes during the reign of Tutankhamun. The commander-in-chief is seen to the right of the block. The inscription records his military exploits in which he re-asserted Egypt's influence in the Levant, Libya and Nubia in the aftermath of the reign of Akhenaten. To the left military scribes record the events, and an African chieftain is about to prostrate himself in front of Horemheb. Below, Egyptian officers and Nubian prisoners, one of whom is being punched on the jaw.

32 (Below) An unnamed Nubian chieftain submits to Horemheb, who is shown on a large scale to the right, holding a staff of office. This relief preserves one of the most vivid representations of an African to have survived from antiquity.

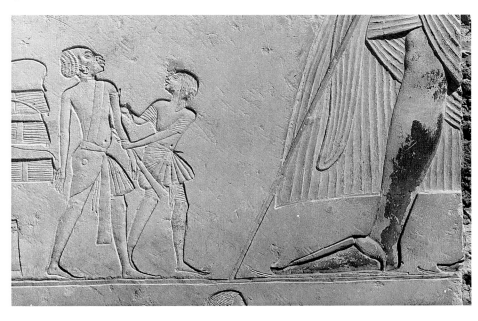

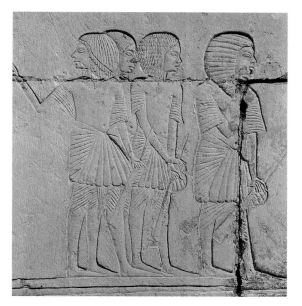

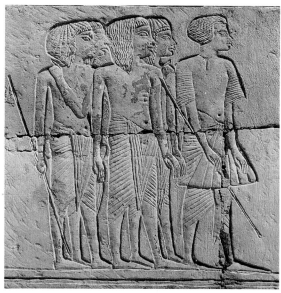

33 *Egyptian military officers in attendance on the commander-in-chief. They hold the wedge-shaped wands characteristic of the late Eighteenth Dynasty.*

34 *Egyptian soldiers witness the submission of Egypt's enemies. The man at the front is more elaborately dressed than the others and is presumably an officer.*

Tutankhamun, so the scenes on the walls of the Second Court probably should be interpreted as punitive expeditions sent out by Tutankhamun's advisers to reassert Egyptian domination and influence in those regions of the ancient world that had attempted to break away in the previous reign.

The submission of the Libyan, Asiatic, and Nubian conquered is presumably meant to be seen as taking place on the field of battle. Military scribes are busily recording on rolls of papyrus the memorable event, or more likely series of events. It may have been the intention at a later stage to edit these field documents and to inscribe the details on a wall of one or other of the cult temples at Thebes and indeed in Memphis. Military conquests were often thus commemorated by the Pharaohs of the New Kingdom – the Asiatic campaigns of Tuthmosis III, Amenophis II, and Ramesses II serving as prime examples. Sometimes stelae were erected in the temples to memorialize pharaonic conquests. Most of the surviving documentation comes from the Theban and Nubian temples. What a wealth of information must have been recorded on the walls of the temples of Memphis! Alas, for the most part we have only the waterlogged remains of the foundations of these gigantic structures, which must surely have rivalled in size and splendour of decoration the much better known Theban monuments.

The scribal scene just mentioned is one of the most vivid and informative in Egyptian art; so realistic is the carving that one can almost see the scribes' fingers moving over the papyrus. The panniers for carrying the scribal equipment are also in evidence. Behind the figure of Horemheb a Nubian, who has perhaps just bent the knee in an act of submission, is hurried away. To

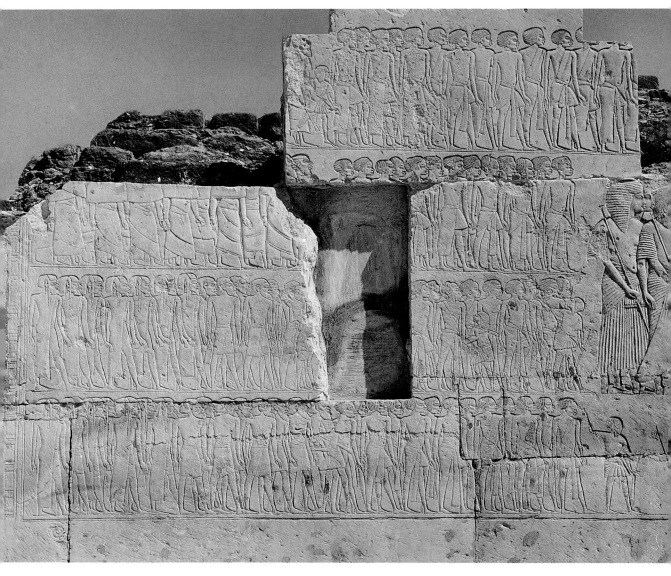

**Military Scenes** *35 Rows of Libyan, Western Asiatic and Nubian prisoners parade before the general Horemheb, who has reasserted Egypt's sphere of influence over territories which had rebelled during the reign of Tutankhamun's predecessor Akhenaten.*

Opposite
*36–41 (Above left) Prisoners from Libya in the reign of Tutankhamun. They are shown with their characteristic coiffure and goatee beards. They wear earrings and long cloaks. Though captives their hieratic pose conveys an impression of great dignity. (Above right) Prisoners from the city-states of Western Asia and Nubia guarded by a young Egyptian soldier. The Asiatics depicted on this and adjoining reliefs may include some who conspired against Akhenaten according to the evidence of the Amarna Letters. (Centre left) Nubians submitting to Horemheb as commander-in-chief of Tutankhamun. More than one physical type is represented. (Centre right) Military scribes record on papyrus rolls the submission of Egypt's foreign foes. Panniers for their scribal equipment are positioned in front of them. (Below left) A young Egyptian recruit punches a Nubian prisoner on the jaw as he is hurried into captivity. (Below right) An Egyptian soldier admonishes a Nubian captive.*

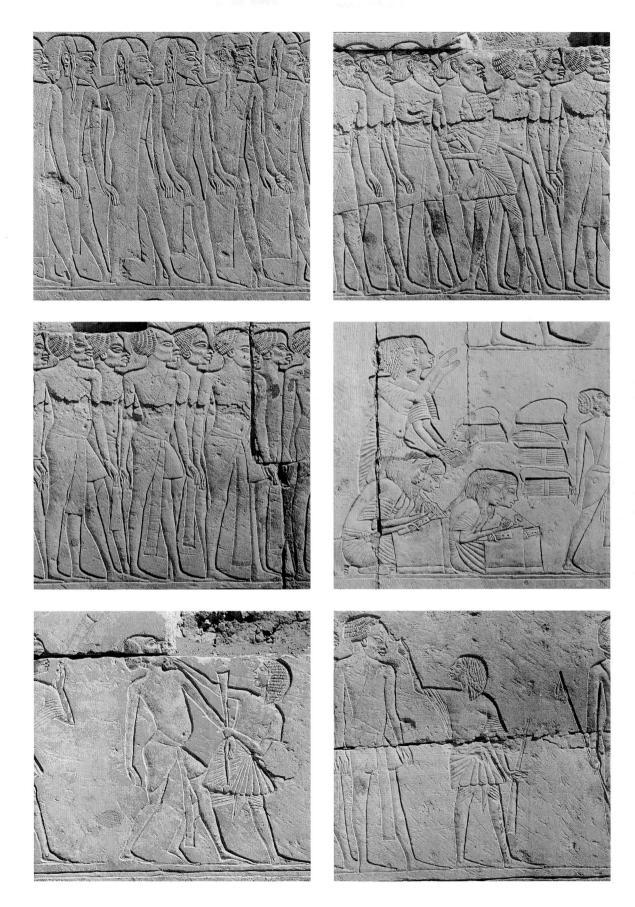

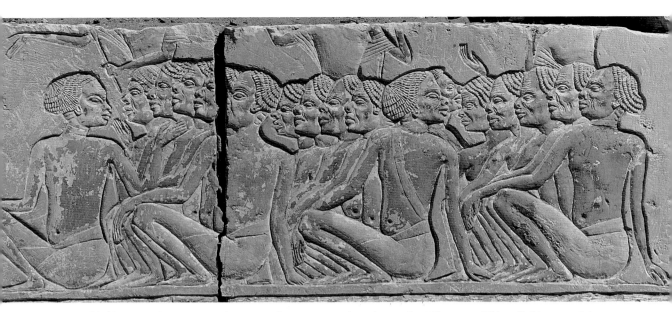

42 *Nubians await transportation to work camps or other places of confinement. This relief is one of the most realistic representations of Southerners to have survived from antiquity.*

emphasize his discomfiture his Egyptian guard is shown punching him on the jaw. On the same wall a Nubian is led forward to make submission, while another is reprimanded by an Egyptian soldier. Further beyond are two groups of Nubians whose personal details – names and perhaps tribal affiliations – have already been recorded. The uppermost register of this scene is on a block in Bologna.

Such scenes as have just been described are valuable illustrations of the somewhat denigrating approach which the Egyptians had towards foes, whether actual or potential. In historical texts Nubians and some Asiatics are not infrequently characterized as 'vile'.

On the far right of our relief the generalissimo's chariot with its grooms and attendants wait for him to leave the reception area. The frieze continues on the south wall.

### The south wall: prisoners as trophies

The series of military scenes is interrupted here by a relief of Horemheb in state (*ill. 43*), with his army scribe Sementawy/Ramose in attendance. A funerary priest is making offering to Horemheb. The upper block is much weatherworn. The hieroglyphic text on it clearly described historical events, doubtless military in character, to judge from the tantalizing fragment mentioning 'regnal year . . .'. Repeated checking of the block in different kinds of light has failed to reveal even the faintest trace of the *actual* year date, which would have been of great importance for placing the events just described in a precisely

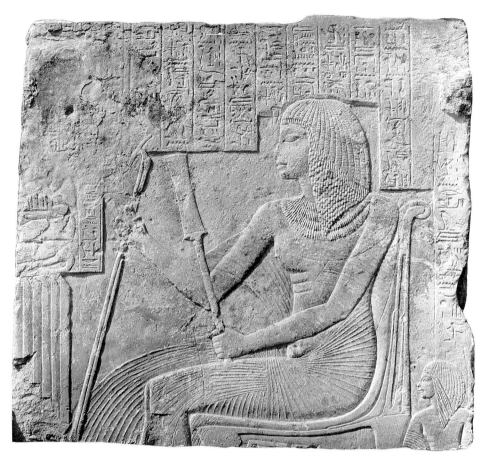

*43 Horemheb seated in state as commander of the army of Tutankhamun. A uraeus has been added to his brow on this relief to signify that subsequently he had been elevated to supreme dignity as pharaoh. Behind him stands his army scribe or personal secretary Sementawy. The latter's name has been almost completely erased and that of Ramose substituted.*

dated context. At least the presence of the crucial phrase, 'regnal year', shows that we are dealing with real, as opposed to symbolic, events. We have to be thankful for small mercies: the reliefs themselves in the Second Courtyard are a remarkable and unique visual record, even in their fragmentary state, of selected episodes in the various campaigns which took place during the reign of Tutankhamun.

Below butchers are seen busily dismembering an ox for the funerary meal. This and the presence of a large pannier or container full of fruits of some kind emphasizes the overwhelming need for provisions to sustain the dead in the next world. Should actual offerings fail, the tomb owner could always rely on the fact that the depictions of food on the walls of the tomb would magically take their place.

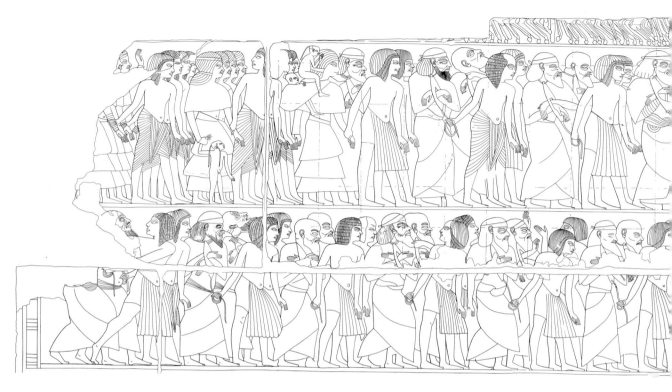

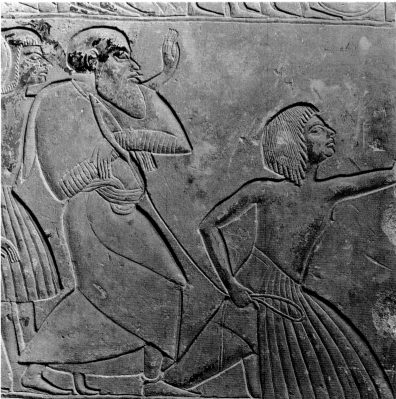

44 (Above) Western Asiatic and Hittite captives paraded by Egyptian guards before Tutankhamun and Queen Ankhesenamun. The wrists of the prisoners are secured by manacles, to which ropes are attached. On the topmost register a melée of horses can be seen, probably forming part of the booty brought back from Asia by Horemheb.

45 (Left) A bearded Western Asiatic led before Tutankhamun.

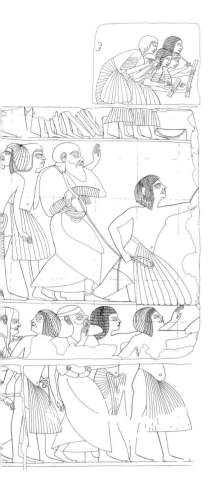

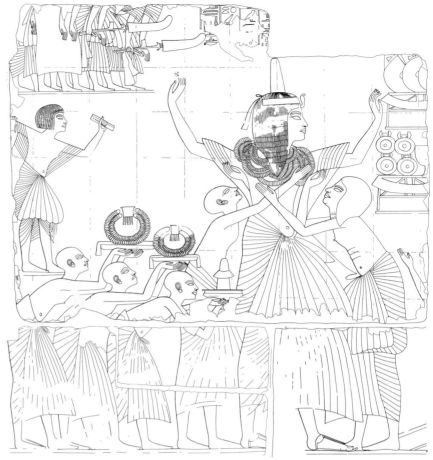

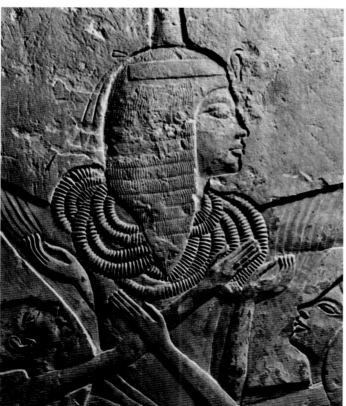

46,47 The victorious Horemheb, decorated with gold collars, reports to Tutankhamun and his queen the results of his punitive expeditions. After his own elevation to the divine kingship a uraeus was carved at his forehead. Behind him attendants hold trays containing more gold collars and a shallow bowl containing a cone of unguent or scented fat, around which a small floral fillet has been fastened.

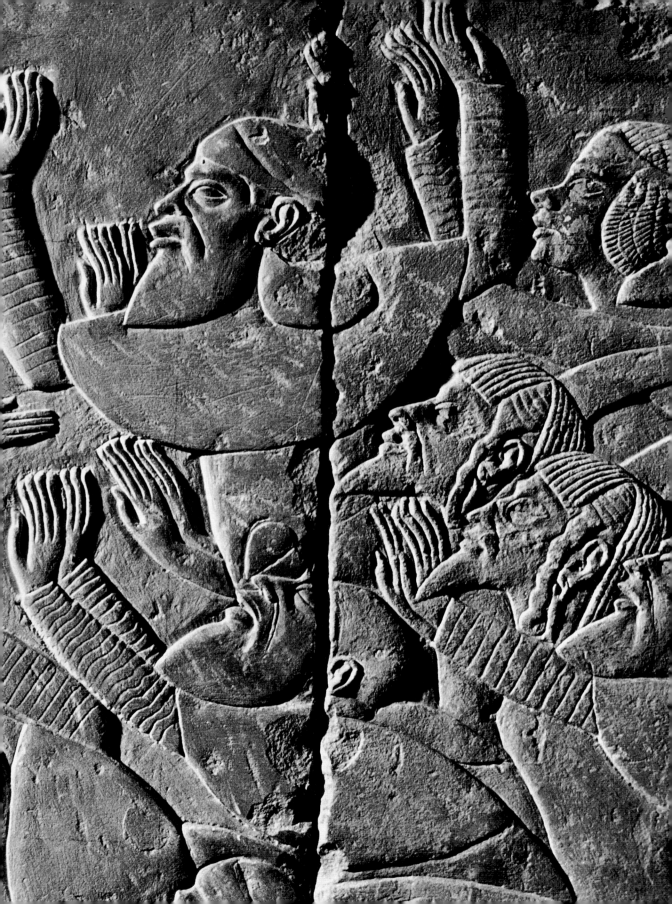

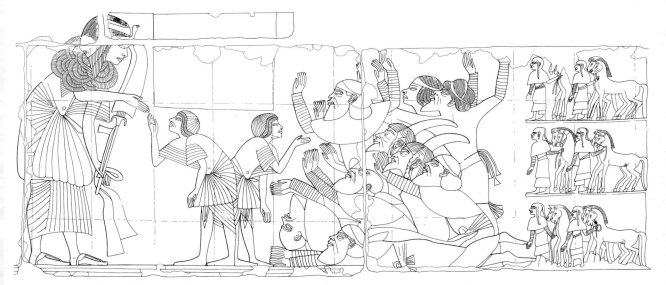

49 *Envoys from Libya and Western Asia petition Tutankhamun in the aftermath of battle. Their request is relayed to the king through an interpreter, who turns to Horemheb, seen on the left. As the highest official in the land, Horemheb acts as intermediary between the ambassadors and pharaoh.*

The main part of the south wall can be reconstituted in truly remarkable detail, thanks to the fact that a whole series of reliefs, long since in Leiden, can be repositioned here.

The scene has changed from the battlefield to the royal palace enclosure, very probably the one in Memphis itself. The young Tutankhamun and his wife Ankhesenamun (third daughter of Akhenaten and Nefertiti) are seated on thrones to the right, with a baldachin above. An attendant hurries down the ramp of the throne dais to the pavement below, where stands the commander Horemheb, loaded with 'collars of honour', made of solid gold. He has just been decorated by Pharaoh for his services to the state, and his faithful servants are adjusting the heavy collars so that they fit comfortably round his neck. Behind him, exhibited as trophies, are paraded long rows of captives, this time only from the Western Asiatic city states, and in one instance from the Hittite dominions. Their characteristic costumes and hairstyles identify them. Perhaps Libyans and Nubians were shown on a part of the wall now lost.

The prisoners, unlike those on the adjacent east wall, are manacled and have ropes round their necks like cattle. Their anguish is best seen on a block found by us in the debris of the courtyard, but joining exactly the left end of the Leiden series of reliefs; the detail of the carving is masterly.

It is clear from the representations on this block that women and children also were carried into captivity in Egypt. The ultimate fate of this particular group will probably never be known, but evidence suggests that foreign captives were sometimes assigned as labourers and brickmakers to the agricultural estates of Amun and possibly other deities. The foreigners may even have formed enclaves in the capital Memphis itself, and may have been the

77

48 *(Opposite) Foreign envoys pleading for clemency at the court of Tutankhamun; scene from the west wall of the inner courtyard of the tomb of Horemheb.*

ancestors of some of the foreign peoples known to have lived in that city in later times, worshipping their own Asiatic deities.

A great deal has been lost to us by the removal or destruction of the upper courses of the wall of the courtyard. Here one would have expected to find a continuation of the text of the historical narrative mentioned above, with perhaps representations of the booty taken on campaign and brought back to Egypt as a gift to Pharaoh and as offerings to the temple treasuries. The presence of spoil is suggested by the lower parts of the legs of a large group of horses, apparently running free. Western Asia was the source of supply of this useful animal, which became increasingly important in military terms from the middle of the Eighteenth Dynasty when the cavalry and chariotry were developed as crucial elements in the Egyptian war machine. Another block which we found recently outside the tomb very probably also forms part of the 'booty' scene. It is a wonderfully accomplished relief showing felines on leashes. Such fierce animals were prized at the royal court, where they were sometimes tied by ropes to the chair legs of Pharaoh's throne, no doubt after they had been tamed and their awesome fangs extracted! We also read in Egyptian inscriptions of wild animals such as lions being corralled, whence they could be picked off at leisure and in comparative safety by the ruler.

The story continues on the west wall of the court.

### The west wall: ambassadors plead for clemency (*ills. 48, 49*)

Here the remains of two distinct scenes can be reconstructed from blocks found still in position and from reliefs in Leiden and elsewhere. The aftermath of the battles or skirmishes implied by the scenes we have already examined on the other walls of the court is now recorded for posterity by the great sculptors who decorated Horemheb's monument. A delegation of ambassadors from Western Asia, Libya, and Nubia, the triumvirate of nations which had tried, evidently unsuccessfully, to throw off the Egyptian yoke, have arrived to beg from Pharaoh the 'breath of life'; in our terms, 'clemency'. They have arrived overland from the Western Desert, from across the Sinai, and from the South; some at least have journeyed on horseback, since we see their grooms and horses waiting to one side. The delegates prostrate themselves in front of Tutankhamun and his queen, who are standing on the palace balcony to the left. The scene is one of the most revealing examples of narrative art surviving from ancient Egypt: the ambassadors, unable to speak Egyptian, make their request for clemency known to an interpreter, who turns round to pass the request to Horemheb, who likewise turns to address the royal couple. Part of the explanatory text survives, but the beginnings of the columns of inscription are lacking:

[Words spoken to His Majesty when] the chiefs of every foreign territory came to beg life from him, by the hereditary prince, sole companion, royal scribe Horemheb. He said, making answer [to the King: . . . foreigners] who do not know Egypt, they are

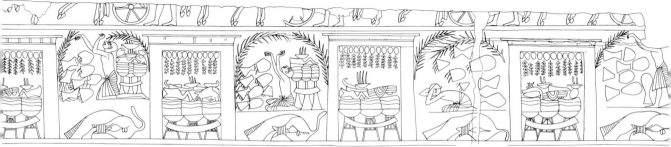

50–54 (Above) *Booths with food and drink, set up for the funeral of the tomb-owner. Red-ware jars have been smashed during the ceremonial, and professional mourners are seen in extravagant attitudes of grief, clearly fulfilling the duties for which they have been paid. (Centre left) A butcher cuts off the head of a sacrificial ox during the funeral service. To the right a booth with fruits suspended from the ceiling and tables piled high with viands for the mortuary feast. (Centre right) A paid mourner, funerary offerings, including meat, bread and a trussed ox, and vases ritualistically smashed during the obsequies. (Below left) A hired mourner, offerings, and vases deliberately shattered as part of the funerary ritual. (Below right) A paid weeper, and offerings, and vases to be deliberately smashed as part of the ritual for the deceased.*

**Scenes of Mourning North Wall**

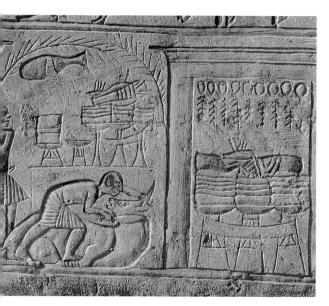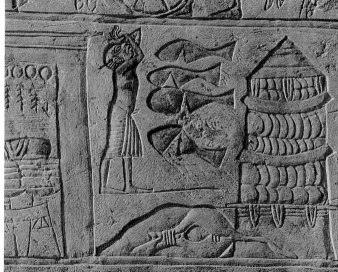

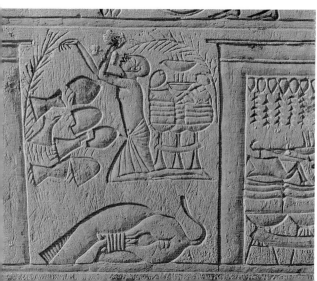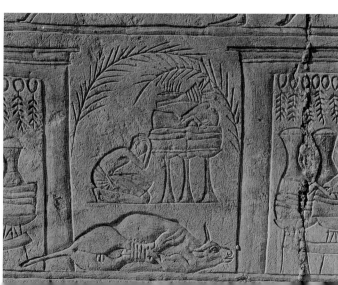

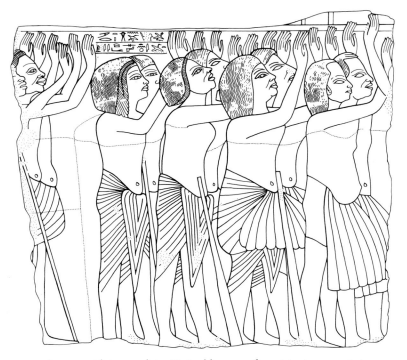

*55 An army platoon salutes Tutankhamun after victorious campaigns.*

beneath your feet for ever and eternally. Amun has handed them over to you. They penetrated [every] foreign territory . . .

Horemheb then addresses the Egyptian officials in the entourage of Pharaoh:

Thus says [Pharaoh to . . . all his officers?] . . . starting from the southern end of Kush (Nubia) [to the uttermost parts of Asia?] . . . Pharaoh has placed them upon your hands so as to guard their boundaries. . . . of Pharaoh according to the custom of the father of your fathers since primæval times. And . . . [it has been reported that?] some foreigners who do not know (how) they may live are come from (?) . . . their countries are hungry, and they live like the animals of the desert . . . the Great of Strength (Pharaoh) will send his mighty arm in front of [his army? . . . and will] destroy them and plunder their towns, and set fire. . .

These tantalizing fragments, in places difficult to interpret and translate, seem to imply that confederacies had been formed against Egypt, but that the rebels had been crushed and their lands devastated by the might of Pharaoh. Horemheb, the great commander-in-chief, was no doubt the instrument of the Egyptian government in the various punitive campaigns, which were necessary, as we have seen, to reassert Egyptian domination of Western Asia and Nubia in the aftermath of the reign of Tutankhamun's predecessor Akhenaten.

I *The aftermath of battle: prisoners from the city-states of Western Asia are led by Egyptian soldiers into the presence of Tutankhamun and his queen.*

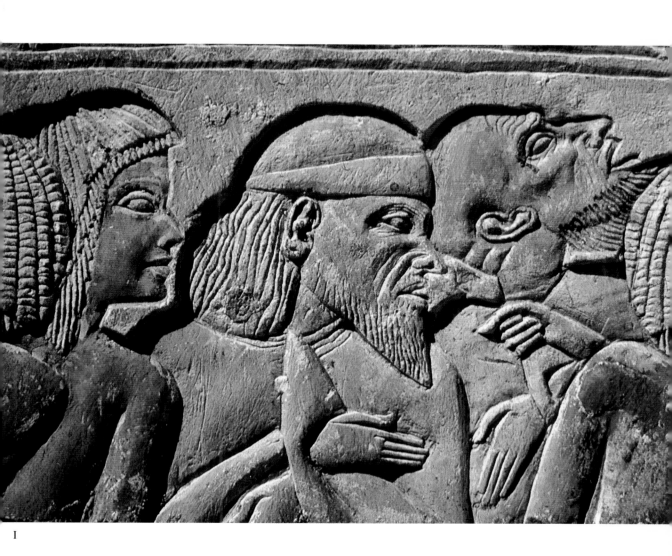

I

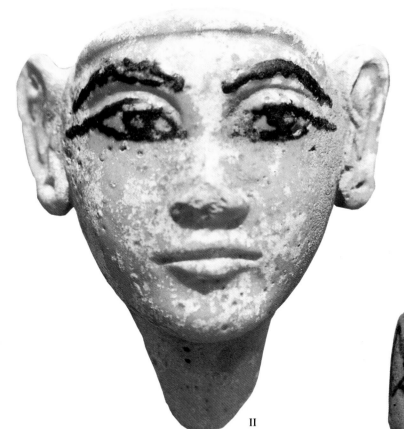

II

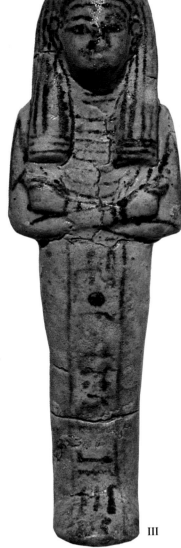

III

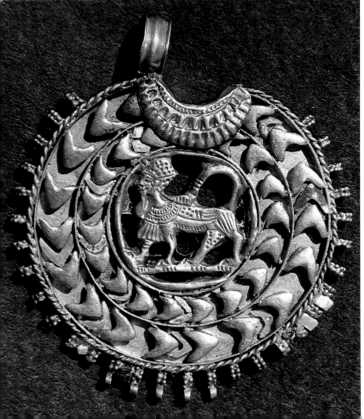

IV

Further along the west wall, on the north side of the entrance to the Offering Room, some surviving blocks show the final episode in the sequence of historical events depicted in the courtyard: the acclamation of the sovereign by the Egyptians and by foreigners. One of the Egyptian soldiers in this scene is afflicted with an umbilical hernia. Interestingly, a short text written above the heads of two of the soldiers gives us the name of their platoon and the title and name of one of their officers: 'Standard-bearer of the regiment "Beloved-of-the-Aten" Minkhay.' The Aten, or disk of the sun, was the deity favoured to the exclusion of almost all others by Akhenaten. This led to the closing of the ancient cult temples and the dismantling of their powerful priestly hierarchies. Aten in turn was by and large repudiated by Tutankhamun and his advisers, and the ancient religious order restored. It is interesting to see that one of the regiments was still associated with the Aten in the reign of Tutankhamun; can it be that Horemheb once commanded this regiment, or served in it during an earlier phase of his military career in the reign of Akhenaten? The officer Minkhay in any case must have been held in high regard by Horemheb, since he is singled out for special mention on the relief.

## North wall: scenes of mourning (*ills. 50–54*)

The north wall of the court has a frieze of well-preserved scenes showing episodes in the funerary ritual, prepared in advance of the tomb-owner's demise. A number of booths or kiosks made of flimsy materials are seen. They contain victuals and drink, the latter in red-ware jars, and form the basic commodities in connection with the preparations for the funerary feast. Similar scenes are preserved in some of the Theban tombs of the New Kingdom, but the Memphite series in Horemheb's tomb is by far the most complete. The frenzied demeanour of the mourners will be noticed, as well as the rather more circumspect attitude of the attendants and butchers. Some of the pots are shown being removed from their stands and later smashed into fragments to conform with the ritual known as the 'Breaking of the Red-ware Vessels'. This episode can be traced back to the remotest times in recorded Egyptian history; and various explanations have been given for its enactment in the funerary liturgy. In the sequence of scenes in Horemheb's tomb bulls are shown being slaughtered and dismembered at the same time as the pots are

---

II *Faience inlay of a human head, possibly from a shawabti figure.*

III *Faience shawabti of the princess Binetanath, daughter of Ramesses II. One of two examples found by the EES/Leiden Expedition in the tomb of Horemheb.*

IV *Gold earring with inlays of glass and faience. In the centre is a representation of pharaoh as a striding sphinx, wearing the Blue Crown or war helmet and a broad collar with pendants. The motif is surrounded by two concentric circles with raised chevrons. The coloured inlays between the chevrons have mostly disappeared. Above, a miniature broad collar, part of the fitting for attaching the heavy ring to the earlobe. The bead pendants which would have been suspended from the lower part of the earring are missing.*

smashed. It seems evident that the two elements are linked. One authority, in describing the Horemheb reliefs, writes:

Both the sacrifice of the bull and the breaking of the *dšrt*-vessels with their Sethian red colour symbolize the annihilation of the god's enemy and, although this is never said in so many words in Egyptian texts, it is quite possible that the water streaming from the jars represents the blood (*dšrw*) flowing out of the bull when its throat has been cut. It seems likely that the destruction of figurines or pottery vases inscribed with the names of enemies and the breaking of the red jars at the end of the offering-ritual are variants of one and the same ritual aimed at the destruction of evil forces lurking beyond the borders of the cosmos. Although the ritual may be described in a technical sense as an act of sympathetic magic it is more likely to be interpreted as a rite of reassurance, enacted to reassure and thereby protect the participants of the ritual when they approach the dangerous borderline between the ordered world and the domain of the powers of chaos. (J. van Dijk)

The funerary scenes are continued on the adjacent north side of the east wall of the court. The upper courses of the north wall are entirely lacking, as elsewhere in the tomb. Here must have been shown, among other things, certain mourning scenes such as the lamentation over the mummy (supported by Anubis or a priest wearing a mask representing that jackal-headed deity) on the part of Horemheb's wife. One block which could well have had a place here turned up in 1986 in the courtyard of the tomb of the army officer Ramose, whose funerary monument is just to the north-west of Horemheb's. It seems to represent Horemheb's first wife Amenia, chantress of Amun, who is also shown on one of the columns in the courtyard. The block, showing a lady of rank in mummy form, supported by the goddess Nephthys, is a major work of art. A priest, whose head has been altered and recut on the relief, makes offering.

A number of other blocks were found *in situ* or loose in the debris of the court. A fragmentary scene on the north end of the east wall shows the interiors of rooms of houses.

### East wall, north side: scenes of private life (*ill. 56*)

Perhaps the rooms just mentioned are those in Horemheb's private villa in the city of Memphis. Various items of furniture, clothing, and equipment are to be seen, and we note servants going about their work. One, a doorkeeper, is dozing, no doubt in the warm sun.

Since the Egyptians never used cupboards (as we know them) they were in the habit of hanging implements, weapons, tools, and similar items on wooden pegs knocked into the mud-brick walls of their houses. In the present relief we observe three pairs of sandals and two bags suspended in this way. In some of the rooms supplies of food and drink are to be seen, including a large chest with loaves of bread. Food, clothing, and other items which we are in the habit of storing in cupboards were habitually kept in boxes, chests, and baskets by the inhabitants of the Nile Valley. A military standard resembling a sunshade is shown in one room.

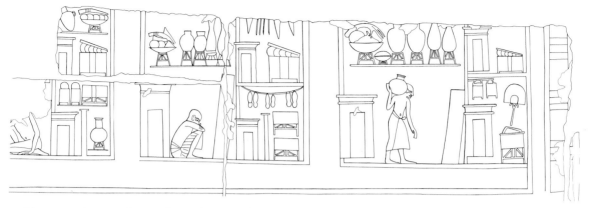

56 *Houses in the city of Memphis in the time of Tutankhamun, showing details of furnishings and equipment. A doorkeeper dozes, and a servant goes about his work. Between the blocks of houses two streets can be seen.*

The houses are similar in plan, showing a large apartment or yard, entered directly from the street, with two rooms to the side. The yard no doubt served as the kitchen area, as in many Egyptian houses to this day. If, as suggested, the buildings depicted on the wall of the Second Courtyard are part of Horemheb's Memphite estate, they give useful clues to the appearance of domestic architecture in that city at the end of the Eighteenth Dynasty.

**Statue emplacements** (*ills. 57–59*)

Two shrines or emplacements for statues are in position in the courtyard, both for double statues of Horemheb and his first wife, who predeceased him. One statue-group, minus the head of Horemheb, was found fairly near the desert surface in the debris of the Offering Room, the other was found embedded in a cross-wall of Christian date in the storeroom or chapel on the north side of the Statue Room. The tomb in the final stage of its history before its rediscovery by us was taken over to be used as dwellings or anchoritic cells, doubtless by monks from the nearby monastery of Apa Jeremias. It was they who must have been partly responsible for the dismantling of the blocks and the smashing of them to burn as lime. The various statues in the tomb were treated in the same fashion.

**The Offering Room**

The focal point of Horemheb's Memphite funerary monument is the Offering Room at the west end of the tomb. It is square in plan and breaks the otherwise rectangular form of the tomb. It would have supported a ceiling of limestone slabs over which was very probably erected a mud-brick pyramid with a pyramidion or capstone in granite, limestone, or another mineral. Small pyramids such as these are seen on contemporary reliefs depicting Memphite tomb-chapels. Although it is virtually certain that the chapel or Offering Room

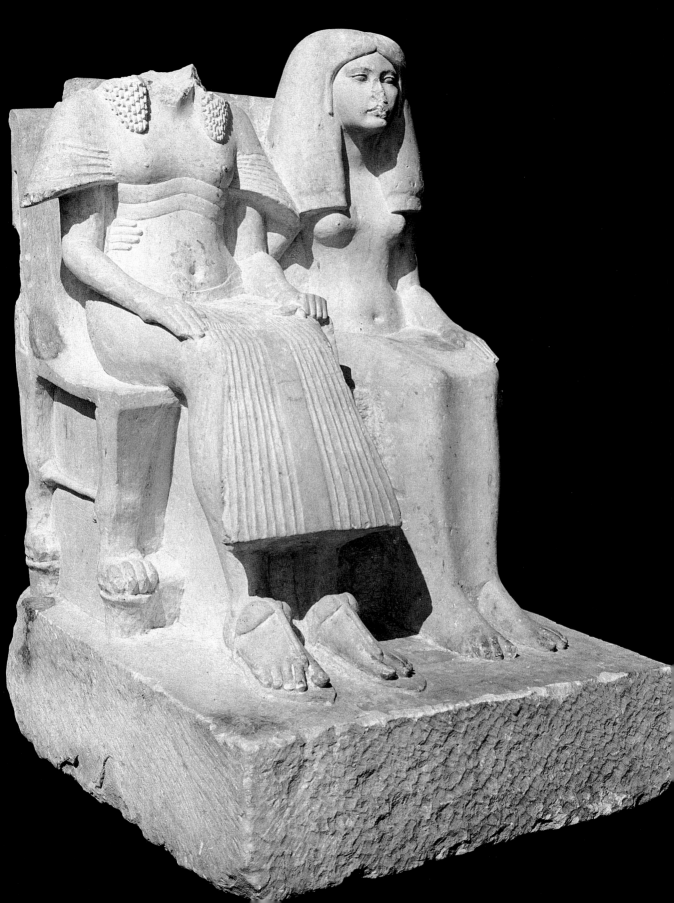

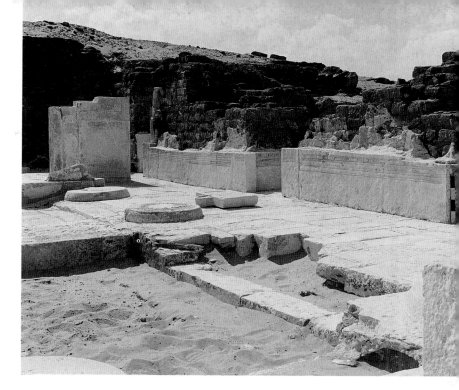

58 View of the southwest corner of the inner court of the tomb of Horemheb, showing the rim of the main tomb shaft leading to the substructure (in the foreground), a statue shrine, and the entrances to the cult room and its flanking chapels. This photograph was taken before the tomb was restored by the EES/Leiden Expedition and the Egyptian Antiquities Organisation.

was finished with these architectural elements we did not find any trace of them in the excavations. Once the cult of the tomb-owner was abandoned, no doubt the roofing slabs of the Offering Room and the bricks used for building the pyramid erected above were carted away for re-use.

In the Offering Room would have taken place the periodic cult services and offerings for the tomb-owner had he been buried in his tomb chamber below. As it was, services must have been carried out for his first wife, and doubtless also for his second (Queen Mutnodjmet), who was interred here as well. When we found it the Offering Room had been practically demolished, only some fragments of reliefs and texts surviving *in situ*. One fine block found nearby

59 A niche originally containing a statue of Horemheb and his first wife, positioned in the southwest corner of the inner courtyard of the tomb. In the foreground is a sunken area or impluvium, which collected and carried away rainwater after storms or flash floods.

57 (Opposite) A seated double statue of Horemheb and his first wife. The sculptor left the dyad partly unfinished, since the inscription on Horemheb's kilt and details of the curls of the wife's wig remained to be carved when the tomb was abandoned on Horemheb's accession to the throne.

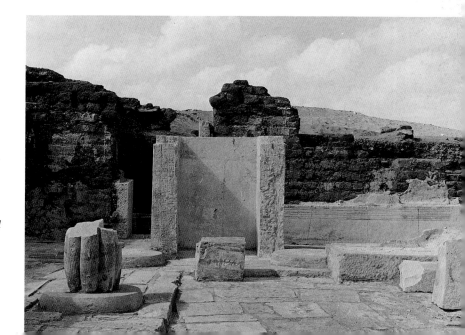

(which proves to join onto another which has been in Bologna since the early decades of the last century) certainly formed part of the scheme of decoration, apparently on the west wall. The conjoined blocks show Horemheb ploughing, sowing, and reaping in the Fields of Iaru, as the Egyptians called this region of the Underworld (*ill. 60*). It was the happy abode of the Blessed Dead, where crops grew to a stupendous height: a veritable paradise. The various areas of the Underworld were guarded by genii, some of whom in the present reliefs are being adored by the tomb-owner. In this instance the uraeus has been added to his brow to signalize his accession to the throne. Very probably all the walls of the Offering Room were decorated with mythological scenes.

### The entrance

The entry to the Offering Room has a tantalizing detail on its southern reveal: a representation of a human foot shown from a curious aspect. It may have belonged to Horemheb's wife or to a musician squatting beside his chair, since the tomb-owner was certainly depicted on the same wall, seated and facing out into the courtyard as if he were waiting to receive guests. A small relief fragment showing his head (with added uraeus) was found some metres away from the tomb at the end of the 1988 season of excavations. The ever-faithful Sementawy/Ramose is seen behind him on the relief *in situ*, the upper part of his figure being completed by a fragment in Baltimore, USA. The opposite north reveal of the doorway preserves the lower part of the legs of Horemheb and a female, presumably his wife (just possibly his mother), moving eastwards into the court, again as if to receive visitors. This emphasizes the close relationship between dwelling and tomb in Egyptian thought, the latter simply being the 'house' of eternity.

### Side-chapels

The side-chapels flanking the Offering Room do not seem to have been decorated, unless their plaster rendering originally was covered with painted mythological scenes. Both chapels had been used in the Late Period for burials.

## The Substructure

The subterranean parts of the tomb are no less interesting than the superstructure, even though they are uninscribed and largely undecorated. As has been mentioned above, the site of the New Kingdom necropolis seems to cover a much earlier cemetery dating back to the Pyramid Age of the late Fifth and Sixth Dynasties. In Horemheb's entrance pylon we found some fine reliefs of this period which certainly derived from demolished Old Kingdom mastaba tombs, the masonry from which was 're-cycled' by the later tomb builders. The architects of these latter tombs too were quite canny. Instead of going to the trouble of excavating new tomb shafts they simply re-employed, and in some cases altered, the shafts and chambers of the original mastabas. Horemheb's

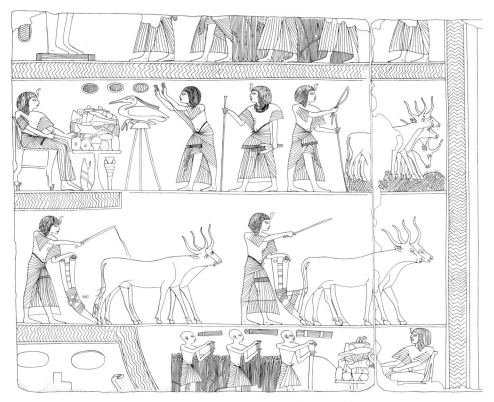

*60 Horemheb ploughing, reaping and threshing in the Elysian fields of the Underworld. A uraeus has been added to his forehead to show that he had acceded to the throne. The Egyptians visualized the Blessed Fields of the Beyond as being a greatly enhanced extension of the agricultural activities they had known in their earthly existence.*

great tomb covers the site of at least two such Old Kingdom tombs: Shaft i (in the First Courtyard), and Shaft iv (in the Second Courtyard), both being the original shafts of the mastabas in question.

### Shaft i and its treasures

This shaft, or rather the rooms leading off it, contained a number of burials of the Nineteenth Dynasty, to judge from the inscribed material found, which included two shawabtis or funerary figurines of the princess Binetanath (one of the daughters of Ramesses II), and a fine heart scarab with a text naming two persons (*ill. 61*). The interments were rich and important, but like all burials of consequence they had been plundered. By a miracle the robbers overlooked a gold earring of unique design, showing an Egyptian king as a sphinx, and decorated with granulation. The bead pendants with which it was once supplied are lacking. Very probably it is the work of a jeweller living in the late

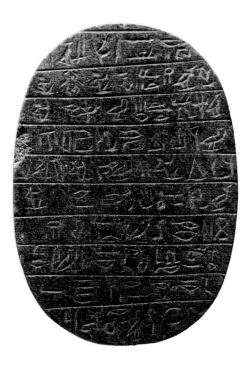

*61 A stone heart scarab engraved with the names of two persons. The scarab itself is an excellent example of its type, carved by a master craftsman. The hieroglyphic text, consisting of a standard extract from Chapter VI of the Book of the Dead, is crudely incised, a common occurrence on funerary objects even of the highest quality manufactured in the funerary workshops.*

Eighteenth Dynasty rather than the Nineteenth, and not necessarily an Egyptian. Aside from the splendid ornaments found in the tomb of Tutankhamun it provides us with one of the finest earrings of the time of that same Pharaoh. It could well have been deposited in Shaft i of Horemheb's tomb as a valued heirloom inherited by the princess Binetanath or another occupant of the burial chamber.

It would not be surprising if precious jewels were handed down from generation to generation, but is the same conceivable for fragile pottery? In the chambers of Shaft i we found quantities of sherds, many of them Nineteenth Dynasty or in some cases Coptic in type (the latter showing that the shaft had been entered in Christian times, when the tomb as a whole was taken over by monks from a neighbouring monastery). Foreign, imported pottery wares were also found here, and these have a fascinating story to tell.

### Imported pottery: its value for ancient chronology

One of several aims I had, when planning work in the New Kingdom necropolis at Saqqara, was to investigate Egypt's foreign contacts. As we have seen, the reliefs in the tomb of Horemheb are illuminating in this respect, but even humble pottery sherds have a crucial role to play. Egyptian chronology provides a basic framework for the chronology of much of the world of the ancient Near East. Foreign pottery wares found in closed or closely datable Egyptian contexts (usually tombs) can themselves be dated by reference to the

Egyptian findspots. In turn these wares can date strata in excavated Near Eastern sites. The process of constructing the chronology has been long and laborious, and the last word has by no means been said on the subject. In Shaft i of Horemheb's tomb fragments of painted Mycenaean pottery were found (reassembled to form three vessels). From the associated Egyptian objects these pots ought to date to the Ramesside Period, but some Aegean specialists would like to date them to the time of Akhenaten, about a hundred years earlier. The problem is not yet resolved, but our hope, now being realized, is that we shall continue to find more foreign pottery in the Memphite necropolis, not just in the uncontexted surface debris (where most of the sherds have been found up till now) but in tomb chambers, the contents of which can be closely dated. This is just one of many research possibilities on our site.

## Late burials in Shafts ii and iii

These are located on either side of the Offering Chapel. We found no traces of burials of the time of Horemheb in them; perhaps they were being kept 'in reserve' for members of his family or entourage. Like practically all the tomb-chambers we have investigated in the area over the years these had been entered in the Late Period and probably even in the Ptolemaic era; indeed, there is the possibility that they were hewn for the first time in the Late Period. Our researches over the past decade have shown that the superstructures of the larger tombs, especially Maya's, have been 'mined' with shafts of the Twenty-sixth and later dynasties. Intrusive burials of quite humble Memphite folk were laid to rest here in these times.

## Shaft iv: Horemheb's intended burial place

This shaft is located in the innermost court of the tomb, and the chambers in the bedrock beneath were designed to house the remains of Horemheb and his first wife, probably the lady Amenia whose name we have seen inscribed on a column in the courtyard above. When in the event Horemheb became Pharaoh, with a tomb at Thebes, his underground complex at Saqqara was taken over for the burial of the mummy of his second wife, Mutnodjmet, who was his consort as Queen of Egypt for at least the first thirteen years of his reign. She died without producing an heir.

The architect of the Memphite tomb was immediately faced with the problem of keeping the subterranean parts of the monument within the confines of the superstructure laid out on the desert surface above. If he had allowed his workmen to hew out the burial chambers beyond these confines there would have been the risk of penetrating into the substructure of an adjacent tomb, even though in the beginning Horemheb's tomb may have been relatively isolated in the desert. Contrariwise, Horemheb's substructure ran the risk of being entered accidentally when another tomb was erected alongside, which, once space was at a premium, was only a question of time. The architect solved this problem by 'corkscrewing' in effect (but not of course in actuality) to the required depth of 28 metres. He achieved his end by a series of shafts, corridors, and stairways. The main shaft itself descends to a depth of over 10 metres, when a high corridor opens off to the south. When we entered it in 1977 we found that much of the stone blocking, which had been put in after the burial (of Mutnodjmet presumably), was still in place. After the funerary priests had arranged the mummy and its equipment in position and the last rites had taken place, the masons charged with the duty of sealing the corridor part-filled it with limestone blocks to the level of the ceiling, and then plastered the exterior before ascending the shaft into the open air. Now it was the turn of the necropolis officials to descend to check that everything was in order. They did so while the plaster on the blocking was still damp, because we found many stamped impressions of their characteristic seal on the plaster. This object, another example of which was used to seal Tutankhamun's tomb and other royal and private tombs of the New Kingdom, showed the jackal god Anubis, guardian of the cemeteries, crouching over bound figures of the nine traditional enemies of Egypt. The mummy of Horemheb's first wife had been buried in the complex some years before, but we have no means of knowing if the corridor was originally sealed on that occasion and the blocking temporarily removed later on for the interment of Mutnodjmet.

The blocking of course had not prevented thieves from entering in antiquity. They emptied the shaft and made a small hole at the top of the blocking just big enough to squeeze through. It was then only a question of time before they found their way, as we did subsequently, to the burial chamber of Amenia and ultimately to the burial of the Queen. Along the way they encountered corridors blocked with stones and rubble, which all had to be partly removed and redistributed underground for ease of access. We found plenty of evidence of the plunderers' activities.

Having located the mummies they broke them up *in situ*, seized what they could in the Stygian gloom of the burial chambers, and hurried back and forth to the comparative light of the open main shaft to examine their plunder and to see what was worth retaining. No doubt they were in the main looking for precious metals and oils, as well as anything that could be sold, re-used, or reworked for profit. The robbers were not interested in objects such as shawabtis, statues, canopic jars, pottery, or purely amuletic figurines in common materials. These are the kind of things we ourselves always find scattered in the underground rooms of tombs or in the debris of the courtyards aboveground. No doubt the burial chambers of large and important tombs were entered and raked over again and again, a kind of gleaning operation once the original harvest had been reaped.

Following in the footsteps of the ancient robbers we know just how long and difficult it is to penetrate underground to the burial chambers. It would have been doubly difficult in antiquity when paving stones had to be removed to find the rims of shafts, the latter often very deep, which themselves had to be emptied of hard-packed rubble. Other shafts and corridors full of stones and blocks had to be negotiated, and all this without the aid of proper light. It is very hard to see how all this activity could have been carried out speedily and in total secrecy; moreover, a number of men and boys would have had to be involved in the operation. If one grants that some precious pieces could have been stolen during the funeral service itself (though with relatives and officials present and watching such objects could not have been large), we must assume that the burial chambers of tombs at Saqqara and elsewhere in Egypt would have been inviolate while the central government – and thus the necropolis administration – was strong and vigilant. We know that this was so for long periods of Egyptian history, but inevitably the necropolis guards became lax and the administration broke down. This was particularly so during the three so-called Intermediate Periods (c. 2181–2040, c. 1782–1570, c. 1069–712 BC), and also in the late Ramesside Period (c. 1185–1070 BC) when most of the royal tombs in the Valley of the Kings and the Queens' Valley at Thebes were broken into and plundered.

In view of the difficulties encountered by potential plunderers, as outlined above, it is to be wondered if some of the robberies in the great private tombs were government inspired. During periods of economic decline and civil unrest the main problem for the central administration was lack of gold. The huge cemeteries, not to mention the royal tombs, were in effect ready-made gold-mines, with large amounts of precious metals and other materials there for the taking. However the plundering was done, and by whom, the effect was to bring once again into circulation bullion that had lain sterile in some cases for hundreds of years.

Let us follow in the footsteps of the original robbers of Horemheb's underground complex, beginning beyond the blocked corridor of Shaft iv, described above.

### The underground rooms

Almost straightaway we find ourselves in a large rough-hewn antechamber, little more than a cave. In the far right corner a second shaft, now empty, drops some 6 metres. At the bottom we could see an entrance doorway. On descending the shaft (we eventually fixed a wooden ladder) we encountered a corridor. The doorway which we saw from above was once blocked and sealed. A tiny trace of a cartouche on the plaster over the lintel is possibly to be interpreted as one of the names of King Ay, successor of Tutankhamun. Since Ay reigned only four years (c. 1325–1321 BC) the date of the burial at the end of the corridor is fixed within that short period. The burial itself was almost certainly that of Horemheb's first wife. The corridor leading to the chamber was blocked after her interment, but the robbers had thrown the stones to one side, penetrated directly to the chamber, removed its precious objects and ransacked the mummy. We found only a few broken pottery saucers on which were written the name of Horemheb as Royal Scribe, and some fragments of shawabti figures. Doubtless these were Amenia's, but the texts on them are greatly faded and virtually illegible; the name, in any case, does not seem to be present. The coffin had been placed in a well-cut pit in the floor. The coffin itself, and other objects in the room, were of wood. The humidity had caused the remnants left behind by the robbers to break down over the millennia, and we found everywhere on the walls and floor and in the rubble a brownish film of decayed timber. Stains in the burial pit showed that during the interment a ritualistic unguent had been poured by the officiating priest over one end of the coffin.

Architecturally speaking the chamber was a great surprise. Before penetrating to it we did not know what to expect, since no great tombs of the New Kingdom had ever been fully excavated before in the Memphite necropolis. Theban precedents indicated that the burial chamber would be little more than an underground cavern with walls, floor, and ceiling roughly dressed or smoothed, and perhaps with a minimum of decoration. Amenia's chamber is rather more elaborate than this. The ceiling is barrel-vaulted, with stripes of painted decoration running lengthwise along it. At each end of the room there is a rock-cut false-door, through which the spirit of the deceased could pass to ascend to the upper parts of the tomb in order to receive the funerary offerings provided by her husband Horemheb, her family and her mortuary priests. A totally unexpected discovery came in the form of a rock-cut shelf or table. This is on the west side of the coffin pit, and is supported on legs in the form of stumpy columns with unusual scalloped capitals. The front of the table, facing the pit, was provided with a cavetto cornice like a shrine or temple. On the table, towards the north end, a small libation basin is inset into the surface. All in all the discoveries in the burial chamber were fascinating, and so far unique in Egyptian funerary archaeology. If this kind of elaborate arrangement was provided for his wife what kind of burial complex could the architect have made for the great commander-in-chief Horemheb himself?

## Horemheb's burial complex

In descending the shaft leading to Amenia's corridor we had already noticed an opening high up in the wall on the north side of the shaft. As expected we subsequently found that this was the entrance that led ultimately, by way of yet another corridor, a third shaft, and a complex of rooms, staircases, passageways, and a pillared hall, to that part of the tomb designed to house Horemheb's mortal remains. We have seen already that he was never buried there. Let us examine this part of the Saqqara substructure.

The third shaft, filled with hefty stone blocks, led by way of a short passage into a large room provided with false doors to north and south, as in Amenia's chamber. Perhaps the room was intended originally as the burial-place of Horemheb, but if so the plan was abandoned and the underground complex

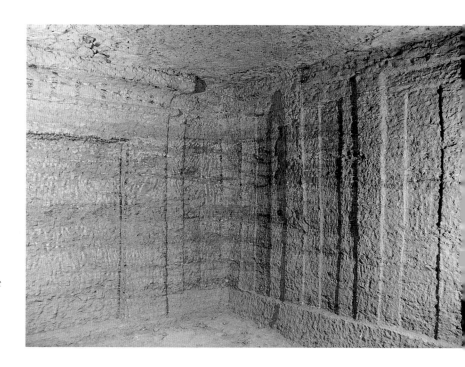

62 *Chamber H in the substructure of Shaft iv of Horemheb's tomb. The recessed or panelled walls are reminiscent of the decoration found on Old Kingdom sarcophagi. To north and south are false doors, with traces of linear decoration in paint.*

extended to form subterranean burial arrangements almost royal in concept. Perhaps the change of plan took place when Horemheb became Tutankhamun's regent. As an added embellishment the walls of the chamber now being described were carved with shallow elongated and recessed panels, resembling the so-called 'palace façade' decoration characteristic of the Archaic Period and Old Kingdom in particular. The 'palace façade' was also carved on the exterior walls of coffins. In the present room the overall effect is to make the chamber itself a gigantic sarcophagus, which would be appropriate if it had been originally designed for Horemheb's burial.

A doorway and stairs in the north-east corner of this room lead down towards another chamber with large but shallow embrasures on either side, originally blocked with stones, some of which are still in position. Such niches, in royal tombs, were intended to house amuletic figures whose function it was to ward off any potential harm to the mummy buried further inside the tomb. The intention was doubtless the same here, even though we found no trace of the figures themselves.

The doorway at the end of the room has an elaborate tympanum or oval-topped panel above, carved in the soft shaly rock. This door was once blocked with stones. Thence we walk through a short passage into a hall, the ceiling of which is supported by four squat pillars. When we first entered it much of the hall was choked with chippings from the original cutting of the underground rooms. These chippings had been set aside by the workmen, and were subsequently used to block the approach corridors, only to be removed and redistributed by the later plunderers. Mixed in with this rubble were quantities of charcoal. We carefully collected every scrap, the total weight being some $5\frac{1}{2}$ kilogrammes. Clearly the charcoal did not get there by chance; at this level we are about 21 metres below the surface of the ground. The probable explanation is that it was issued to the workmen who were cutting out the rooms from the bedrock. Charcoal is mentioned as having been distributed to the masons who cut the corridors in one of the royal tombs at Thebes, but there is still some doubt as to how the charcoal was used on that occasion. One suggestion is that it may have been burned to break up the rock and to make tunnelling easier, though only with risk to the workmen because of the fumes. Charcoal may have been so employed in the Valley of the Kings, but the rock at Saqqara is very much easier to remove with the conventional chisel. Some strata are so soft that the stone can be picked away with the fingers. Neither can the charcoal have been used in Horemheb's underground chambers to keep the masons warm. As the present writer knows only too well, the temperature at that depth is a fairly consistent 80 degrees Fahrenheit (27 degrees C), and the air is humid. Possibly the charcoal was used in some way for lighting, or in connection with the funeral service carried out at the burial of the mummy.

The pillared hall, when fully cleared of the accumulation of rubble, proved to be an impressive chamber, and totally unprecedented for a private tomb in the Memphite necropolis. Even so, this was not yet the last room in the substructure, because the destined burial chamber was to have been situated beyond the pillared hall. The workmen were still cutting the doorway for it when orders were given to down tools, perhaps on Horemheb's accession to the throne. The masons' diorite pounders, used in bruising the rock so that it could be speedily removed with a chisel, were thrown to the ground, where we found them, alongside the projected doorway, some three-and-a-half thousand years later.

By the time Horemheb came to the throne on the death of his erstwhile army colleague Ay, about the year 1321 BC, his great Memphite tomb was virtually complete; one chamber of it already contained the mummy of his first wife. Some historians believe that Horemheb married his second wife, Mutnodjmet, to legitimize his accession, she allegedly being the sister of Queen Nefertiti. There is no evidence to prove either assertion. The name Mutnodjmet is not particularly rare in the late Eighteenth Dynasty, and even if she were the sister of Nefertiti her marriage to Horemheb would have had no effect on Horemheb's legitimacy or candidacy since Mutnodjmet (who is depicted in the private tombs at El-Amarna) was not herself of royal blood. In any case, whatever her antecedents Mutnodjmet could have been married to Horemheb a little before he became Pharaoh.

The Memphite tomb in its finished state, like a miniature temple and with its splendid reliefs in pristine condition, must have been the finest private tomb of the age. When Mutnodjmet the Queen died what more natural than that she

THE TOMB OF HOREMHEB

should be buried in the tomb prepared for her husband when he was the chief official of Egypt under Tutankhamun? The Memphite tomb of Horemheb was not of course a royal one, either in plan or intention, but its underground arrangements were certainly more sumptuous than any tomb made for a queen consort of the Eighteenth Dynasty. Horemheb therefore seems to have determined to make her burial in Saqqara; his Memphite tomb may even have been in sight of the royal palace down below in Memphis.

## Mutnodjmet's burial

Since the rooms leading off the pillared hall were not even begun, a shaft was sunk between two of the pillars and a very rough and totally undecorated chamber was hewn out. There would have been plenty of room for a sarcophagus here, as well as the usual funerary furniture and equipment fit for a queen. Larger items would have been positioned in the hall above. All that we found were large quantities of broken amphorae and pottery storage vessels that would have contained foodstuffs and wine for Mutnodjmet during her sojourn in the Underworld. These potsherds had a story to tell, as we shall see.

We had already found, near the bottom of the main shaft giving access to the rooms we have been describing, a fragment of an alabaster vase inscribed with a funerary text for the chantress of Amun and King's Wife Mutnodjmet, as well as pieces of a statuette of her. We were thus already alerted to the probability that Mutnodjmet, even though a queen, was once interred here. The funerary vase in particular, since it bears her name and titles, would hardly have been used for the burial of some other person. Another piece of evidence that Mutnodjmet was buried in the Memphite area comes in the form of one of her canopic jars, now in the British Museum, the provenance of which is said to be Memphis. It is significant that the dealer who provided details of the provenance should have mentioned Memphis, where there were no known royal tombs of the New Kingdom, rather than the Valley of the Kings (or Queens) at Thebes, which in a sense would have been more logical.

Let us return for a moment to the pillared hall. As we cleared it, broken fragments of human bone began to appear around the rim of the shaft leading to the burial chamber. I myself collected every minute fragment because of the potential importance of the material, for once not leaving such delicate work in the hands of our skilled workmen. Expert analysis subsequently showed that the bones represented part of the skull and other portions of the body, including the pelvis, of an adult female who had given birth several times. Furthermore, she had lost all her teeth early in life, and was therefore only able to eat soft foods for much of the time. She died in her mid-forties, perhaps in childbirth, for with her bones were those of a foetus or newborn child.

The plunderers had evidently dragged the two mummies, mother and child, from the burial chamber below, and broken them open in the pillared hall above. Further robberies at a later date must have dispersed some of the bones.

The balance of probability, taking into account the evidence of the objects inscribed for Mutnodjmet, is that the adult bones are those of the queen herself, and that she died in attempting to provide her husband the Pharaoh with an heir to the throne.

When we sorted through the sherds in the burial chamber itself we found two pieces of pottery from wine amphorae, bearing ink dockets. Both bore the name of Horemheb, one with his prenomen, the other with his nomen. The prenomen was one of the five names assumed by the Pharaoh on his accession. His nomen was another of these, and the name by which he had been familiarly known before his assumption of the divine kingship. The former, or prenomen, text is the longer and in many ways the more important document, since it provides us with the probable date of the death of Mutnodjmet as well as the highest certain regnal year of her husband the king. The inscription reads as follows: 'Year 13 [1309 BC], third month of the inundation season. Very good quality wine from the vineyard of the estate of Djeserkheprure [Horemheb], beloved of Amun – life, prosperity, health! – in the house of Amun.' The docket also gives, as was customary, the name of the vintner and the district where the grapes were grown. So almost the last item we recorded and removed from the tomb of Horemheb provided us with new historical material, and augured well for the future, when we hoped to clear other large and important tombs of officials of the time of Tutankhamun and his successors in the Memphite necropolis.

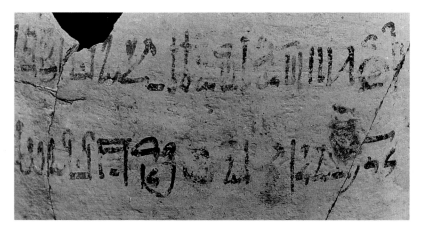

63 An hieratic text written in ink on an amphora from the main burial chamber in the tomb of Horemheb. The inscription is dated to Year 13 of Horemheb as pharaoh, and describes the contents of the vessel as being 'very good quality wine'. The name of the vintner and the place where the grapes were grown are also given in this important document.

V (Opposite) Detail from a painted coffin lid found in a cache of coffins and reed-mat burials in the tomb shaft of Iurudef.

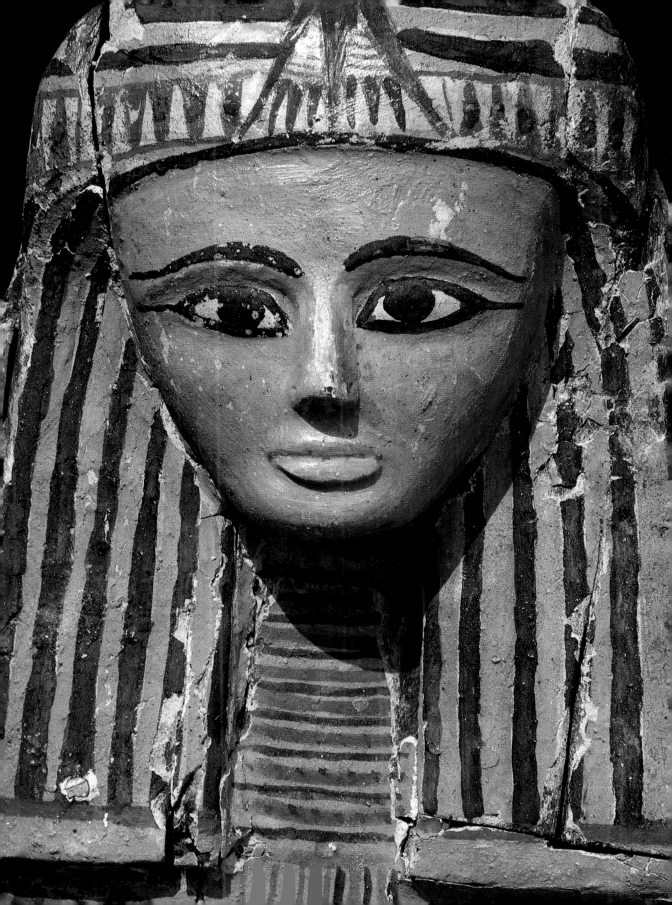

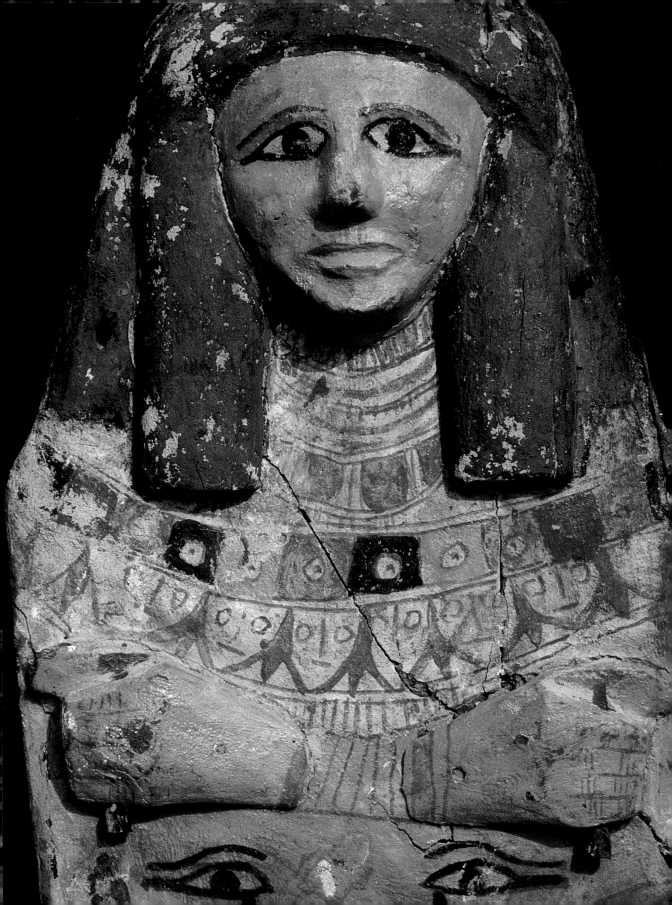

## CHAPTER FOUR

# THE TOMB OF TIA AND TIA: A ROYAL MONUMENT OF THE RAMESSIDE PERIOD

Horemheb's death in 1293 BC left the throne vacant. Being childless, before his death he had selected as his successor an old army colleague, Paramessu, who ascended the throne as Ramesses I, the founding father of a new dynasty, the Ramessides.

The new Pharaoh's reign was brief – only a year and a half. His son and successor was Seti I, a warrior king, one of whose tasks was to consolidate Egypt's frontiers and to strengthen its hold on its satellite dominions in Western Asia and in the south. In this he was evidently successful, and was able to bequeath to his son Ramesses II an immensely powerful and wealthy state on his death in 1278 BC. The arts flourished too in his fairly brief reign. His tomb in the Valley of the Kings is the most magnificent monument there; his alabaster sarcophagus, a masterpiece of the sculptor's craft, was brought to London in the nineteenth century, and can be seen in Sir John Soane's Museum in Lincoln's Inn Fields. Seti's mortuary temple at Abydos is one of the grandest buildings surviving from the ancient world. The subtlety of the relief carving is beyond praise. The artists, as always, are anonymous, but I believe it is likely that they were trained in the reign of Horemheb and in some instances even earlier: in the Abydos temple are many echoes of Memphite art as seen in the private tombs at Saqqara dating from the end of the Eighteenth Dynasty.

One such tomb was that of Horemheb but, since he became Pharaoh, never used by him. Years after his death it became, as we have seen under Ramesses II, grandson of Paramessu-Ramesses I, the focus of a funerary cult for the dead and deified Horemheb, the putative ancestor (in that he promoted Paramessu) of the new Ramesside dynasty. What more natural than that the princess Tia, sister of Ramesses II and granddaughter of Paramessu, should choose for the site of her tomb a plot adjacent to that of Horemheb in the desert at Saqqara?

## The princess and her husband

Tia married an administrative official of high rank, apparently not a relative, who curiously bore the same personal name as herself. There are indications,

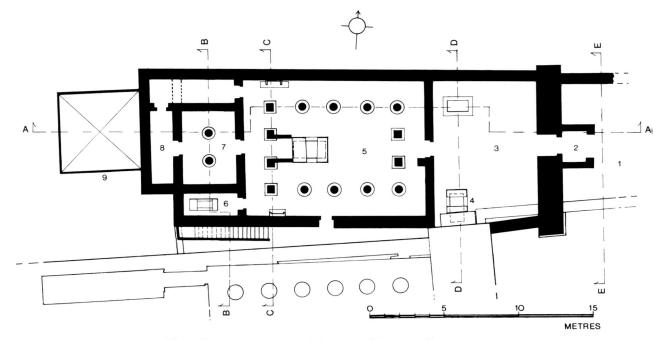

64 *Plan of the superstructure of the tomb of Tia and Tia.*

from our current excavations, that the great Memphite officials of the late Eighteenth Dynasty chose not to build their funerary monuments cheek by jowl, but preferred to leave convenient open spaces of desert around and between each. A measure of privacy was thus assured. The spaces were soon in-filled during the succeeding dynasty when ground in the necropolis was again becoming scarce. The architect of the tomb of Tia and Tia found a plot only partly occupied immediately adjacent to the north of Horemheb's tomb. The site must have been chosen quite deliberately by the princess and her husband to link themselves in some way to the great general, later Pharaoh, who had promoted their ancestor to royalty. It is not unlikely that the cult of Horemheb was instituted in his Memphite tomb about the same time as the architect was positioning the foundations of the tomb of the Tias.

Until our discovery of the tomb of Tia and Tia in 1982 it had been assumed that all members of the royal family in the New Kingdom (apart from the family of Akhenaten) were buried in the Valleys of the Kings and Queens in far-off Thebes. The finding of a prestigious Ramesside royal tomb in the Memphite necropolis was something of a surprise to us, but its presence there is a further indication of the importance of Memphis in the New Kingdom.

The tomb of Tia and Tia differs in many respects, both architecturally and iconographically, from the tombs of the grandees of the late Eighteenth Dynasty, though the basic elements of design are retained. Limestone was used throughout, but what shoddy workmanship is evident! Hardly a wall is straight, and there are scarcely any true right angles. Poor quality or faulty stone was employed, the defective areas being masked with plaster, which has fallen away in many places. The walls of the tomb are themselves not of solid stone, but are in the form of limestone orthostats set up side by side in parallel rows, the spaces between being filled with rubble and chippings. No doubt everything looked spick and span for a few years, but once the cult of the tomb owners fell into disuse – we do not know when this happened but it was probably within a hundred years or so of their decease – plunderers moved in and stripped the walls of much of the reusable stone, leaving for us a few fragmentary walls, a relatively well-preserved side chapel, and a 'mock' pyramid. The presence of the last in a New Kingdom Memphite monument was unexpected.

## The architecture of the tomb

Architects in ancient Egypt were experimenting all the time. If we turn to the individual architectural elements in the tomb of Tia and Tia we see the following: a paved forecourt leading by way of a small portico to a massive pylon gateway, giving onto an open court. A doorway in the centre of the west wall of the latter gives access to a large colonnaded area with a deep shaft in the middle, leading to the burial chambers. The roof of the colonnade of the courtyard was supported by a series of columns and piers, the latter square in

65 *View of the superstructure of the tomb of the Tias looking towards the west. In the foreground are the outer court and pylon, awaiting excavation. To the left is the tomb of Horemheb, and in the far distance the low-lying outlines of the Third Dynasty pyramid enclosure of Sekhemkhet.*

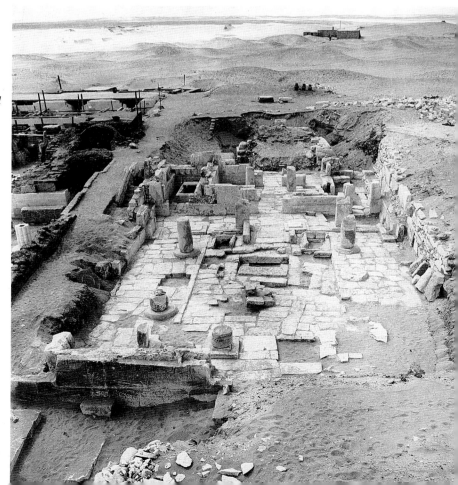

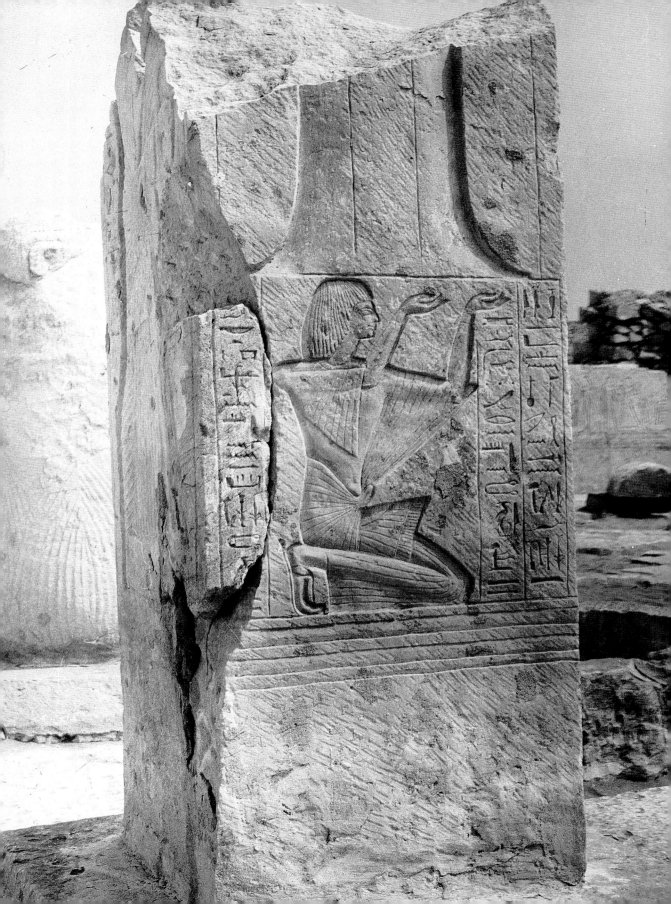

section, as will be seen from the accompanying plan. The west wall, with a central doorway leading into an antechapel with two columns, is flanked by side rooms. The most intimate part of the tomb as always is the cult room, where was positioned a great funerary stela, of which we found only fragments. The antechapel and cult chapel in effect form a single large room, with projecting walls on the west side partly masking the holy-of-holies where the mortuary priests would have officiated in the cult of the tomb-owners. The final element is a pyramid, its east face abutting onto the back wall of the cult room.

Some of these elements we have seen in Horemheb's tomb, and we shall encounter them elsewhere in the necropolis as we examine the tomb-chapels we have excavated over the past few years. Some things are new, however, and indeed innovatory. For instance, the idea of a porch or portico seems to have been introduced into the architectural repertoire of the Memphite tombs in the Nineteenth Dynasty. Such was lacking in the tomb of Horemheb; neither was it present in the tomb of Maya, with which we shall deal later. Egyptian colleagues, currently excavating important tombs of the New Kingdom on the desert edge to the east of our work, have also found porticoes in the Ramesside monuments they have uncovered.

The porch is the first element we see in the tomb of Tia and Tia. It is much destroyed, and only the lower part survives. It introduces visitors into the main pylon entrance of the structure, the jambs bearing representations of the princess's husband. The reveals or side walls of the entrance bear large-scale figures of the tomb-owner's brother, Ramesses II. The outer court beyond is largely destroyed. Two private tomb-chapels were located here. The northern-most is entirely destroyed, and the substructure and bedrock were in such a terrible condition that it was too dangerous to excavate. The remains of the southern chapel show that it belonged to one of the prominent members of the entourage of Tia and Tia, a scribe and steward called Iurudef. We shall see him depicted or named in several places in the main tomb. The presence of the two private chapels within the confines of what was in effect a royal tomb is indicative of the status of their owners. Though not members of the royal family themselves they had important connections at court through Tia and Tia.

The shaft and chambers of Iurudef's tomb were crammed with coffins and other material, and proved to be one of the most productive areas we have excavated in Saqqara in the past decade. We shall examine these shortly.

## The inner courtyard

Passing through a second pylon gateway, greatly destroyed, we emerge into a large open court, once colonnaded. The square-sided piers in it are interesting because on some of their faces Tia (the husband) is seen supporting the so-called *djed* pillar. Though depictions of the *djed* in a funerary context are well-

66 (*Opposite*) *The tomb-owner Tia raises aloft the* djed *column, the upper part of which is missing. His titles and those of his wife, one of the two sisters of Ramesses II, are given in the accompanying text.*

known, the tomb of Tia and Tia for the first time gives us examples, still *in situ*, of the piers on which the *djeds* are depicted. The exact nature of the *djed* is not fully understood; it may represent a lopped tree (for instance, part of a trunk of a palm) or possibly a notched stake. The king himself carried out a ceremony known as 'the erection of the *djed*-pillar', which was performed in honour of the Memphite god Ptah; Osiris, god of the Underworld, was also associated with the fetish. Officials (like Tia) would no doubt vie with one another for the honour and prestige of taking part in any ritual connected with the *djed*, not least those living and working in the Memphite area, in which Ptah was the pre-eminent deity. From the circumstance that our piers were found in their original locations it has been possible to study the orientation of the depictions, and this will further enable scholars interested in religious symbolism to work out the correct orientation of the unprovenanced and stray examples in the museum collections. Assuredly the orientation was significant to the ancient Egyptian architects and tomb-owners who, from the funerary and ritualistic standpoints, left nothing to chance.

Almost all the revetment or decorated wall surfaces of the court have gone. Some loose blocks found in the debris (actually placed neatly to one side in antiquity for eventual removal) have given us the opportunity of reconstructing part of the north wall. On it Tia (the husband) is shown adoring the goddess Isis. In fact, the various loose reliefs and cornice fragments we unearthed during the work have shown conclusively that the overall scheme of decoration in this tomb emphasized its marked resemblance to a mortuary temple. Because it *is* a royal tomb – since the princess Tia by birth, and her husband by marriage, were members of the royal house – we would not expect the same kind of iconographical representations as we find in tombs of government officials and private citizens. It is natural that the divine royal family should be shown worshipping the state gods, a theme stressed in the Memphite tomb of the Tias.

Part of the east wall of the court is well preserved, and on it we see Tia and Tia adoring and offering to Osiris, Horus, Isis, and Atum, the last-named an ancient god of Heliopolis. A gift of seven sacred oils is presented to the first-named deity.

When we cleared this court in 1982 we found two statues in position there: a triad in the south-east corner and a dyad against the east wall near the door. Since statues were focal points of the funerary cult the discovery itself was not especially remarkable, because all tombs of note were furnished with statuary. What renders these particular examples unusual is the fact that they are unfinished. The mason has barely roughed them out, but his ultimate intentions are certain: one would have emerged as a triad of deities (Ptah, Sekhmet, and Nefertem would have been appropriate in a Memphite setting), the other would have become a double statue, conceivably of the tomb-owners. Traces of red ochre on the stone, serving as markers, show where the skilled sculptor would have aimed his chisel. One would have expected that such notable tomb furnishings would have been finished in a workshop – in this case

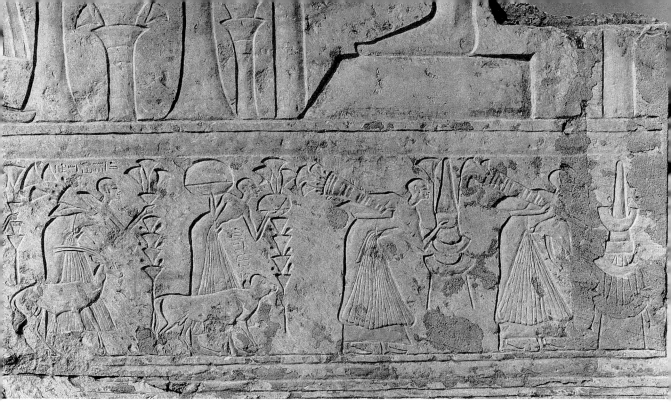

67 *A procession of offering bearers moves towards the offering room of the tomb of Tia and Tia. A calf and a young oryx form part of the sacrifice. Above, the tomb owner worships a deity.*

in nearby Memphis or just possibly in an atelier somewhere in the Saqqara necropolis. But since all the carving of tomb reliefs and inscriptions in tombs was done *in situ*, on blocks previously placed in position and 'dressed' by the masons, it would not surprise me if the Tia tomb statues were to have been completely worked in the monument itself. The preliminary roughing-out of the stone would have taken place in the quarry, to minimize the problem of weight and transport.

Most of the revetment of the south and north walls of the court is stripped away; the robbers in antiquity were particularly active in this tomb. We found the bottom part of a stela against the south wall. Its counterpart, originally forming part of the north wall, has been in the Egyptian Collection in Florence since the nineteenth century, and was doubtless extracted from the debris of the tomb by antiquities hunters.

The west wall of the courtyard shows offering-bearers, carrying their produce or leading sacrificial animals towards the main cult-chapel. This is one of the commonest iconographical themes in Egyptian tombs, but here, as always, the skill of the individual artist was brought to bear on a subject that theoretically was hackneyed. Some of the offering-bringers are shown leaning forward in a curious cringing posture. The beasts they bring for slaughter have endearing, even comical, expressions on their faces (*ills. 67–70*).

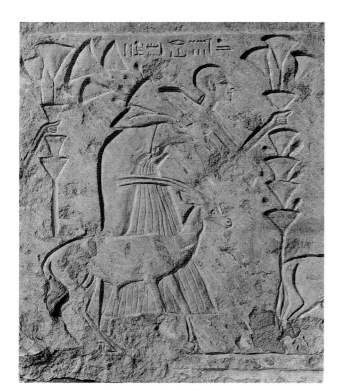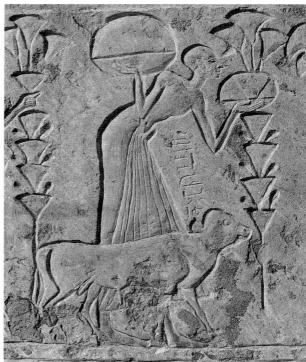

68,69 Details of ill. 67 showing (left) 'the servant Tjeneramun', who was in the entourage of Tia and Tia, and (right) the cringing pose of one of the offering bringers, who is named as 'the servant Djed-amun-nakhtu'.

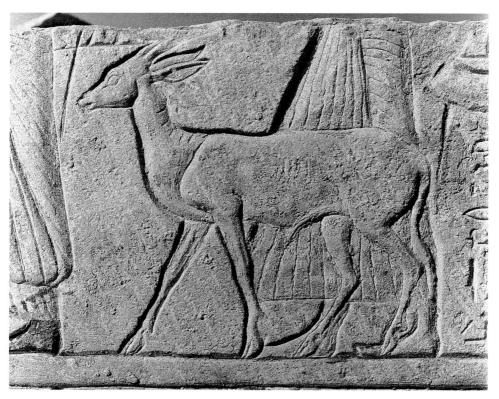

70 A young oryx is led forward to be sacrificed at the altar in the offering room of the tomb of Tia and Tia.

## The antechapel and cult chapel

We need not linger too long in the antechapel and main offering room of the monument, since most of the architecture in this part of the tomb was dismantled in antiquity. The south wall of the antechapel, though, is decorated with scenes showing the royal family, and gives us the name of one of the two daughters ([Mut]metennefer) of Tia and Tia, otherwise unknown to history.

The ancient stone plunderers were adept at dismantling the monument we are describing. Why they should have spared one room (on the south side of the antechapel) is a mystery, but robbers are habitually unsystematic in their work for several reasons: the availability of labour, the pressing factor of time, the possibility of being apprehended in the act, are but some. By chance, therefore, in the tomb of the Tias there survives to our time a remarkable chapel, not complete, but with a good deal of its decoration intact, which throws welcome light on the cult of the distinguished tomb-owners. It is situated adjoining the south wall of the antechapel.

## The Apis chapel (*ills. 71–74*)

On the left or south wall as we enter we see Tia and Tia in their funerary barge, which is being towed by another. Their ultimate objective is the ancient sacred site of Abydos, the centre of the cult of Osiris, god of the Underworld. In theory, but doubtless not too often in practice, the deceased was supposed to be transported to that place to worship at the temple of Osiris, or 'the staircase of the great god', as the texts so often call it. In the case of the Tias we see them not as mummified corpses under a funerary canopy but as living persons (or conceivably as statues). They are seated in state, their faithful steward Iurudef in attendance. The royal couple were clearly horse lovers: on board the towing barge are their two steeds in a specially constructed miniature stable. The vessel itself is manned by a captain or lookout, steersman, and matelots, some of whom are clambering about in the rigging. A few of them are named, lending actuality to the scene, and they may well have been in the employ of Tia and Tia in real life. Below, in the waters of the Nile, we see fish, a crocodile, birds and aquatic plants. This part of the relief is very reminiscent of certain river and marsh scenes in mastaba tombs of the Old Kingdom. The gifted artist of our relief, working in a New Kingdom 'genre' tradition, probably had access to one or other of the great Saqqara tombs of the Fifth or Sixth Dynasties (already ancient monuments in the time of Ramesses II when the tomb of the Tias was being decorated). The mastaba of Mereruka, just to the north of the pyramid of Teti, is one of several examples in the necropolis. Such aquatic scenes, though unusual in the New Kingdom, are not uncommon in the Old Kingdom.

Opposite, on the north wall of the chapel, a very well preserved scene shows Tia and Tia behind a lavishly bedecked offering table, adoring a procession of deities, including some of those associated with the Abydos cemetery. The

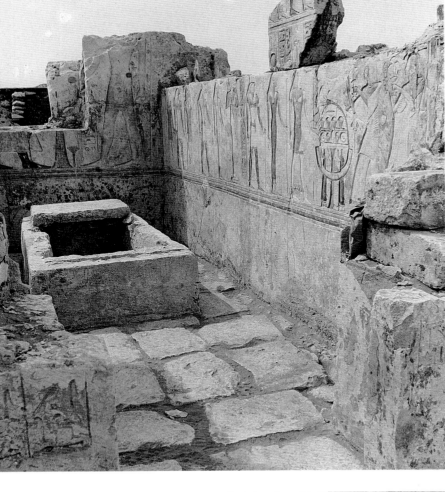

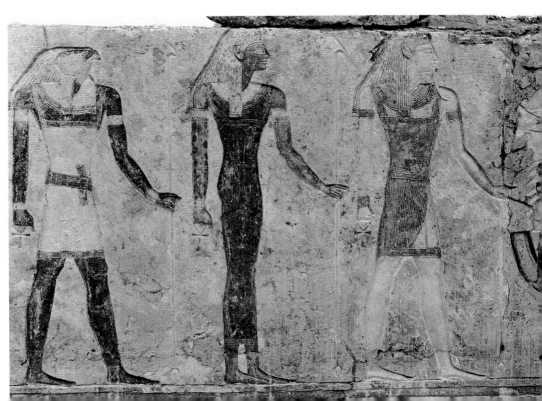

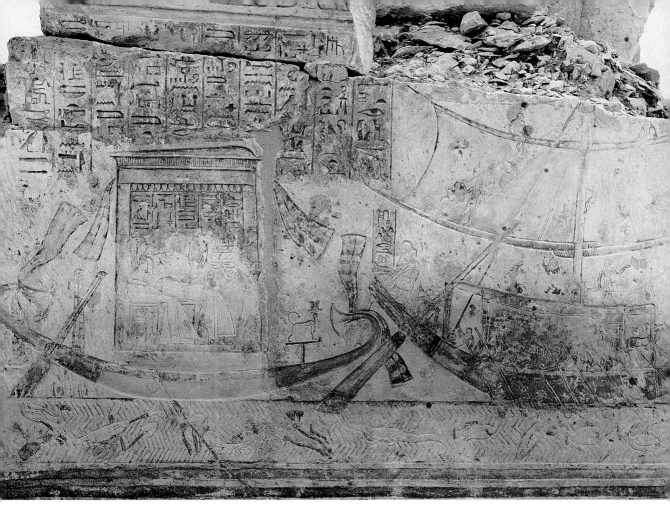

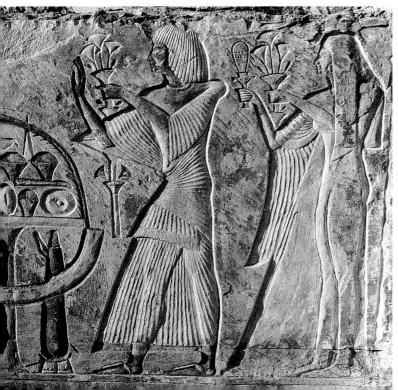

71–74 (Opposite, above) *Chapel A in the
tomb of the Tias, looking west. The plinth
at the back of the room originally
supported a statue of an Apis bull, a
limestone fragment of the hindquarters of
which was discovered at the entrance to the
chapel, in the foreground to the right.*
(Above) *Tia and his wife make a voyage
along the Nile to Abydos as part of their
funerary ritual to worship at the temple of
Osiris. They are seated in the boat to the
left, in a shrine positioned amidships. Their
vessel is being towed by another, manned
by rowers. The Tias' faithful servant
Iurudef stands in the stern of the leading
boat, which also contains a miniature stable
with two horses.* (Opposite, below) *Part of
a procession of deities. The gods Osiris-
Andjety, Isis and Horus are depicted on this
part of the relief.* (Left) *Tia and Tia,
standing behind an altar loaded with
offerings, adore the procession of deities.
Both hold bouquets, and the princess also
shakes a sistrum, a musical instrument, in
honour of the gods.*

carving and painting on that part of the relief adjacent to the entrance is remarkably fine, and recalls contemporary work in the temple of Ramesses II at Abydos. Indeed, the same artists could have executed both series of reliefs.

Much of the decoration of the north wall was, however, once masked by the statue of a bull, almost life-size and mounted on a plinth in the centre and towards the back of the chapel; we found a fragment of the hindquarters of the bull statue near the entrance. The artists, knowing full well that it would be difficult for any officiant or visitor to squeeze past the statue once it was in position, skimped their work on the adjacent north wall (possibly too on the relevant part of the south wall, though this has mostly gone). The figures of the gods here are rather summarily carved, and the pigment is applied in a slovenly fashion.

Though none of the surviving texts in the chapel alludes to it the bull must represent Apis, the incarnation of the great creator god Ptah of Memphis. After death and burial in the catacombs of the Serapeum (within twenty minutes' walking distance north-west of our site) the Apis became the Osiris Apis (or Osirapis, the Serapis of the Greeks), and his cult was one of the most potent in Egypt, particularly in the later stages of its history. The presence of Apis in a royal tomb in the Memphite necropolis is exciting, and throws new light on the mortuary cults as practised in the Ramesside Period.

The catalogue of fascinating new facts given by the excavation of the tomb of Tia and Tia, however, is not yet exhausted. The substructure, which was totally undecorated and hardly more than a cavern in the rock, certainly housed the burials of the princess and her husband, and there was room besides for other members of the family. Curiously, though, we found no inscribed objects here for the Tias' children. As usual, the plunderers had done their worst. Fragmentary objects were recovered, and from them we were able to build up a picture of the tomb furnishings, originally no doubt sumptuous. A shawabti figure of an unusual type, with glass inlays, was one of the pieces encountered, and there were several fragments of a handsome granite sarcophagus inscribed for the princess's husband. A sizeable piece of the same object had found its way, in the nineteenth century, into the Egyptian Collection of the Ny Carlsberg Glyptotek in Copenhagen, and actually joins onto one of the fragments we found below ground in 1982.

### The pyramid

Apart from the Apis chapel the most intriguing architectural feature we found connected with the tomb of the Tias was a pyramid, and it is to this that we turn before quitting the monument. The pyramid, roughly built of rubble encased with limestone, is set somewhat askew and to the west of the offering chapel of the tomb. It occupies part of a demolished courtyard of the tomb-chapel of Ramose, which we shall glance at in due course. One may well ask what a pyramid, not usually associated with New Kingdom tombs, is doing in this

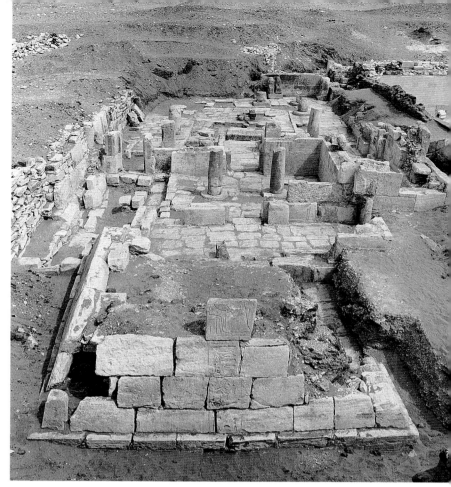

75 *The tomb of Tia and Tia: view of the superstructure looking eastwards in the direction of the Nile and Memphis. In the foreground is a small pyramid, partly preserved, built behind the offering room. When this photograph was taken the outer court and main pylon entrance of the tomb towards the east had yet to be revealed.*

context. Pyramids are of course the archetypal funerary monuments of kings and other royalties of the Old and Middle Kingdoms (and of the Nubian rulers of the Twenty-fifth Dynasty). Like so much else connected with the royal funerary cult the pyramid, or at least a miniature version of the more famous and grandiose examples, was taken over by private persons in the New Kingdom. In the Theban necropolis tiny chapels topped by mud-brick pyramids were erected on the surface above the rock-cut chambers of the tombs. In the contemporary Memphite necropolis, where the free-standing tombs were built in the form of small temples as we have seen, the pyramid, still in mud brick, was built atop the stone roofing slabs of the main chapel at the west end of the structure. This is quite clear from representations of Saqqara tomb-chapels in Eighteenth Dynasty reliefs. In the succeeding Ramesside period, when important tombs were built wholly of stone, the pyramid was transferred from the chapel roof (where it would have been too heavy) to an area of ground adjacent to the west. Such is the case in the tomb of the Tias. Egyptian colleagues, digging to the east of us on the edge of the escarpment, have similarly found stone pyramids attached to the large Ramesside tombs they have cleared over the past decade.

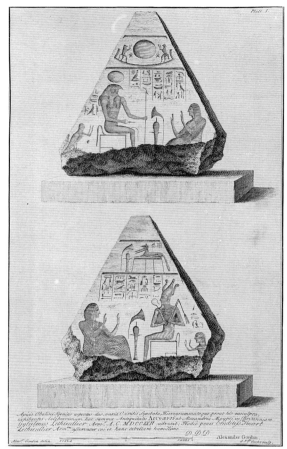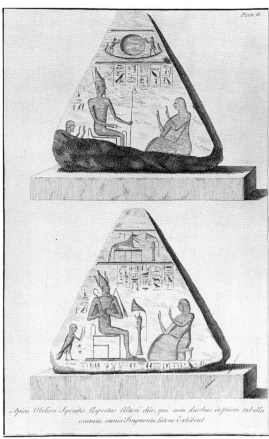

*76 The four sides of the lost pyramidion of Tia and Tia, as drawn and published in the eighteenth century by Alexander Gordon. Originally it was positioned at the apex of the pyramid constructed behind the offering room of the tomb.*

The New Kingdom tomb pyramid was a 'mock' one, in that no provision was made for a burial inside it. Indeed, the examples so far excavated at Saqqara are of solid masonry with a fill of rough stones. However, the tomb chambers below ground ideally ought to have been situated directly beneath the cult room and its associated pyramid. An essential part of the latter was the pyramidion, or capstone, on which the rays of the sun alighted in the early morning.

### The lost pyramidion of Tia and Tia (*ill. 76*)

By a curious chance of history the capstone of the pyramid of the Tias has been known to science since the eighteenth century. It was first published in 1737–9 in a collection of plates, without printed text, by a Scottish traveller and author,

Alexander Gordon. Indeed, the pyramidion, which was brought to this country from Alexandria in 1722, must be among the earliest Egyptian antiquities to have reached Great Britain. Gordon illustrates each of the four sides of the pyramidion, and although the engravings were made a hundred years before the decipherment of hieroglyphs, at a time when scarcely anything was known about Egyptian art and architecture, the signs on the published drawings are fairly easy to make out. There is no doubt that Tia and Tia were the owners of the pyramidion, and that it must originally have come from their Saqqara tomb. The pyramidion was referred to in publications more than once down to the end of the eighteenth century, after which it disappears from history. The last recorded 'sighting' was in 1792, by which time it was standing in the garden of the residence of Sir James Tylney Long, Baronet, at Wanstead in Essex. At that juncture it seems to have served as an item of garden furniture. The house was demolished long ago and the estate swallowed up in a vast modern cemetery covering many acres. Can it be that the long-lost pyramidion of Tia and Tia, carved in the thirteenth century BC in the reign of Ramesses the Great, Pharaoh of the Oppression, has been incorporated into the decoration of a nineteenth-century tomb in England? It is not impossible, though all efforts to locate the pyramidion have so far been fruitless. This means that for the first scientific publication of the tomb of the princess and her husband, which is now being written, we shall have to refer to, and make illustrations from, a volume known to few scholars and published exactly two and a half centuries ago! This is a timely reminder that the material and monuments Egyptologists are recording today may well be the only source of reference for future generations.

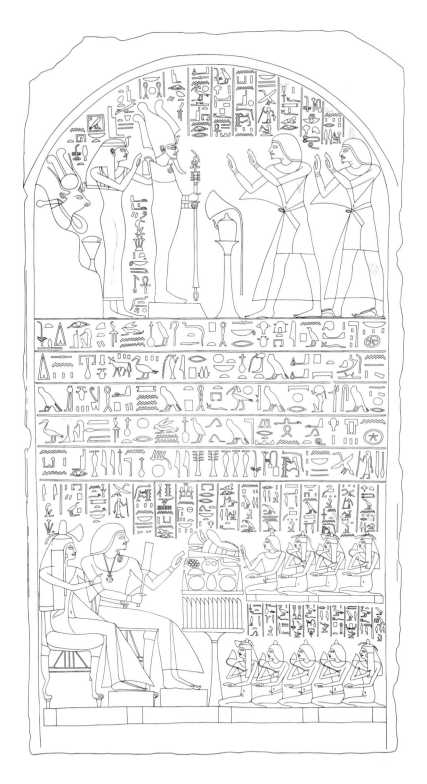

77 *Stela of Paser. In the lunette or upper part the owner and his brother Tjuneroy worship Osiris, Isis and Hathor, lady of the Southern Sycamore, a temple in Memphis. In the register at the bottom Paser and his wife Pypwy are seated in the presence of their family. From this stela the beginnings of a genealogy of a prominent Memphite family can be constructed.*

CHAPTER FIVE

# MINOR TOMBS IN THE MEMPHITE NECROPOLIS

We have seen how the great tombs of the New Kingdom in the Memphite cemeteries are full of information on various aspects of public and private life as well as the Hereafter. But one of the objectives of our mission has been to shed light not only on the careers of high administrative officials and army officers of rank but also on minor functionaries and craftsmen.

It was to be expected that we would find the burials of relatives and dependants in and around the tombs of the great ones. We were surprised, though, to find tomb-chapels of persons ranking relatively low in the administrative hierarchy built side by side in the necropolis with some of the most prestigious funerary monuments of the New Kingdom, such as those of Horemheb, the Tias, and Maya. It will be interesting to see if this state of affairs is restricted to the small area of the desert we have opened up so far or whether, as I suspect, it will apply over the entire necropolis.

From the surviving texts in the minor tombs there is no indication that their owners were related to the great officials. They may in real life have been neighbours or dependants in the city of Memphis, and simply perpetuated this circumstance in the next world. Some of them could have been on the 'payroll' of the family of the deceased, serving as mortuary priests and attendants at the tomb after the death of the great tomb-owners. The texts in the small tomb-chapels do not hint at this. All the ones we have excavated so far are inscribed with the names and titles of minor officials and tradesmen, but in theory there would have been nothing to prevent them taking on the duty of making offerings of food, drink, and incense at the high officials' tombs on the stipulated feast days.

Though we found that the burial chambers of the small tombs had inevitably been robbed in antiquity – some of them must have contained objects made of precious metals and other commodities worth plundering – the superstructures on the whole have survived reasonably well. There was not a great deal of stonework in them worth demolishing for re-use, and the stone in any case was usually not of high quality in the first place. In this respect the architecture of the small tombs contrasts with the fine limestone revetments of the monuments of the high officials, at least those of the late Eighteenth Dynasty. Those of the Nineteenth, though outwardly splendid when in a finished state, were in fact jerry-built of somewhat inferior limestone, which easily flaked and fractured on continuous exposure to the elements.

Let us examine the small New Kingdom tombs we have found so far in the Memphite necropolis, to see what kind of information they yield on the inhabitants of Memphis in the period of a century and a quarter spanned by the reigns of Tutankhamun and Ramesses II. We shall study them not in the order in which they were excavated but in chronological sequence.

### The tomb of Ramose, a military man

Ramose's chief title was a military one – he was deputy of the army – and he seems to have lived at the end of the Eighteenth Dynasty, so he was a contemporary of Horemheb and Maya. His mud-brick tomb originally consisted of two large open courtyards with an offering room at the west end flanked by two chapels: the archetypal Memphite New Kingdom tomb plan in fact. The stone elements in the building were stelae, door jambs, and door sills. The offering room too was lined with slabs of limestone, but whether these bore texts or scenes we shall never know because they have all been stripped away. A flake was found loose in the debris of the tomb, with Ramose's name and title written in red: the sculptor's chisel has never touched it. This may be an indication that Ramose died prematurely and before his funerary monument could be finished. The main stela or focus of the funerary cult may well have been still in position in the offering room in the last century. At any rate it was taken from Saqqara, probably in the 1820s, and is now part of the fine Egyptian Collection in East Berlin. It bears the name and titles of Ramose, who is seen above in a shrine supported by the jackal-headed god Anubis or a priest representing him. It is always satisfying to be able to assign a precise provenance to a piece in a collection, but how did we know that the Berlin stela was part of Ramose's tomb? The answer is: because we ourselves found the lower part of another stela of his in position against the west wall of the outer court of his tomb. The fragment is exceedingly pitted and weatherworn, so much so that at first we despaired of reading anything on it. Soon, however, our philologist was able to make out certain elements of the name and title of the owner on the bottom line of the inscription. It was then easy to check in reference works to see if any other pieces or objects from Ramose's tomb were known. The Berlin stela, which has the same name and titles as our stela fragment, could thus be re-allocated to the newly excavated Saqqara monument. It is very unlikely that Ramose would have set up his stela anywhere else. From such a patchwork of information we are beginning to build up a corpus of knowledge about the tombs and their owners, from material found *in situ* and from pieces found in the last century and now in museums all over the world.

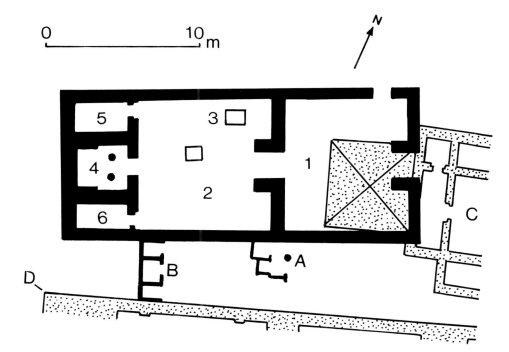

78 Plan of the superstructure of the tomb of Ramose, showing its relationship to the tomb-chapels of Khay (A), Pabes (B), Tia and Tia (C) and Horemheb (D). (1) Outer court, mostly overbuilt by the pyramid of the Tias. (2) Inner court with main shaft in the centre. (3) Shaft which gave access to the substructure of the tomb by way of a robbers' tunnel in 1986. (4) Offering room. (5,6) Side chapels.

For the maintenance of the cult of the dead and for the repair of the tombs the deceased officials relied on their relatives if they had any and on their paid mortuary priests. Ramose's tomb fared rather badly some time after his death. The outer court was taken down brick by brick, and over the site was erected the stone pyramid of the princess Tia and her husband, members of the royal family of Ramesses II. It would be pleasing to think, though we cannot prove it, that the Ramose whose tomb we have found was the same Ramose who is named in the adjacent tomb of Horemheb. In the latter's tomb he is called the private secretary of Horemheb as well as scribe of the army. If the two Ramoses are identical, which is not at all unlikely, by the time he came to prepare his Saqqara tomb he had risen somewhat higher in the echelons of the army, perhaps through his association with the greatest military man of his day. There can be no certainty in the matter. Indeed, earlier in this book, we speculated whether the Ramose in Horemheb's tomb was none other than Paramessu, the future Pharaoh Ramesses I.

We have a very good idea, now that we have cleared Ramose's tomb, of the architectural layout of what is probably a typical Memphite tomb-chapel of an official of middle rank in the time of Tutankhamun and slightly later. Ramose's funerary monument is a much simplified version of the tombs of his great

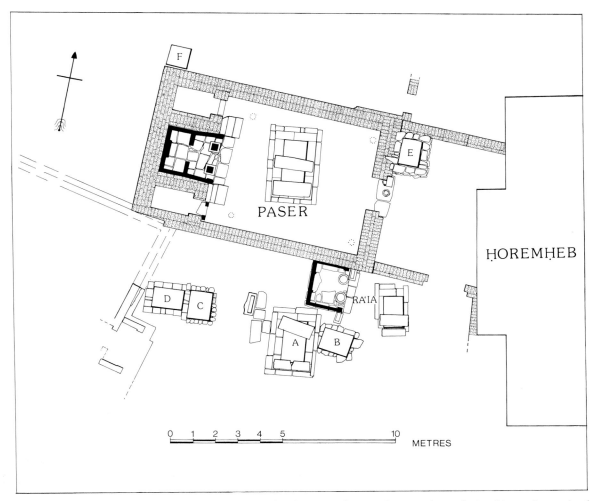

*79 Plans of the superstructures of the tomb-chapels of Paser and Raia, showing their relationship to the tomb of Horemheb. The letters A to F represent shafts of tombs which have been demolished in antiquity.*

contemporaries Horemheb and, as we shall see, Maya. There must be dozens of tombs like Ramose's buried under the sand in the Saqqara necropolis, awaiting location and examination. One of the two shafts in the main court of his tomb breaks into the subterranean parts of a neighbouring monument, and our investigations here in 1986 and later have opened up a very exciting new chapter in the history of Memphis and indeed of the history of Egypt as a whole, in the time of Tutankhamun. This discovery is dealt with in Chapter 6.

### The tomb of Paser

Paser, who was a builder in the reign of Ramesses II, came of a well-known Memphite family, well-known that is in his own day and, curiously enough, in modern times. This arises from the fact that a large stela, giving details of Paser and his family, has been known to Egyptologists for a century and a half. This stela, clearly from Saqqara even before we reassigned it to the tomb-chapel we are about to discuss, entered the British Museum Collection in 1835. Scholars have been interested in it from the fact that Paser was shown on the stela to be the brother of a certain lector-priest, Tjuneroy, whose tomb we have yet to find, although it must be somewhere in the area of Paser's. Before we examine the importance of Tjuneroy's burial place, let us glance at the monument of his brother, which we located and cleared immediately to the west of Horemheb's tomb in 1980.

Paser's monument is somewhat later in date than Ramose's tomb-chapel, but in plan it is not at all dissimilar. Like Ramose's it is built of mud brick, though with only one open court rather than two. At the west end of the court is the expected cult chapel or offering room, flanked by side chapels. We found that this part of the tomb had been demolished, and the limestone revetment of the offering room was smashed and scattered around. We were able to reassemble it, and as with Ramose's tomb we can now easily picture the original appearance of a typical Memphite tomb-chapel of a person of middle rank, this time in the reign of the long-lived Ramesses II. This tradition of tomb building at Saqqara thus had a history of at least a hundred years. Later

*80 The tomb-chapel of Paser, looking west in the direction of the offering room, central stela, and side chapels. The large stela on the right was purchased in 1835 by the British Museum. In the foreground is the shaft leading to the burial chambers, with two covering slabs still in position.*

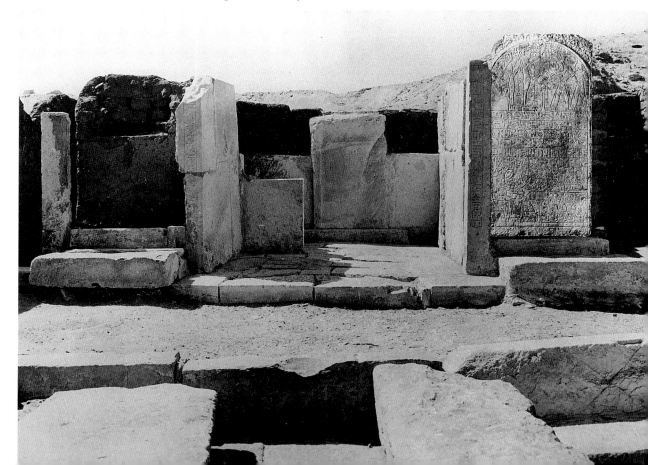

## GENEALOGY OF PASER

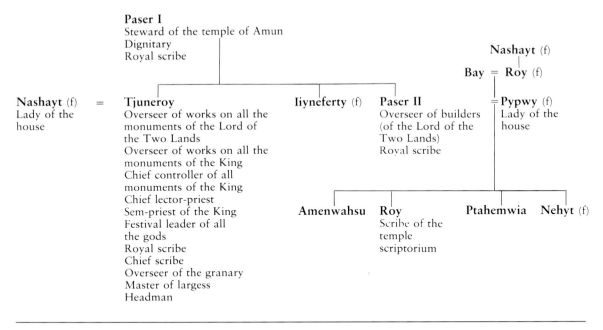

Ramesside tombs, as we shall see, appear not to have conformed to such a standard or uniform plan, and moreover were built, by and large, of limestone rather than of mud brick.

It would have been expected that a builder with connections at court (through his brother Tjuneroy) would at least have finished his own tomb before his death. Evidently Paser did not. The large stela which we found thrown down, but which was originally fixed to the west wall of the cult room, was decorated in outline only. The sculptor who should have completed the work made only a few desultory attempts to chisel some of the outlines. And this stela was supposed to be the focal point of Paser's funerary cult after his death! Perhaps he was too busy building other officials' tombs at Saqqara to be in a position to supervise the completion of his own monument efficiently. Or of course he may have died prematurely, and his family neglected to complete the stela. In any case Paser had at least two other stelae, in front of each of which would have been a table for offerings. One of these stelae we are still lacking; the other, which stood on the north side of the court against its west wall is the stela in the British Museum, referred to above. A photograph, superimposed on the architecture of the court after we had restored it (*ill. 80*), shows how it would have looked in Paser's own day.

By careful clearing and brushing in the court in which the stela stood we were able to show that originally four small trees or bushes were planted there, one in each corner. The foliage on these would have given welcome shade to the spirit of Paser, as well as to the spirits of his family who were buried with him.

The Egyptians visualized the 'shade' of the deceased as being a small human-headed bird. As such it was able to flutter up the tomb shaft to observe the comings and goings in the world above, forsaken, reluctantly no doubt, by the deceased.

The underground part of Paser's tomb was simple in the extreme: rough-cut rooms with no decoration at all, in which the sarcophagus of the owner and his funerary goods were placed. These rooms had been ransacked at an unknown date after the death of Paser, and the complex was re-used for burials of impoverished Memphite citizens, apparently mostly during the Thirtieth Dynasty, the last royal house of purely Egyptian origin (fourth century BC), or slightly earlier.

## Tjuneroy, a prominent Memphite citizen

Inscribed slabs from the tomb of Paser's brother Tjuneroy entered the Cairo Museum Collections in the last century. Evidently they came from the Saqqara necropolis, but the tomb was never properly cleared and recorded, and its exact position remains unknown to this day. The fact that the most important part of the tomb-chapel was a list of Egyptian kings from the First Dynasty down to the reign of Ramesses II, in whose reign Tjuneroy flourished, renders important a monument that might otherwise be commonplace. The most complete list of Egyptian rulers known to scholars is the Turin Canon of Kings, so called because the tattered and fragmentary papyrus on which the names of the kings are written is housed in the Egyptian Collection at Turin. It too dates from the reign of Ramesses II, as do most of the other surviving Egyptian king-lists. The Ramesside royal family was *parvenu*, with no known royal ancestors, and it is not surprising that the proud and powerful dynasty would wish to attach itself to the potent pharaohs of the past. Mortuary cults of deceased kings were established by Ramesses II, and the selective list of monarchs inscribed in Tjuneroy's Saqqara tomb was no doubt drawn up on the orders of the royal court at Memphis. One of Tjuneroy's main duties was to officiate as chief lector-priest of the dead and deified rulers. As with other king-lists certain pharaohs, such as Hatshepsut, and Akhenaten and the other monarchs tainted by Atenism (including Tutankhamun), were excised from the official canon of rulers. The slabs on which the royal names are carved, as now mounted in the Cairo Museum, are out of context, and it would be of considerable interest to see how the king-list fitted into the overall scheme of decoration of Tjuneroy's monument, and indeed to see what other details of his family and his official duties were recorded there. Perhaps we ourselves will be lucky enough to locate the tomb in the future. It would not be surprising if families were buried near one another; Tjuneroy's monument ought not to be too far from his brother Paser's. The four canopic jars that once contained Tjuneroy's viscera are in the Brooklyn Museum, New York, so it looks as though the tomb-chambers were entered in the last century, unless the jars were found in the debris of the superstructure of the tomb. In any case it is doubtful if the clearance of

Tjuneroy's tomb-chapel was systematic, and there must be other valuable data there waiting to be uncovered. It would be instructive to see, for example, if the post of lector-priest of the ancient kings passed from father to son in Tjuneroy's and Paser's family, or indeed if any other of Tjuneroy's several administrative titles were inherited by any descendants he may have had. The genealogy on p. 122 demonstrates how the beginnings of a family tree can be built up on the evidence at present available, both from our own work in Paser's tomb and from documents known previously.

From the size of his tomb one gets the impression that Tjuneroy's brother Paser was not a builder of the first rank – one of those charged with the construction of a mighty temple or of a royal monument, for example. Rather, he probably spent his life in day-to-day contact with building workers constructing houses perhaps, both of the living and of the dead, and was involved with minor public works. After a lifetime in this profession he would hardly have wanted to find himself in the next world in the position of a day labourer digging canals, irrigating fields, or humping hods of bricks in a building site. This was a risk that even high officials ran; but all functionaries, Paser (and doubtless Tjuneroy) among them entered the Netherworld confident in the belief that their shawabti (substitute labourer) figures would do all these things and more on their behalf.

### The tomb of Raia, a Memphite musician (*ills. 81–88*)

The tiny stone-built chapel of Raia is tacked onto the south side of the outer wall of the court of Paser's tomb. Raia held the position of chief of singers of Ptah-lord-of-Truth in the city of Memphis. Very little is left of the great temple of the creator god Ptah, the scene of Raia's daily activities; a few tumbled stones, practically submerged in water for part of the year, are all that remains of one of the largest religious buildings in ancient Egypt.

So small is Raia's tomb-chapel that a visitor (or an officiant in former times) can just about stand upright in it; a mortuary priest would have had room to perform his ritual functions with hardly any room to spare. The chapel itself is square, the front being open, with two columns set askew in the entrance. A stela set against the west wall is an integral part of the decoration of the tomb. The roof no doubt consisted of slabs of limestone laid flat, which in turn supported a small brick pyramid. We now know this to have been a characteristic architectural feature of tomb-chapels of the Ramesside Period in the Memphite necropolis, and there must have been a veritable 'forest' of small pyramids in the Saqqara cemeteries in the reign of Ramesses II, the period in which Raia lived, and even earlier, in the late Eighteenth Dynasty. Raia was a contemporary of Paser and Tjuneroy, though whether he was a relation of those officials or a neighbour of theirs in the city of Memphis is unknown. It is to be suspected that there was some relationship from the fact that Raia's tomb adjoins Paser's. There is no reason to doubt that the two tomb-chapels are

## The Tomb-chapel of Raia

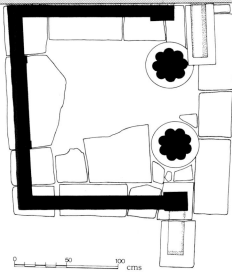

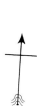

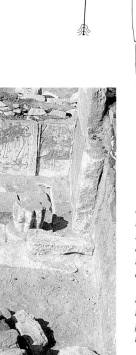

82 (Left) *The tomb-chapel of Raia, looking westwards. The pit giving access to the substructure is in the foreground, with one covering slab still positioned over the rim. In the upper left are the remains of other destroyed tomb-chapels.*

81 (Above) *Plan of the superstructure of the tomb of Raia. The thick wall shown above is part of the south wall of the contemporary tomb of Paser.*

83 (Below) *Offerings are made to Raia and his wife Mutemwia by their lector-priest Shedamun. A monkey clambers in the struts of Mutemwia's chair. The costumes worn by the tomb-owners are typical for the Ramesside Period.*

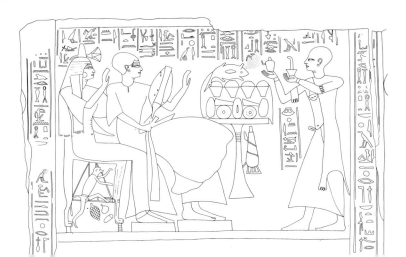

exactly contemporary, even though Raia's stands on a bed of rubble slightly higher than the foundations of Paser's monument. This probably has no chronological significance, but was the result of the levelling of the ground in preparation for erecting the walls of Raia's chapel.

For so small a tomb the decoration is of considerable interest, and being almost complete gives us a good idea of the original appearance of the monument. We have seen earlier that Memphite tomb-chapels previous to the reign of Ramesses II conform more or less to a type; from the reign of Ramesses II a number of different tomb types emerged, of which Raia's is the first of its kind to be excavated at Saqqara. Only time will tell if such chapels were frequently built in the necropolis. If they are commonplace, and if they are as well-decorated and informative as Raia's, a treasure-house of knowledge about the inhabitants of Memphis in the Ramesside Period awaits us under the sands of the desert.

The existence of Paser was already known (from the British Museum stela) even before the discovery of his Saqqara tomb. Raia, on the other hand, was unknown before our discovery, though there is just a chance that a stela from Abydos (now in Liverpool) of a like-named musician, Raia, was erected at an earlier stage in his career in a cenotaph near the temple of Osiris, ruler of the Underworld.

On the north wall of his Saqqara chapel we see Raia and his wife Mutemwia receiving offerings from their funerary priest. Below, the tomb-owner and his family adore a statue of the jackal god Anubis. A calf is being led forward for sacrifice. Mutemwia bears the title chantress of Amun, a common one for women of rank in the New Kingdom who, though important in the temple hierarchy and in the home, had no place in the administration of Egypt as a whole. There were several chapels of Amun in Memphis, and we must imagine that Mutemwia functioned in one or other of these. Her duties would have consisted of singing and probably playing a musical instrument to entertain the god, represented in his shrine by an image. The statue of the deity was itself sacrosanct and screened from vulgar gaze, the Pharaoh and the purified priests alone being permitted to cast their eyes upon it.

The focal point of the funerary cult of Raia and Mutemwia (for she was buried in the subterranean parts of the tomb with him) was the stela forming the west wall of the chapel. The upper section is partly missing. On it the tomb owner was shown worshipping Osiris, behind whose seated figure stand Isis and Nephthys, sisters of the deity. Below, Raia and Mutemwia are themselves receiving offerings. This bipartite arrangement of a gravestone, the edges usually in the form of a frame with a cornice above, is typical for Saqqara in the Ramesside Period.

On either side of the stela the tomb-owner, on a large scale, adores the deity and presents in one instance a pectoral for the decoration of the image of the god. The scenes we have outlined so far are *de rigueur* and thus commonplace in Egyptian funerary monuments. What lends the tiny chapel its special interest is the south wall, virtually complete; it shows Raia performing his official duties in the temple of the great creator god Ptah, the shattered foundations of which, as we have seen, survive in part in nearby Memphis.

Above, in a very well-preserved register, Raia, chief of singers, is playing the harp before statues of Ptah and the cow-headed goddess, Hathor-Lady-of-the-Sycamore. The workmanship is very fine and much colour is preserved. The scene is given added interest from the fact that the performer is shown as a blind man, whereas on the opposite north wall he is shown possessed of normal eyesight. Almost without exception harpists in Egyptian art are shown as blind; sometimes this must have been because they were so in actuality, since musicianship was one of the few professions in antiquity a blind man could profitably follow. There is some evidence to indicate however that sometimes *symbolic* blindness is involved in Egyptian paintings and reliefs. The reasoning behind this is that, as has been noted above, only the 'purified ones', including the divine Pharaoh, could gaze on the image of the deity. Some reliefs of the Amarna Period from the great temple of the Aten at Karnak even show musicians blindfolded, probably so that they would not be struck blind if their eyes happened to alight accidentally on the *benben*-stone, the symbol of the Sun in his holy-of-holies in the temple. If we assume that our worthy was not blind, as I think we must, he and his choir, carrying out their pleasant duties in the sanctuary of Ptah at Memphis, must have positioned themselves in such a way that the deity was able to enjoy the performance (the door of his shrine being open) without being seen. In Raia's tomb a most unusual detail is preserved: the choir (or part of it) is depicted, in the bottom register of the scene being described. There they are shown as mourners at the funeral of Raia. They are all male, and are shown with the slit eyes of the blind, but whether they were thus afflicted in real life we cannot tell. They are named, and fragments of the song which Raia was singing before Ptah in the register at the top of the scene are also preserved, but the only sentence of the broken text that yields much sense is '. . . we do not detest the mooring-post'.

To the right of the blind mourners part of the obsequies of the deceased are shown. Such scenes are commonplace in Egyptian tombs as might be expected. Yet the artist almost always gives the episode an individual touch. The craftsmanship of the scene in Raia's tomb is surprisingly good for so small a monument. The mummy of the deceased is being received by Anubis (or by a priest representing him), preparatory to being placed in the tomb-chamber below ground. Mutemwia, with one arm touching her husband's side and with the other throwing dust over her head, is reluctant to let him go. To the left some of the dead man's surviving family, and no doubt paid professional mourners, are weeping and wailing and, like Mutemwia, throwing dust over themselves. Since the embalming process took seventy days, and Raia had thus been dead almost two and a half months, one wonders just how genuine such gestures and displays of grief would have been. In any case, the scene would probably have been carved in advance of Raia's death.

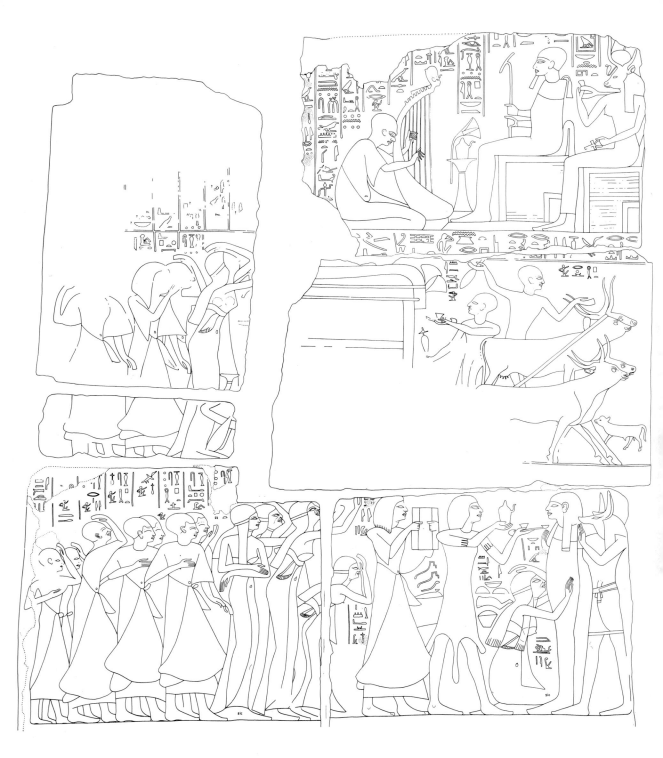

84 In the topmost register of this relief Raia is depicted as a blind musician, playing the harp before statues of
Ptah and Hathor in one of the temples of Memphis. Below, the tomb-owner's catafalque is drawn into the
Netherworld by oxen. In the bottom register Mutemwia embraces the mummy of her husband, which is
supported by Anubis or a priest representing him. Other priests perform the Opening-of-the-Mouth ritual on
the mummy, whereby Raia would be enabled to breathe, speak, eat and drink in the afterlife. Female mourners
and members of the temple choir also take part in the ceremony.

## The Tomb of Raia
## South Wall

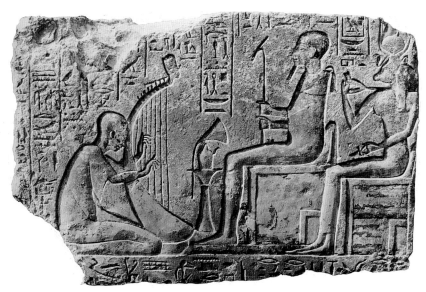

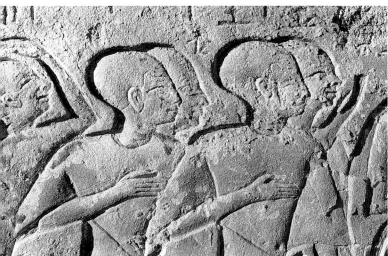

85 (Above) *Raia before Ptah and Hathor. The god holds his* was *sceptre, while the goddess extends her necklace with one hand and with the other holds an* ankh, *the sign of life. Detail of ill. 84.*

86 (Left) *Blind members of the choir from one of the Memphite temples, assisting in the obsequies of Raia. Detail of ill. 84.*

87 (Below) *Part of the burial service of Raia. His lector-priest Shedamun ritualistically opens his mouth and purifies him with water, while the requisite spells are recited from a papyrus by an assistant. Detail of ill. 84.*

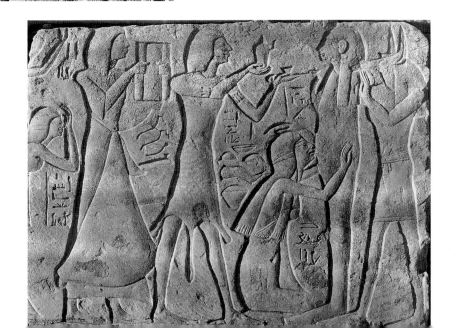

An essential part of any Egyptian funeral was the ritual known as the Opening-of-the-Mouth of the mummy. This ceremony ensured that the deceased would be able to perform all the functions with that organ that he had while he was alive, including breathing, speaking, eating and drinking. Raia duly made provision for the service of the necessary priestly officials, and we see them performing their tasks in front of the mummy. One holds a libation vessel and offers incense, another is unrolling a scroll or service book from which was chanted the magical formulae that would effect the opening of the mouth. Miniature adzes and a serpent-shaped wand, together with the chest in which they were stored, are shown between the priests.

In the middle register of the wall is a damaged scene which showed Raia in his coffin on a catafalque, being drawn by oxen to the Netherworld. The accompanying text welcomes the deceased into his new abode: 'To the West, to the West, O praised one, to the West, to the West, the place of silence, the district of Truth.'

On the north wall of the chapel the tomb-owners are receiving libations and incense. In the register below Raia and Mutemwia adore a figure of the jackal god Anubis in a shrine, as we have noted. Accompanying them are female members of their family. Such details as these give very useful clues as to the composition of Memphite families in the New Kingdom. More often than not they are women, presumably unmarried and living in their brothers' households. In the shafts associated with this small tomb was the usual complement of funerary furnishings, including an exquisite inlay of a human face.

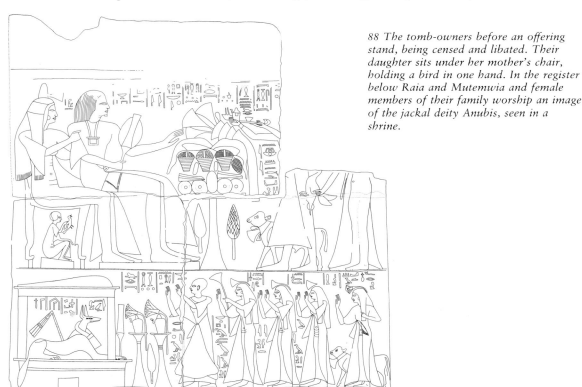

88 The tomb-owners before an offering stand, being censed and libated. Their daughter sits under her mother's chair, holding a bird in one hand. In the register below Raia and Mutemwia and female members of their family worship an image of the jackal deity Anubis, seen in a shrine.

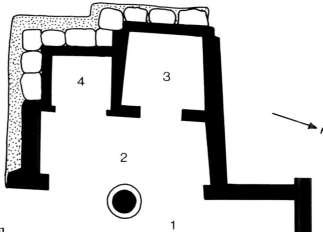

89 *Plan of the superstructure of the tomb-chapel of Khay. (1) The forecourt. (2) Antechapel. (3,4) Chapels.*

90 *(Below) A scene in a goldworkers' atelier in Memphis, with Khay superintending the activities and holding a long cane. One craftsman is working a pair of foot-bellows.*

## The tomb of Khay, a Memphite technician

In 1986 we uncovered behind the tomb of Tia and Tia the remains of a bipartite or two-roomed chapel of an official named Khay. He was probably a contemporary of Paser and Raia, living in Memphis in the reign of Ramesses II. His main title was goldwasher of the Lord of the Two Lands, and as such he had an important function to perform in connection with a precious mineral that was crucial to the Egyptian economy. Much of Egypt's gold at this period – the metal that made her so powerful and much courted by the other nations of the Near East – was to be found in the eastern desert, where it was fairly easily accessible. Another source was Nubia, the vast country to the south, whence it came in the form of tribute and doubtless also as a medium of exchange for much-coveted Egyptian goods. Khay thus had a responsible job, but whether he carried out his duties under the burning sun in the arduous conditions of the eastern desert he does not tell us. Probably his role was superintending the treatment and refining of the mineral once it reached the workshops of Memphis. In his little tomb-chapel, in the room to the south, he depicts a scene in just such an atelier. We see material being smelted in a pan, the heat from the fire being increased by the use of foot bellows, manipulated by hand. To the left a craftsman wields a pair of tongs, while above two others (one named as a chief of craftsmen) are busy at work. On the right side of the scene two men are scooping the mineral into pans. Khay, leaning nonchalantly on a cane, oversees all the activities.

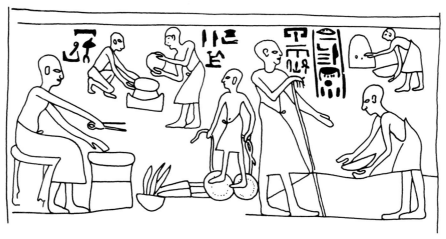

In the upper registers of the wall Khay and his wife worship Osiris and the sun-god, Re-Harakhty. Below, Khay, supporting a pan on his left shoulder, adores Hathor, Lady-of-the-Southern-Sycamore (a temple in Memphis).

The relief is crudely carved (as so often in genre scenes in Egyptian tombs), but is very revealing for all that, and shows us among other things an activity that must often have taken place in the government factories in Memphis. It is to be hoped that the present expedition of the Egypt Exploration Society, working in the town-site in an industrial area of the Ramesside Period, will locate just such a smelting workshop.

Other walls in the tomb-chapel are carved with the customary ritualistic scenes that were always shown in Egyptian funerary monuments – including the worship of the gods, and the offering of provisions to the tomb-owner and his wife. By magical means these activities would continue in perpetuity. One wall in the south room of Khay's tomb gives us details of his family, who are all named and represented. Such reliefs, banal perhaps at first sight, help to build up a picture of the domestic setting of the deceased and at the same time add more names to the prosopography, or 'Who was Who', of Memphis in the New Kingdom. Another wall, in the north room, shows his funeral, with an interesting detail added for good measure: a schematic representation of his actual funerary chapel at Saqqara, before which his mummy stands for the last rites. The roof of the chapel is shown topped by a pyramid which, being of mud brick, would have been one of the first elements to be demolished when the tomb-chapel proper was partly dismantled in antiquity. We did not find the capstone or pyramidion; it could still be somewhere in the vicinity, or it too could have been carted away as building material.

Some pieces of Khay's funerary equipment were found down below in the burial chambers, mixed in with a great deal of later intrusive burials and objects. It seems that his coffin was decorated with gold leaf; the latter may have been one of his perquisites of office; few officials, other than those of high rank, would have had access to this prized metal. Most of it was hacked off by the despoilers of his tomb – even tissue-thin gold leaf was worth collecting for melting down – and we found only broken pieces of Khay's coffin. It must once have been splendid. Some shawabti figures of his were also recovered.

One of the people named in Khay's tomb was his son Pabes, and we were fortunate enough to find his funerary chapel just behind his father's. It will be instructive to see whether such family groupings of tombs will be common throughout the necropolis.

### The tomb of Pabes, a Memphite tradesman

Pabes, or Pabasa, seems from the inscriptions in his badly preserved tomb-chapel to have been engaged in trade. His monument again furnishes us with a new 'type' for the Memphite necropolis in that it is tripartite, having three rooms. The middle one served as the cult place, the much weatherworn

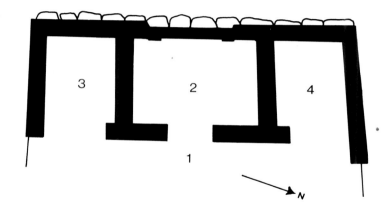

91 *Plan of the superstructure of the tomb-chapel of Pabes. (1) The forecourt. (2) Offering room. (3,4) Side chapels.*

92 *(below) A dockyard scene in Memphis. In the upper register labourers bring goods to be weighed, including an ingot. Below, a ship with masts lowered is drawn up at the quayside. Genre scenes such as this are full of vitality, though often crudely carved in comparison with more conventional scenes in Egyptian tombs.*

remains of a stela still surviving against its west wall. The workmanship of all the Ramesside monuments we have cleared so far at Saqqara is shoddy. The tombs are built of poor quality limestone slabs roughly mortared together, the whole being masked by a liberal application of plaster.

The overall effect, when the tombs were first put up, would have been attractive, but such monuments quickly fell to pieces once the plaster between the blocks disintegrated, and the winds and weather did the rest. Pabes' tomb is a particularly good example of this state of affairs. Yet there remained quite a lot to record when we found it in 1986.

From our point of view, apart from adding his name and occupation to our ever-increasing catalogue of Memphite personalities of the New Kingdom, the most interesting scene in his chapel is on the north wall of the north room. The relief is much fractured and weatherworn, but on it we see what must be part of the dockyard of Memphis. Ships are drawn up and produce of many kinds

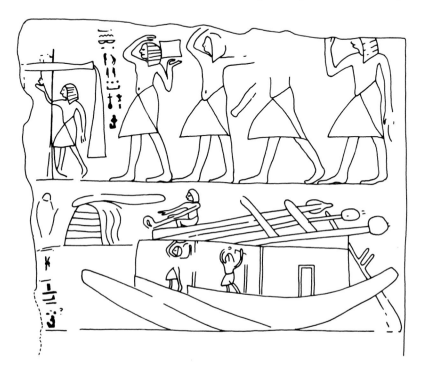

including at least one ingot, is being unloaded onto the quay. These materials must surely be part of the goods dealt with by Pabes in the course of his duties.

The location of the dockyard at Memphis in the Ramesside and earlier periods is unknown. Documentary evidence from the time of Tuthmosis III, in the middle of the Eighteenth Dynasty, shows that it must have been a flourishing concern. Surely, even from the beginnings of dynastic history, the quays of Memphis, the capital city, must have been hives of industry. Recent excavation work by the Egypt Exploration Society has produced clues to the location of the site of the Roman dockyard, but as we have seen earlier the Nile has been gradually shifting eastwards since antiquity, so the site of the quay of the Classical Period need not be the same as the one that was operating when Pabes was a tradesman loading and unloading his wares there. Still, the representation in his tomb, schematic though it is, is a valuable addition to knowledge, and we are hoping for more scenes showing minor officials, merchants, and craftsmen at work as we uncover other tomb-chapels in the necropolis in the years to come.

Pabes' tomb-chambers were plundered, and as in the tomb of his parents the subterranean parts had been taken over in late dynastic times as a burial place for humbler Memphite citizens. We found a few fragments that were part of his equipment for the next life, including the ubiquitous shawabtis.

To conclude our examination of the minor tombs we turn finally to a monument of a member of the entourage of the princess Tia and her husband. We have already seen him depicted in the tomb of his royal master and mistress. His own tomb-chapel is extraordinary for two main reasons: first, because of its location, and second because of the enormous amount of material recovered from the burial chambers, which were on two levels, cut out of the bedrock.

## The tomb-chapel of Iurudef

Throughout the course of history the rulers, nobles, and great officials in the Near East and elsewhere had, in their palaces and villas, trusted confidants who ran their households with efficiency and discretion, and kept a vigilant eye on their estates. This was certainly the case in ancient Egypt, where tomb inscriptions and stelae frequently vaunt an official's devotion to his lord. Though Iurudef unfortunately has not left us any biographical text in his tomb-chapel, almost entirely destroyed, we get a clear indication from other clues of his standing in the entourage of two of the most important persons in Memphis, and indeed in Egypt as a whole, in the Ramesside Period: Tia and Tia, sister and brother-in-law of Ramesses the Great himself.

We have already seen Iurudef officiating at one of the funeral rituals of the royal couple – the ritualistic Voyage to Abydos – and he is depicted a number of times elsewhere in the tomb of the Tias. So trusted was he that he was accorded the rare privilege of a burial place and funerary chapel within the confines of what was in effect a royal tomb in the Saqqara necropolis, that of Tia and Tia.

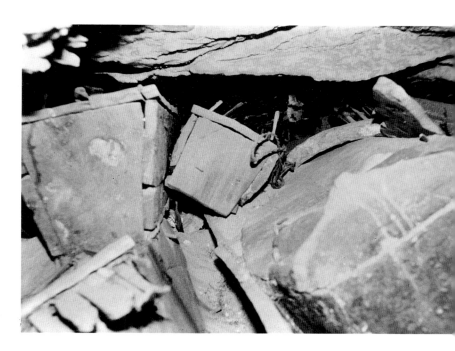

93 *View looking into one of the burial chambers of the tomb-chapel of Iurudef. This illustration shows the difficulty faced by the excavators in clearing the cache of coffins and associated burials.*

We found Iurudef's tomb shaft in 1984 when we were clearing the outer court of the main tomb. All that remained above ground was an inscribed door post of limestone and some pieces of masonry. The rim of the tomb shaft was soon revealed, with a couple of the covering slabs still in position. This fact did not, however, give rise to hopes on our part that the subterranean rooms would be undisturbed since Iurudef's death. Our previous work had shown that all the shafts of the tombs we had excavated had been emptied and the chambers entered. An intact burial of any consequence is hardly to be expected since, at Saqqara in particular, the whereabouts of the tomb-shafts of the major monuments was usually fairly evident. The contents of tomb-chambers here and throughout the rest of Egypt were safe from spoliation only so long as the necropolis administration was vigilant and the central government authority efficiently run.

We decided to probe Iurudef's tomb-shaft while we were excavating the tomb of the Tias, just to see what would face us in the following season of work. The removal of a few basketfuls of sand soon revealed damaged but painted coffins, seemingly of Late Period date (though we subsequently revised our opinion), propped upright against the sides of the shaft as if they had been removed from the burial chambers below to facilitate access. Our other interpretation at that time was that the coffins had been lugged to the surface by the robbers, pillaged of any valuables they contained, and then thrown back down the empty shaft. Although it was rather a dispiriting sight at least we now knew there *was* material below, though later in date than the time of Iurudef. The question remained: was there anything of his and his family's funerary furnishings left, or was everything that had been lovingly placed in the chambers for their use in the Netherworld broken up and thrown out when the shaft and rooms were re-used in later times?

The efforts of our workmen soon revealed, at a depth of 5 metres, entrances leading to chambers both on the north and the south. And what a sight met our eyes! The rooms were crammed from floor to ceiling with coffins, some of the lids gaping open. Burials were also to be seen in reed mats, and there were loose skeletons, the skulls grinning balefully at us from the gloom. It was a veritable charnel-house, but as we quickly realized also a treasure-trove, not of precious items but of new information on an extensive group of inhabitants of Memphis, practically undisturbed since they were laid to rest, probably three millennia ago.

The shaft itself continued below the 5-metre level, so we could expect more coffins and more skeletons further down. We were clearly faced with a major logistical problem in dealing with such a mass of skeletal and funerary material, so it was decided to postpone the clearance of all the chambers until the following season, 1985. We blocked the entrances to the rooms, refilled the shaft to the brim, and calmly continued the excavation of the tomb of Tia and Tia, the objective of our 1984 campaign.

It will now be necessary to anticipate a little to say that in the following year we emptied all the rooms at the 5-metre level and continued down the shaft to the second or 9-metre level, where more rooms opened off, but this time only on the south side. All the chambers, upper and lower, had been hewn out for the interment of Iurudef and members of his family, which must thus have been quite extensive. Before discussing what we were able to find out about the post-Ramesside inhabitants of Memphis and their funerary customs, from the intrusive burials in the upper chambers of Iurudef's tomb, let us first glance at the material in that monument that could be assigned to the primary interments – those of Iurudef and his relations in the time of Ramesses II.

The Egyptian collections of the world are full of funerary objects of New Kingdom date, most of them probably from the Theban necropolis. Quite a number, however, can be assigned to the Memphite area on the basis of iconography and particularly inscriptions. Although some of the material derives from controlled excavations, a large proportion of the material was acquired in the last century, in particular from antiquities dealers. No certain details of provenance or even of date can be expected from objects purchased in this fashion. Thus quite a formidable amount of research has still to be carried out on the many classes of surviving funerary objects. The quantity and quality of the furnishings, including the amuletic material, placed in a tomb naturally varied according to the status and means of the deceased. Our excavations at Saqqara are uncovering each year many New Kingdom objects. A large

94 (*Opposite*) *Serpentine shawabti figure of Iurudef, showing him in the dress of daily life rather than as a wrapped mummy. On his chest is a* ba-*bird, symbolizing the spirit of the deceased. The* ba-*bird had the ability to fly out of the tomb-chamber into the world of the living, and was thus a vital link between the deceased in his coffin and the outside world.*

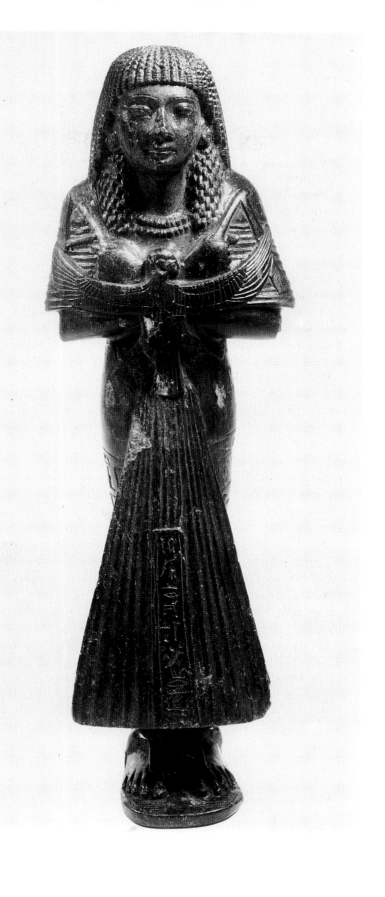

number of these, although not in the exact position in which they were placed in antiquity, nevertheless are datable. In not a few cases a very precise date can be allocated to them. Over the years we hope to build up information on an extensive corpus of objects of all kinds, including pottery, which will ultimately form a valuable basis for comparison with the rather vaguely dated material in the museum collections. The objects from Iurudef's tomb are a case in point. We know for certain from inscriptions and reliefs in the tomb of the Tias that he flourished in the reign of Ramesses II (c. 1279–1212 BC), but whether he was born under that king's father Sety I is uncertain. As an additional proof of his date – but hardly needed in the present instance – a scarab of Ramesses II was found in one of the rooms of his underground complex.

Every official, or indeed any private citizen of means, had to provide himself with 'standard' pieces of funerary furniture, which included obvious items such as a coffin or sarcophagus in wood or stone, canopic jars for the viscera, shawabti figurines, probably in a specially-made box, a heart scarab, possibly in a pectoral, amuletic figures, food provisions in pottery vessels, drink, and ideally a copy of the Book of the Dead. The last was needed as a guide to the hazards of the Underworld. The other objects placed in the tomb were by and large optional extras, and might include objects used in daily life such as jewellery and pieces of domestic furniture, often somewhat battered and worn from use.

Of the objects listed above Iurudef could boast, among other things, a fine coffin of an unusual type (with an openwork design), some shawabtis, including a masterpiece of the figurine-maker's art showing Iurudef in the dress of daily life rather than as a swathed mummy, and a well-made pectoral in faience, the heart scarab missing. Curiously, we found no trace of canopic jars either for him or for the other persons buried with him. From the skeletal material found scattered in the various rooms underground our physical anthropologists were able to tell us how many burials were involved: at least thirty-four. Some of the bones were tiny charred fragments, because the upper set of chambers had been fired, either by the original plunderers or by the later citizens of Memphis when they came to place their deceased relatives there, as we shall see further in this chapter. The firing may have been a purificatory act. By good fortune the inferno had the effect of preserving some of Iurudef's funerary objects, which we found in quite good condition under the layer of ashes. All that these needed was cleaning and conservation at the hands of our restorer.

Since the reliefs in the small chapel above ground had almost all disappeared, the shawabtis naming members of Iurudef's family, which we found in the chambers below, are particularly valuable for garnering some information at least on his relatives, some of whom may have been depicted and named on the missing reliefs. The shawabtis give us the names of the lady Akhes (who may have been his wife), the scribe Ba-anti, the songstress of Amun-Re Bakwerel, the lady Hener, and the scribe of the treasury Tia. This scribe was presumably a namesake of Iurudef's master, the husband of the princess Tia. Even before our discovery a stela naming Iurudef was known. It must have been found in Saqqara in the nineteenth century, and is now in the Oriental Museum of the University of Durham. Rather battered and chipped, it was not studied in any detail until recently. At first glimpse it is just an ordinary funerary stela or gravestone, of which thousands survive from ancient Egypt. Examination of its worn surface, however, shows that in the upper register the princess Tia and her husband are shown adoring the seated Osiris, while in the lower register Iurudef and his father Pekhoir worship an image of the Hathor-cow placed on a pedestal. Iurudef's father Pekhoir (which means 'The Syrian') is otherwise not known; in fact he has two names, the other being Amenemhab. The original position of the stela is something of a puzzle; it does not seem to belong to Iurudef's chapel. We can only suppose that it was set up somewhere in the tomb of the Tias, perhaps in another small tomb-chapel now demolished, which was the counterpart of Iurudef's and built opposite his on the north side of an outer court of the main tomb. At any rate, Iurudef is seen to be associated with the royal couple, who were his patrons in his lifetime, even in the Netherworld. He would have benefited from their funerary cult in a very positive way during the ritual known as the Reversion of Offerings. This was a custom, familiar to us from temple services, but no doubt applicable also to the private funerary cult, whereby food and drink which had been placed on the altars would revert to the living. In the temples the victuals were first offered to the gods resident in the shrines, then to the royal ancestors (represented as statues), and then finally would revert to the officiating priests and their dependants. Iurudef and his family would likewise have derived benefit from the mortuary cult of Tia and Tia, after their spirits had magically consumed the delicacies placed on the altars in their tomb. A whole network of the living could thus be provided for, as well as the deceased's relatives buried with him, and this happy state of affairs was supposed to continue in perpetuity.

## The later burials

Though strictly outside our terms of reference, since they date to a much later period in Egyptian history, we must examine now the intrusive burials in the upper chambers of Iurudef's tomb, which we have alluded to more than once in the preceding pages.

Most of our knowledge of the life and customs of the ordinary people or poorer classes of ancient Egypt derives from the reliefs and inscriptions left behind by the upper echelons of society: the royal family, the nobility, the ubiquitous official classes. Not infrequently a man's servants and labourers would be depicted on the walls of his tomb, busily going about their duties in a great official's household, on his estate, or in his government office. Very often such humble people are named, and an indication is given of their responsibilities; even snatches of their conversation are inscribed on the reliefs in the tombs. But as regards their customs, religion, interests, diet, and general lifestyle we are not particularly well informed. That is why, when a discovery such as the cache of coffins and the remains of relatively unimportant folk in Iurudef's tomb is made, it should be an occasion for rejoicing rather than lamentation. It is often forgotten that Egyptologists are not solely concerned with the unearthing of treasures or works of art. Our own satisfaction, in the case of the Iurudef cache, was tempered by the sobering thought that we had a most difficult task on hand.

If the ancient undertakers or morticians had been systematic in the placing of the coffins in the chambers our job would have been relatively simple, though manœuvring cumbersome (and as we discovered, fragile) coffins out of the rooms and up the shaft was not easy. On reflecting that what went down ought in theory to be able to be brought out and up, we set about making a kind of wooden cradle on which the coffins, as well as reed-matting burials and individual unwrapped skeletons, could be placed and hauled to the surface. The system worked reasonably well, and the rooms were emptied without mishap, though there were some difficult moments when we thought that one or other of the ancient citizens of Memphis was going to slither off the cradle and crash back down the shaft amidst a shower of wooden splinters and mummy wrappings.

Since the placing, or rather haphazard wedging, of the coffins in the rooms had a chronological significance (though we are still not sure if all the material was cached at one time or over an extended period) it was important to record the juxtaposition of the various coffins and loose burials. This was a formidable task, when it is considered that many of the receptacles had split open – or their lids had been prised off – and some burials had disintegrated completely. The difficulty of working in a very confined space, ankle-deep in fine mummy dust, was an additional hazard. Nevertheless the task was successfully brought to a conclusion in a season of two-and-a-half months' work. The Expedition now has a series of wooden coffins, some quite elaborate, others very simple, for study and analysis.

The reader may well ask: why is the study of such coffins important, and are not our museums full of examples of them already? We shall now attempt to answer these questions.

### The coffins

The public collections are certainly plentifully supplied with examples of coffins of most periods of Egyptian history, but most of them – at least those normally exhibited – are 'museum-pieces', in that they are finely made or have elaborate, sometimes beautiful, decoration. Such coffins must always have been the prerogative of a minority of the population of Egypt: the well-to-do, official, and priestly classes. Humbler folk buried their dead in roughly-made and often crudely painted coffins, or in reed mats. With one or two exceptions our newly excavated material belongs in these classes, but the types of coffins we found fall into categories that have hardly been studied at all; indeed, excavators in the past have tended to throw such material aside, especially if damaged, as being of no scientific or intrinsic interest, assuredly a somewhat blinkered view. The result is that we ourselves, in studying the new finds and preparing them for publication, have experienced problems in finding parallel and dated material from the Memphite area and indeed from other parts of Egypt.

In the innermost chamber of the southern group of rooms in the upper level of Iurudef's shaft we found two large coffins side by side, with a pottery vessel between them. The pot is the only clue we have to the date of the cache of coffins, but here again we are up against a problem. Until recently Egyptian ceramology – the study of pottery in all its manifestations – was an undeveloped science in comparison with ceramic studies of other regions of the ancient Near East. Pottery was, of course recorded during excavations in Egypt, but often in rudimentary fashion so that the results were sometimes uninformative. Much sherd material was regularly discarded as being of no account. There were several reasons for this, which happily is now a thing of the past. One is that pottery sherds accrue on an Egyptian dig in truly alarming quantities, and with limited expertise and budgeting in the past have, with some exceptions, been left unrecorded and unpublished. Computer techniques have alleviated the problem of storing information about pottery and its distribution throughout a settlement site or in a cemetery; even so, more often than not the recording of sherd material is selective, even on a well-conducted excavation. Egyptologists have few reliable corpuses of pottery against which to compare and date their own new finds. The solitary and crucial pot just mentioned has not proved particularly easy to date with precision; our current feeling is that it was made, and presumably deposited between the two coffins, in the Twenty-first Dynasty (c. 1069–945 BC). This would accord with our own impression of the date of the coffins, parts of which, in particular the wigs of the head-pieces, are reminiscent of dated Twentieth Dynasty or late Ramesside coffins and statuary. When our research is complete it should be possible to assign a reasonably precise date to our material. In the meantime we have recorded in great detail the individual coffins, so that curators of museum collections and other interested scholars will eventually have for the first time an extensive corpus of coffins made for humble inhabitants of Memphis at a precise moment in the history of the city.

When we were recording the coffins in the field we were concerned with two main aspects: technological (how they were made) and iconographical (how they were decorated). The study of the few objects found inside the coffins, and the mummies and skeletons themselves, came later.

It may surprise the reader to learn that although much is known about ancient Egyptian technology there is still an enormous amount to be found out. For instance, few of the objects from the greatest find ever made in Egypt – the

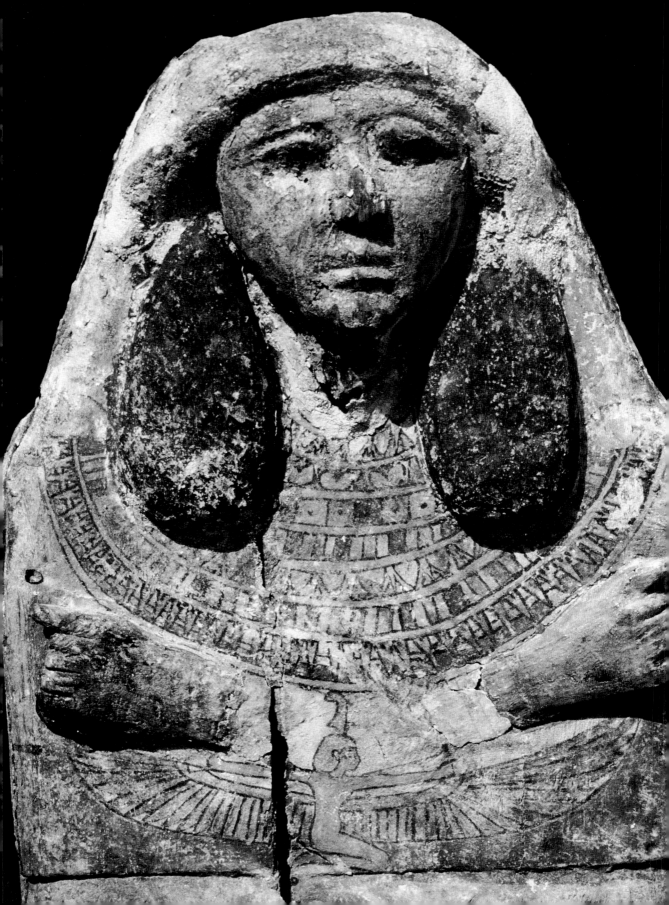

treasures of Tutankhamun – have been analyzed in detail to see how the craftsmen put them together. Until recently the technology of coffins was an almost totally neglected field, yet the study of the carpentry of such objects tells us a great deal about the work methods of the ancient craftsmen. We have yet to analyze the wood from which our specimens were made, but the carpenters are hardly likely to have used expensive imported timbers even if such were available in the Twenty-first Dynasty. Almost certainly they made do with local material. The workmen were adept at joining small pieces of planking together, using wooden pins sharpened at one end. Nails of metal were never employed. The result is a kind of patchwork, the technique used in all our coffins. The bits and pieces so joined were covered with a layer of plaster, sometimes only on the exterior, which was then painted or roughly decorated with figures of deities and religious symbols. The craftsmen were accustomed to putting to good use any stray pieces of wood found lying around, since sturdy timber was always in rather short supply in Egypt. It is not improbable that some of the fragments used in the coffins we found are earlier in date than the Twenty-first Dynasty. There must have been many remnants of plundered burials in the necropolis in ancient times just as there are to this day. In Saqqara it is not uncommon to find fragments of wooden coffins on the surface of the sand, warped and turned almost rock-hard by the blistering sun, but certainly dating as early as the fourth and early third millennia BC (the Archaic Period and Old Kingdom).

We will not attempt to describe all the coffins we found in the shaft and chambers of Iurudef, but will fix our attention on four specimens which may be regarded as representing the whole cache. The scheme of decoration is best grasped by reference to the illustrations. The first coffin is one of the two found in the innermost emplacement, as described above. The face is its most distinctive feature; indeed, the head-pieces of the entire group provide us with a veritable portrait gallery, though the craftsmen could hardly have intended the features to represent those of the actual owners of the coffins, since these were not made to order but were mass-produced in the funerary workshops. In a real sense such 'icons' are the forerunners of the much better known Faiyum portraits of the second century AD, most of which have been expertly published. Specimens of the latter can be examined in most Egyptian collections.

The coffin with which we are dealing probably dates as we have seen, from the Twenty-first Dynasty, or just possibly the very end of the Twentieth Dynasty. It is uninscribed, like most of the coffins in the cache, emphasizing the fact that the owners were quite humble citizens of Memphis, probably without any rank in the administrative hierarchy. Only one coffin has yielded a personal name, Imyptah, curiously enough the only record of such a name in Egyptian sources. A few coffins are inscribed with mock hieroglyphs.

The second coffin is by far the most elaborately decorated of the whole group, and in style and decoration is reminiscent of the very large cache of

95 (Opposite) *Decoration on one of the many coffins found in the burial chambers of the tomb-chapel of Iurudef.*

painted coffins of priests and priestesses of the gods Amun and Montu, found in the nineteenth century at Thebes, a number of which date to the Twenty-first Dynasty. The overall impression given by our specimen is quite sumptuous, but close examination shows that the iconographical detail is very bizarre, and the texts which were supposed to identify the owner and assist him in his perilous progress through the Underworld are mumbo-jumbo! A few of the signs can be identified as genuine hieroglyphs, otherwise they bear hardly any resemblance to the true Egyptian sign-list. All these facts are of great interest, and can mean only one thing: the craftsmen who decorated and inscribed the coffin (and the others with garbled texts), as well as the patrons who commissioned them (or more likely who purchased them 'off the shelf' in a funerary workshop) were illiterate. Such workshops specializing in the manufacture of mortuary equipment, probably closely associated with embalmers' emporia, must have been commonplace in Egypt, but not one has ever been found. It is greatly to be hoped that the current excavations taking place in Memphis will eventually uncover one. Every town of consequence must have had such an embalming place and workshop, and it is not difficult, since our museums are full of grave goods of all periods, including coffins, to conjure up a picture of what took place there. Indeed, some New Kingdom tomb paintings and reliefs actually show the embalming house, though not the individual stages of the process in which the desiccation of the corpse was achieved, nor the various individual layers of wrappings being placed on the mummies. Likewise, numerous items of funerary furniture are quite often represented in the paintings on the walls of the tombs.

The craftsmen who decorated our coffins were no doubt working from models, which over the years would have become worn and battered so that their iconographical detail was almost unrecognizable. The painters would also have been provided with standard funerary texts which they could use as guides when labelling the figures of the gods and inscribing the lids of the coffins. These models too would have become virtually useless with age. In the end the painters, unable in any case to understand the hieroglyphic script, would have been reduced to the expedient of making up their own signs as they went along! This is shown very forcefully in the third coffin of our selected group. Without any doubt the 'hieroglyphic' inscription painted on it is the most debased ever to have been found in Egypt. I feel that had the inscribed lid of the coffin been an isolated and unprovenanced piece in the hands of an antiquities dealer it would have been rejected as modern by any expert to whom it was submitted for an opinion. Indeed, when we found it in Iurudef's tomb an Egyptian colleague remarked that the coffin looked as if it had been made only the week before in the Khan el-Khalili, the covered bazaar in Old Cairo, where spurious antiquities are made in quantity for sale to the gullible tourist. All these facts throw a most vivid and interesting light on the attitudes and work methods of the ancient Egyptian funerary craftsmen who were mass-producing goods for an undiscriminating clientèle.

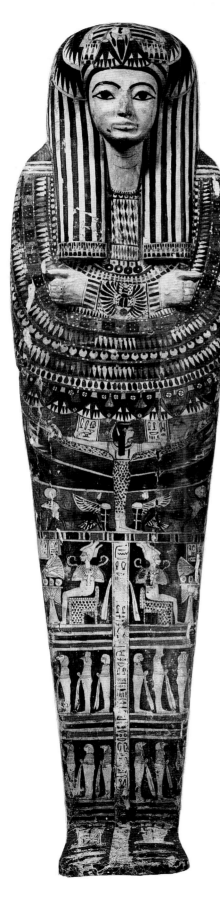

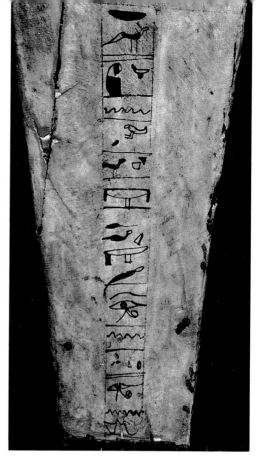

Cache of Coffins

96 (Left) *Painted coffin from a deposit of coffins and reed mat burials in the tomb of Iurudef. The hieroglyphic inscription down the front of the lid is garbled and without meaning.*

97 (Above) *Detail of a coffin found in the Iurudef cache, one of many intrusive burials in that deposit. The 'hieroglyphic' text is without meaning.*

98 (Below) *Undecorated coffins of children and babies, a poignant reminder of infant mortality in ancient Egypt. The burials were intrusive in the tomb-chambers of Iurudef.*

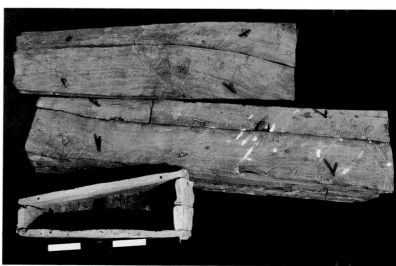

Finally, we examine a very poignant object: the coffin of a small child. Many of the skeletons found in the Iurudef cache were those of children. This indicates the rate of infant mortality in Memphis and doubtless throughout Egypt in the first millennium BC. Very few of the dead in our cache were wealthy enough to carry grave goods with them into the next world, a clear indication of their relative poverty. Ancient plunderers had penetrated the shaft and removed a few of the coffins, as we saw earlier. The lids of some of the others were eased off. The robbers must have quickly realized that they were wasting their time: there was nothing worth taking. One aged man interred in the cache carried with him into the next world two walking-sticks, no doubt the very ones he used when hobbling round the streets of Memphis. Another burial had a curious object which we had a little difficulty at first in identifying; it seems to be the handle of a whip. Yet another coffin had a broken black-ware pot, of a type dating to c. 1600 BC. Several examples of such vessels have been found in Saqqara, and many elsewhere in Egypt and the Sudan. Such pottery, with incised linear and dotted decoration, was made in Palestine, the contents no doubt an oil or unguent not available in Egypt itself. Our pot was already an antiquity when it was re-used in the Twenty-first Dynasty.

The skeletons and their dentition are still being studied. They form valuable material for investigating the health, diet, life expectancy and diseases of quite an extensive group of ordinary folk – as many as a hundred – at Memphis in the first millennium BC. Some of the bodies were mummified in a rudimentary fashion, but in these instances the wrappings were reduced to black powder. The Expedition has now collected for study and analysis masses of human skeletal material, mostly from intrusive burials deposited in the burial-chambers of the tomb-chapels of the New Kingdom. This material, the actual physical remains of the inhabitants of ancient Memphis and the surrounding villages, is potentially a major source for the anthropologist. Already, in addition to the expected bone fractures, we have evidence of calcification of glands and arteries, dental diseases and severe tooth wear, not to mention arthritis, the curse of our own times, and these only at the outset of our investigation.

CHAPTER SIX

# SEARCHING FOR
# THE TOMB OF MAYA

While our colleagues of the Egypt Exploration Society expedition, supported by Memphis State University, have surveyed the ruinfield of the city of ancient Memphis (and are now excavating there) our team, as we have seen, has been concentrating its efforts in an area of the high desert to the west of the city. In the city were the royal palaces, the temples, administrative offices, government workshops, arsenals, and dockyards. The officials and others who lived and worked in Memphis in the New Kingdom built their funerary monuments in the Saqqara necropolis.

Parts of some of these tomb-chapels were seen by the great Prussian scholar, Karl Richard Lepsius in 1843, during his epigraphic mission to record the standing monuments of the Nile Valley. The tomb of Maya, treasurer in the government of Tutankhamun and his two immediate successors, was one of those seen by Lepsius in the stretch of desert to the south of the causeway of the pyramid of Unas. The office of overseer of the treasury was always one of the most important in the pharaonic administration, and the holder was responsible for the day-to-day running of the finances of the state and for the efficient distribution of the enormous revenues of the country, mainly in the form of agricultural produce and minerals, especially gold. In the late Eighteenth Dynasty, when Maya was living, the office of treasurer was of immense prestige and importance, particularly as he must have had daily contact with Pharaoh and was able to influence major policy decisions in the sphere of government. Apart from his colleague Horemheb, Maya was the most important man in the realm. It is curious that we hear very little of the two viziers or chief ministers of Egypt during this period. Technically Maya must have functioned under the vizier of Lower Egypt, based in Memphis.

The most important source of information about his status, his career in the administration and his family life is his tomb in the Memphite necropolis, to which we shall shortly turn. One or two other sources throw some light on his activities, though the great mass of documents for which he was undoubtedly responsible as one of Pharaoh's chief ministers has disappeared for ever. There is plenty of evidence to show that the ancient Egyptians liked to take their favourite reading matter with them into the Netherworld (thus many literary texts survive). Dedicated bureaucrats may even have given instructions for specimens of their own penmanship to be deposited among their tomb furnishings and equipment. Alas, such priceless evidence would not have survived long in the humid conditions underground in the Saqqara necropolis! The drier conditions further south in the Theban area are more conducive to the preservation of papyrus documents. Even so quite a number of copies of Books of the Dead and other written material of the New Kingdom certainly stem from the Memphite tombs. The explanation probably is that in some cases these were stored in containers (possibly pottery) that protected them from the damp, or that the tombs were robbed relatively soon after the interments, and any documents stored below ground would have found their way to the drier desert conditions of the courtyards above.

There is just a chance that we actually have a specimen of Maya's own handwriting. In one of the rooms of the magnificent tomb of Tuthmosis IV in the Valley of the Kings at Thebes there is to be seen the following handwritten text: '. . . Command of His Majesty (may he live, be prosperous and healthy!) to commission the fanbearer on the King's right hand, overseer of the treasury, chief of works in the necropolis, leader of the festival of Amun in Karnak, Maya . . . to restore the burial of King Tuthmosis IV, true of voice, in the august house [the royal tomb] on the west of Thebes.' The instruction is dated to the 8th regnal year [1314 BC] of King Horemheb, so that Maya was still active and flourishing well into the reign of his erstwhile colleague. Evidently tomb robbers had disturbed the burial of Tuthmosis, and Maya, as part of his official responsibilities, had to check the contents of the tomb, doubtless to make good any deficiencies, and then re-seal the entrance. One of his more onerous duties as treasurer must have been to assemble the great trove of objects, both ritualistic and personal, that was placed in the tomb of the young Pharaoh Tutankhamun, who died unexpectedly early. We have an inkling of Maya's closeness to the king from the fact that he was accorded the rare privilege of presenting certain funerary figurines inscribed with Tutankhamun's name and his own as part of Pharaoh's tomb furnishings. For instance, a particularly fine shawabti figure for the king's use in the Underworld was dedicated by Maya, who recorded the fact in a text engraved on the soles of the feet of the figurine, thus ensuring his own immortality. Furthermore he presented a beautifully worked effigy of the king in the form of the god Osiris, extended on a funerary bier. This object is inscribed: 'Made by the servant who is beneficial to His Majesty, who seeks what is good and finds what is fine, and does it thoroughly for his lord, who makes excellent things in the Splendid Place, overseer of building works in the Place of Eternity, the royal scribe, overseer of the treasury Maya.' The inscription continues: 'Made by the servant who is beneficial to his lord, who seeks out excellent things in the Place of Eternity, overseer of building works in the West [the Necropolis area], beloved of his lord, doing what he [Pharaoh] says, who does not allow anything to go wrong, whose face is cheerful when he does it [presumably his duty] with a loving heart as a thing profitable to his lord.'

Loud must have been the lamentations of officials like Maya on the death of the divine Pharaoh! They must have wondered if their positions were safe at the hands of the next ruler. Maya, as we have seen, survived into the reign of Horemheb, and had, no doubt been retained in office after the death of Tutankhamun by that Pharaoh's successor, Ay.

A recently discovered stela fragment gives us a unique glimpse into another of Maya's administrative responsibilities, and one that could not have endeared him overmuch to his fellow citizens. The text reads: 'Year 8, third month of the winter season, day 22, under the Majesty of Horus . . . son of Re [Tutankh]amun, given life. On this day His Majesty commanded the hereditary prince and count, the fanbearer on the King's right hand, royal scribe, overseer of the treasury Maya . . . to tax the entire land and to institute divine offerings [for] all [the gods] of the land of Egypt . . .' The rest of the stela is missing, but it might well have gone on to explain the reason why a tax should have been levied throughout the land at this time, rather late in the reign of the young king. Perhaps this was the occasion for an official celebration of the fact that the great cult temples, which had been closed under Tutankhamun's predecessor Akhenaten, were now repaired and fully operational. Maya, as treasurer, would have played a crucial role in the reorganization of the revenues of the temples, which had been seized and diverted by the agents of the 'heretic' Akhenaten.

Over the years, from the time of the discovery of Horemheb's monument in 1975, the Expedition had not forgotten Maya, whose tomb we had sought at the outset of our mission. From clues already available the relocation of his tomb would surely provide us with valuable material to augment the information we already had about Maya's life and career, as well as other facts to compare and contrast with tombs and funerary objects which we had previously found in the necropolis.

## The tomb is found

At the beginning of February 1986, in excavating one of the shafts in the courtyard of the tomb of an army officer, Ramose (his tomb is described above), we found that we were able to enter the subterranean parts of a tomb adjacent on the north through a robbers' tunnel. The desert at Saqqara is honeycombed with such underground passages, and we ourselves had encountered many in our work in the necropolis over the previous decade or so. With very little doubt all the great tombs at Saqqara had been entered and robbed in antiquity. The superstructures of the monuments, as we know from our experience, had been partly dismantled for re-use. Plundering and dismantling activities are however by their very nature haphazard, and even the activities of nineteenth-century collectors and looters were unsystematic, and no true excavation was undertaken in the early years of that century at Saqqara. In creeping through the passage leading from Ramose's tomb our hopes were not high that we should find anything of real consequence, other than the usual undecorated chambers of another large funerary monument. The thought of finding inscriptions or other material that would identify the tomb-owner was hardly in our minds.

Of paramount importance in excavating underground are the quality and stability of the bedrock and the purity of the air. Once these were pronounced tolerable we began to investigate the substructure of the tomb adjacent to Ramose's. Clearly the newly discovered tomb had burial chambers on two levels; at this stage we were still in the upper, where rock-cut loculi or emplacements with some fragments of skeletal material were to be seen. So far there was no evidence of New Kingdom burials. Plastered into the corner of one room of the upper level we noticed something rather odd: small blue shawabti figures of Late date, no doubt placed there for the benefit of one or other of the burials in the adjacent loculi. It is exceedingly unusual, if not unique, to find funerary figurines fixed to the walls of a burial chamber. Normally they were placed either with the mummy or were housed in a special box provided for the purpose and placed alongside the sarcophagus.

In the same room where we noted the shawabtis a deep shaft was to be seen empty of debris, leading to a second level. A day or two passed until on 8 February I decided to try to establish the ownership of the 'new' tomb by descending the shaft, at the bottom of which a door opening off to the north could be discerned. My hope was that we might be able to establish the identity

*99 View looking north from the tomb-chapel of Pabes (foreground) into the courtyard of the tomb of Ramose. A shaft in the latter (indicated by an arrow) gave access to the substructure of the tomb of Maya in 1986. In the distance is the Step Pyramid of Zoser.*

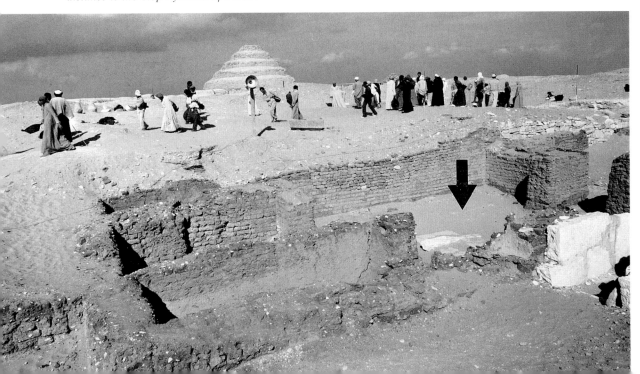

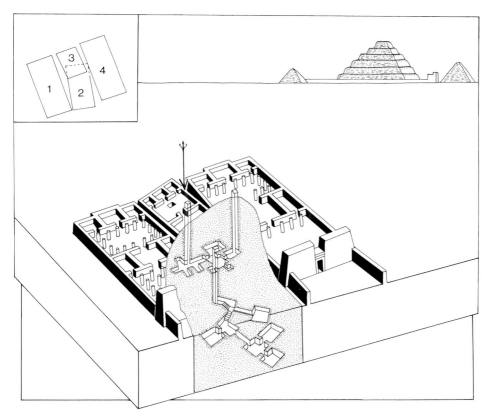

*100 Schematic drawing showing the shaft and substructure of the tomb of Maya and Meryt, and one of the shafts (arrowed) in the inner court of the tomb-chapel of Ramose. This shaft gave the current expedition access, by way of a plunderers' tunnel, to Maya's underground chambers in 1986. In the distance, to the north, the Step Pyramid of Zoser and the pyramids of Unas and Userkaf. Inset: (1) Tomb of Horemheb. (2) Tomb of Tia and Tia. (3) Tomb-chapel of Ramose. (4) Tomb of Maya.*

of the tomb-owner, or at least a member of his family, from inscribed objects which we might expect to find lying around in the debris.

It took only a few minutes to get into the shaft and to peer into the doorway at the bottom. From here a stairway could be seen curving round and downwards, the steps choked with rubble. Our lamps showed us two rock stelae cut into the walls to left and right (we had seen two others in the burial chamber at the top of the shaft). A moment or two passed while we negotiated the stairway, being careful not to disturb anything on the way down. The ancient robbers must have passed this way on leaving the burial chambers (we did not expect to find these undisturbed) and there was always the chance that they had dropped something in their anxiety to escape into the fresh air above. The ancient plunderers must have been in a great hurry to secrete their finds and to avoid the risk of detection by the necropolis authorities; the chances are, however, that these latter were sometimes in league with the tomb-robbers. On that February morning we ourselves were not in a particular hurry, not expecting to find anything dramatic, and being concerned at that stage with the prosaic business of manœuvring into position the cable from our generator, located on the desert about 25 metres above our heads. A second or two passed; my Dutch colleague and I held the light-bulb above our heads and gazed down beyond the stairway. We were totally unprepared for the sight that met our eyes: a room, full of carved reliefs, painted a rich golden yellow!

### The painted room

The ancient Egyptians were in the habit of lavishing much of their resources on their 'houses of eternity', as they called their tombs. Curiously, though, they tended to neglect the decoration of the burial chambers of their funerary monuments, which often were hardly more than rough-hewn caverns in the ground. By contrast the chapels and courtyards on the desert surface above were covered with painted reliefs and inscriptions, as we have seen in the tombs already described. After the interments were in position the underground burial chambers were never meant to be seen again by mortal eyes, whereas the buildings above ground would be the setting for the mortuary cult of the deceased, theoretically for ever. It was a complete surprise, therefore, when my Dutch colleague and I found ourselves confronted by finely painted reliefs in the newly discovered underground chamber. The accompanying texts identified the tomb-owners as Maya and Meryt. A corridor blocked with rubble opened off to the east.

Once we had discovered the substructure we knew immediately that over our heads, on the desert surface above, was the superstructure of the long-lost tomb of Maya in which Lepsius had stood one hundred and forty-three years before. Two choices faced us: we could empty the blocked corridor and penetrate through to the burial chambers (where all kinds of exciting finds might await us) or we could seal the area and the shaft we had discovered by chance and postpone the excavation of the substructure to a future season of work. Most people – the Press certainly – were rather astonished when I opted for the latter expedient. How could we possibly contain our impatience for twelve months or more (in the event it turned out to be longer)? The reasons are straightforward, even prosaic: archaeologists are not treasure hunters, the work underground would in any case need careful forethought and planning, and it was logistically more sensible to work from the desert surface downwards rather than the reverse. Furthermore, we had already begun a campaign of excavation that season, which was yielding interesting scientific results (described in Chapter 5), and it would be wrong, I thought, to abandon this work in favour of something that might be more 'spectacular'. So after the initial excitement had died down we resumed our activities in the small tomb-chapels of Khay, Pabes, and Ramose.

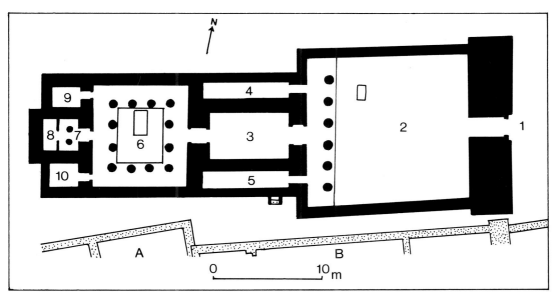

*101 Plan of the superstructure of the tomb of Maya and Meryt. (1) Forecourt. (2) Outer courtyard with colonnade. (3) Statue room. (4,5) Side chapels. (6) Colonnaded inner court with shaft leading to the burial chambers. (7,8) Offering room with projecting side walls. (9,10) Side chapels. (A) Outer court of the tomb of Ramose. (B) Inner courtyard of the tomb of the Tias.*

## The 1987 season

In 1987 we had the rewarding prospect of clearing the courtyards and chapels of Maya's tomb, and to stand where Lepsius had stood in 1843, and probably to gaze on some of the reliefs he recorded all those years ago. From his published plan it was clear that he had seen only a part of the inner court of what must have been a grandiose monument, on a par with that of the tomb of Horemheb.

Logically it would have been preferable perhaps to have located the east end or pylon entrance of the great monument, and then work systematically westwards towards the offering room and chapels, rather as we did with Horemheb's tomb. There was no clue on the desert surface as to where the entrance would be (though we guessed it would be roughly on a line with the pylon of Tia and Tia; our 1988 season of work was to show that our hunch was correct). Again, it is always desirable to be able to work from the known to the unknown, and we were aware that the main shaft of the tomb, beneath which we had stood in 1986, would be located within the second or inner courtyard of the tomb, the very court partly exposed in 1843 when Lepsius was in Saqqara. I thought it would be instructive to clear that court as a preliminary, to check to see what reliefs and other material remained, and to compare the surviving reliefs with the drawings published by the great Prussian scholar. The accuracy of his epigraphic work had never been tested, at least in the case of the Maya reliefs.

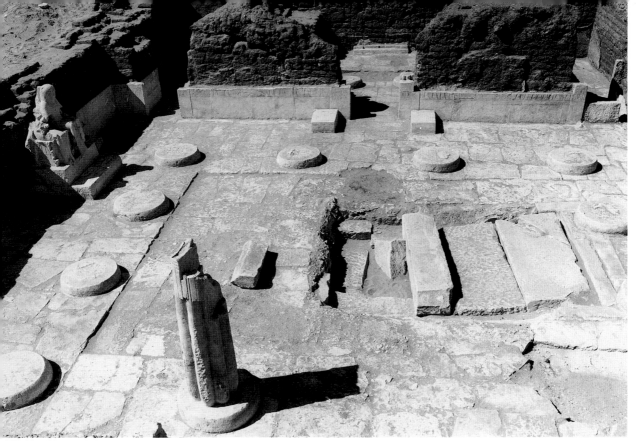

*102 View of the inner courtyard of the tomb of Maya and Meryt, looking westwards into the offering room and flanking chapels. The column and statue group to the left were seen and recorded by K.R. Lepsius in 1843. In the centre is the main shaft of the tomb, with three covering slabs in position, giving access to the substructure.*

Accordingly we set to work early in 1987, and before long had exposed the tops of the mud-brick walls of the inner court, the main cult room and its flanking chapels. As always the chief task was to clear away the huge amounts of superincumbent sand and debris that covered the architectural remains. Once this was done we could see that the part of the tomb now exposed was almost exactly similar to the corresponding area of the contemporary and nearby tomb of Horemheb; evidence, in fact, for the existence of a 'standard' tomb plan in the late Eighteenth Dynasty.

In a matter of days the inner courtyard, cult chamber and side chapels were completely free. It was an odd sensation to see the reliefs which Lepsius had admired gradually emerging from the sand as our workmen emptied the court. It quickly became evident, however, that quite a number of the wonderful blocks he had recorded were no longer on the walls or in the debris. Some reliefs positioned on the south wall had been taken down and sent to Berlin by Lepsius (as well as copying for posterity the standing monuments of the Nile Valley he was also engaged in collecting material for the great state museum in Prussia). These blocks survived unscathed in Berlin until the Second World War. During the bombardment of Germany they were very badly damaged by fire, so that only calcined fragments remain to this day, a timely reminder that the great treasures of antiquity (or indeed of more recent times) are not necessarily safe even if they are housed in a museum collection. Fortunately a set of good photographs of the Berlin reliefs was made earlier in the present century so that, together with the drawings made by Lepsius' copyist, there is an adequate record of the material. These reliefs, and the others we found in 1987 and 1988, will be described below.

What of the reliefs that had disappeared since 1843? It must be supposed that they were taken away from the tomb some time after Lepsius made his record of them, and that they went into the lime-kilns of local villagers, like so much from the Saqqara cemeteries in the last century.

## The statue-group

Lepsius had noted a double statue or dyad of Maya and his wife Meryt set against the south wall of the inner court, in front of the reliefs which subsequently went to Berlin. The dyad was in rather a damaged condition even when Lepsius saw it (to judge from his drawing). We found it thrown face downwards in the courtyard, thus revealing its base. Perhaps it had been treated in this cavalier fashion by the workmen who had received instructions to remove the reliefs for transportation to Prussia. The men who did it unwittingly gave us a valuable bonus, which we should never had had if the

*103 A column in the inner court of the tomb of Maya, found by the EES/Leiden Expedition overturned and shattered. Lepsius saw it in situ in 1843, and it has now been repaired and repositioned.*

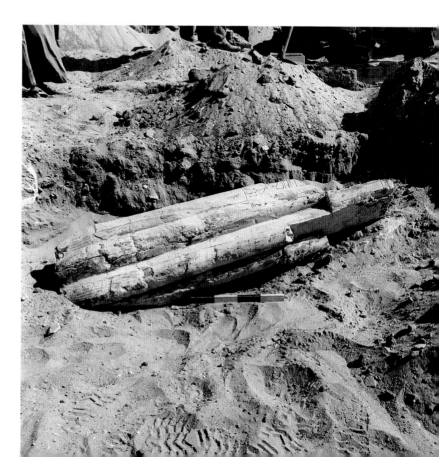

statue had been left upright in its proper place: the statue is carved from an Old Kingdom relief block, dating probably from the Fifth Dynasty (c. 2375 BC). The underside shows part of a scene of offerings, carved in delicate low relief. This was the first of many indications that the workmen who were constructing and decorating the tomb of Maya obtained much of their building material from existing monuments. We have found that many of the paving blocks and the reliefs forming the inner revetment of the courtyards derive from Old Kingdom monuments. From inscriptions carved on some of them it seems clear that a number of the blocks (perhaps most) come from the causeway of the pyramid of Unas, a few minutes' walk northwards of the tomb. One wonders if other New Kingdom statues now in museum collections, but originally from the Memphite necropolis, are similarly made from Old Kingdom blocks.

### The columniation

On Lepsius' plan of the inner court of the tomb a solitary column is drawn. This was one of twelve which supported the roof of the colonnade that ran round each of the four sides of the court and protected the reliefs on the walls underneath. Again, after Lepsius' departure in 1843 someone pushed over the column. We found it in 1987 shattered into several pieces, and in a very sad state. Our restorers, however, soon put it together again.

An inscribed panel bearing Maya's name and titles was carved on one side of the column, orientated towards the main axis of the tomb. When Lepsius saw it the panel was complete; in 1987 part of it was lacking. In 1988, when we came to excavate the deep shaft nearby in the centre of the courtyard we found the missing fragment of text. The finding of the panel fragment part way down the shaft indicated that the shaft itself must have been emptied in the nineteenth century, something which we should not otherwise have suspected (since we found no other evidence). Lepsius does not mention the shaft in his report.

### The cult chamber and side-chapels

The main cult room on the west side of the court was originally decorated with reliefs, and we can only speculate that they showed, as was customary, religious or funerary themes. They were all stripped away for re-use in antiquity, and for the most part all that survives are the setting lines at pavement level. A large stela, the focus of the cult, was set against the west wall. This too has gone, only the base remaining, but enough to give us a good idea of the stela's dimensions. The flanking side-chapels were decorated with painted

VII *Maya adoring Osiris: a block from the Memphite tomb of Maya, carved in delicate low relief. The raised hand of his wife Meryt, who accompanies him, may be seen behind his shoulder.*

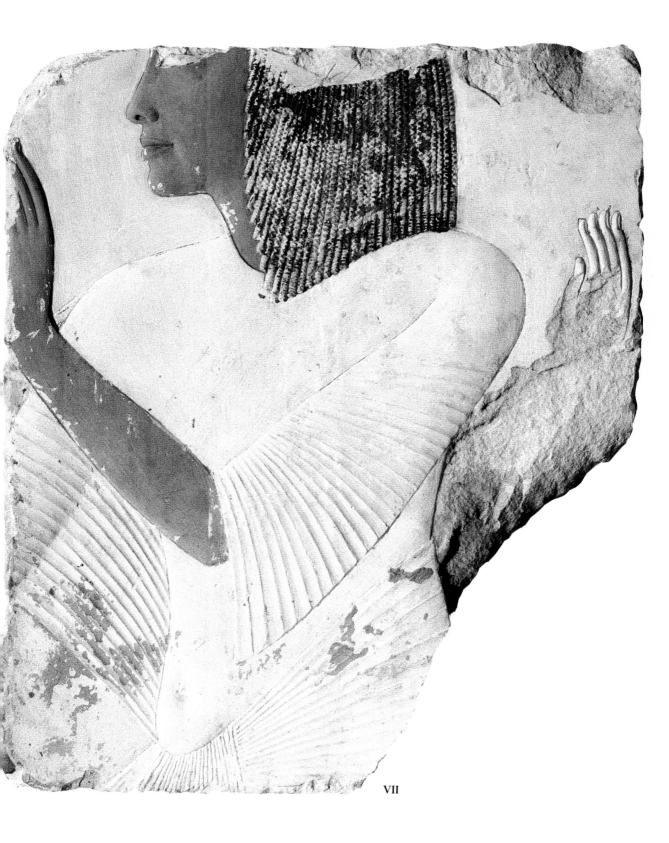

VII

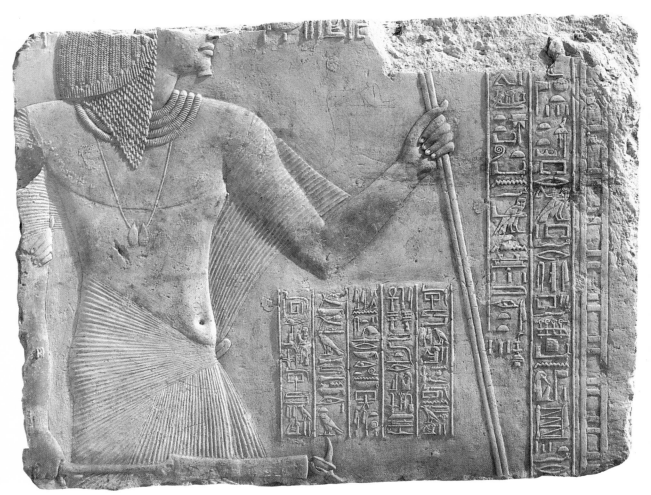

VIII

scenes on a mud-plaster base, like so many of the chapels in the Theban necropolis, but only minute traces of the paint remain. The side-chapels were once vaulted in mud brick, whereas the cult-room would have had a flat ceiling of limestone slabs, which in turn supported a small brick pyramid, Horemheb's tomb providing an exact parallel. The reveals or entrances to the chapels still bear the remains of scenes of offering-bringers, bearing in perpetuity the choice products that would, by magical means, have been placed on the altars in the chapels if the actual food-offerings failed. We shall see, as we examine the reliefs in Maya's tomb, that there is more emphasis than usual in the wall decorations on the provision of food and drink offerings. To judge from the number of large storage vessels found below ground in the tomb chambers Maya and Meryt were well provided for on that score. The emphasis on offerings contrasts in some respects with the scheme of decoration in the neighbouring tomb of Maya's colleague Horemheb. In the latter tomb, as we have seen, the great commander stresses aspects of his career. Maya, by contrast, is somewhat reticent about his administrative activities and private life, at least to judge from the extant reliefs in his Memphite tomb. Perhaps Horemheb had more to crow about, while Maya went about his life, and carried out his duties, with a minimum of display and fuss. Though the feeling is completely subjective, I get the strong impression that Maya and Horemheb, though close colleagues and even perhaps intimate friends, each had a different personal 'style', originating in their background and upbringing.

## Maya blocks from the Apa Jeremias monastery

I have mentioned more than once that the builders of the New Kingdom funerary monuments in the Memphite necropolis were in the habit of dismantling existing monuments at Saqqara in order to re-use the blocks. This was happening right down into the Christian period and even later. An English archaeologist, J.E. Quibell, excavating between 1908 and 1910 in an important Coptic monastery a little to the east of our site, found that the architects had, in the fifth century AD and later, dismantled a number of New Kingdom tombs in the nearby cemetery. The monastery itself was eventually abandoned on the advent of Islam, fell into disuse, and was itself plundered for stone. If Quibell had had the luck to find the buildings of the monastery more or less intact he would doubtless have been able to reconstruct, from the blocks of which they were partly composed, quite a number of New Kingdom monuments! As it is

VIII *Maya holding his staves of office. He wears a magnificent full wig, a necklace consisting of four rows of dozens of gold disk beads, and a pendant on a chain, as well as a finely pleated garment. A small ceremonial beard is attached to his chin. This block was in position in the tomb of Maya when Lepsius visited the site in 1843. The EES/Leiden Expedition found it lying in the debris.*

we have only the pieces which survived after most of the rooms in the great Coptic settlement had been plundered and stripped of stone. The blocks that remained until the present century, fortunately for us, included at least twelve reliefs from the tomb of Maya and Meryt. These are now in the Cairo Museum. All the blocks found in the Apa Jeremias monastery have given new insights into New Kingdom art in the Memphite area, and they also furnish clues to the presence of tombs of important administrators in Memphis in the period spanned by the reigns of Tutankhamun and Ramesses II.

As we excavated the inner courtyard we were struck by the fact that though only a small number of reliefs survived in position (at the lowest level of the east, south, and west walls), some of them must have been there when Lepsius recorded the tomb in 1843 – yet he took no account of them. This is hard to explain, since he assuredly saw them. Perhaps his time was limited, so he may have given instructions to record only what he himself regarded as being of prime importance.

Our own discoveries and rediscoveries of reliefs, those found by Quibell, and Lepsius' drawings of scenes which have now been destroyed or have disappeared, mean that we can form a very good idea of the scheme of decoration of the inner court of Maya's tomb, and it is to this area of the monument that we shall now turn.

### The inner court of the tomb

The scenes in this part of the monument are almost without exception conventional in content, but none the less interesting for that. They illustrate themes that were *de rigueur* in any Egyptian tomb of note, and mainly have to do with provisions for the mortuary cult of the owners, and the depiction of funerary objects that would have been useful to Maya and Meryt in their abode in the Netherworld. All this is in marked contrast to the inner court of the tomb of Maya's contemporary, Horemheb, where unique historical scenes were carved by a masterly hand. Maya's reliefs are certainly major works of art, but as I have stressed he seems a little reticent about revealing or recording for posterity very much of his private life, personal beliefs, and administrative responsibilities. By and large only the lowest courses of limestone revetment remain in position in the courtyard (so much is lost here) that we have to recognize that we may be arguing from silence.

The true position of the Maya blocks found by Quibell in the Monastery of Apa Jeremias has yet to be worked out satisfactorily. They seem to come originally from the inner court. Since there are no 'joins' with blocks found *in situ* by Lepsius and later by us in 1987 (by which time some of the reliefs recorded by the Prussian scholar had disappeared) we cannot yet be sure on which wall or walls they were mounted. Only one of them need detain us. It shows Maya and Meryt seated, with three attendants censing and bringing offerings. On the same block Maya is shown worshipping the cow of Hathor in

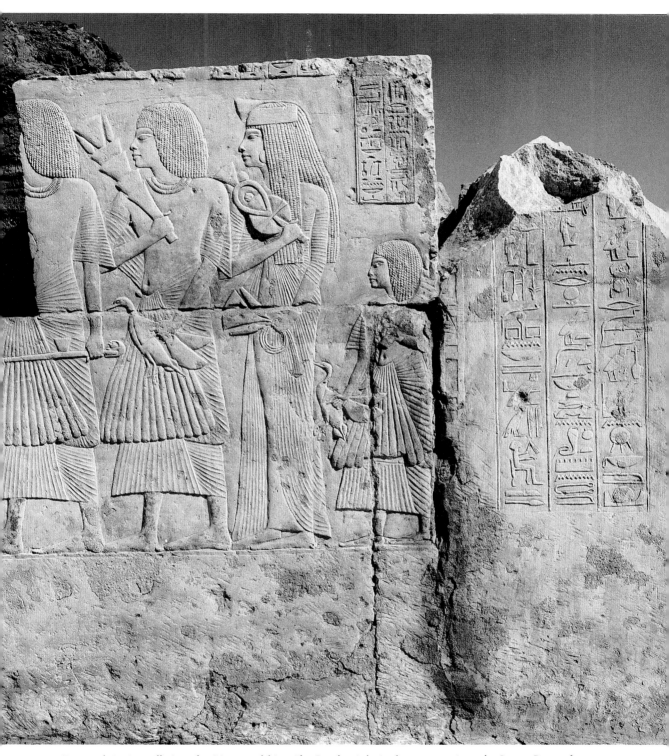

*104 Bearers bringing offerings for Maya and his wife. On the right is the entrance into the Statue Room from the inner court of the tomb.*

a barque. Almost the sole insight we have into the tomb-owner's administrative duties (apart from the inscriptions recording his official titles) occurs also on the same relief: Maya is shown supervising the registration of Western Asiatic captives and of humped cattle brought in by herdsmen. It is not unlikely that these prisoners were among those depicted in Horemheb's tomb, subsequently handed over by the great military commander to his colleague the overseer of the treasury, so that they could be allocated to work projects or other duties for which he had responsibility.

On other blocks found by Quibell or recorded by Lepsius hymns to the sun, and to the moon, as well as a depiction of Hathor being offered to in a shrine, emphasize Maya's predilection for scenes which were religious in content.

On the south side of the courtyard Lepsius saw a magnificent series of blocks depicting Maya's funeral procession. Officiants are dragging seated and standing statues of the tomb-owner, and they are followed by men with jars and chests. Mourners are also present. Maya's coffin, as well as a kneeling statue of the great official, are being dragged into a courtyard of his funerary monument. These were the scenes removed to Berlin by Lepsius.

We ourselves were lucky enough to find some blocks forming the east wall of the inner courtyard, either in position or in the debris. The best preserved reliefs show offering-bearers in front of Maya and Meryt, a work of art carved in delicate low relief like so many of the scenes in the monument.

## The Statue Room and chapels

Once we had completed the excavation of the inner courtyard of the tomb and its associated chapels our workmen were directed to move eastwards. Before long they had uncovered a large room, originally housing two statues (or possibly dyads), flanked by side-chapels. The latter were undecorated, and had been re-used in the early Christian period as dwellings, just as in their counterparts in the tomb of Horemheb. In the southern chapel a large stela was still in position upright against the west wall. Frustratingly for us it was completely blank. The excitement, as the round top of the stela began to emerge from the sand, can be imagined. Could this prove to be the long biographical text giving details of Maya and his family, for which we had been hoping? Perhaps the text had been painted on the stela (as a time-saving factor); at any rate, no trace survived to our day. But our hope of finding some biographical information was soon to be forthcoming. The stela in the north chapel flanking the Statue Room had been removed in antiquity.

The Statue Room, which as we now know is roughly in the centre of the superstructure, must have been the focus of a statue cult. Two emplacements for images of the tomb-owner (and possibly his wife) are still to be seen on the west side of the room, which itself was originally vaulted in mud brick and was very dark. Clouds of incense wafted by the mortuary priests in the direction of the statues would have made it a very stuffy chamber.

*105* (Opposite) *Dyad of Maya and Meryt, originally in position in their Memphite tomb. It was removed to Europe in the early part of the nineteenth century. Unlike many Egyptian statues this dyad is virtually in pristine condition.*

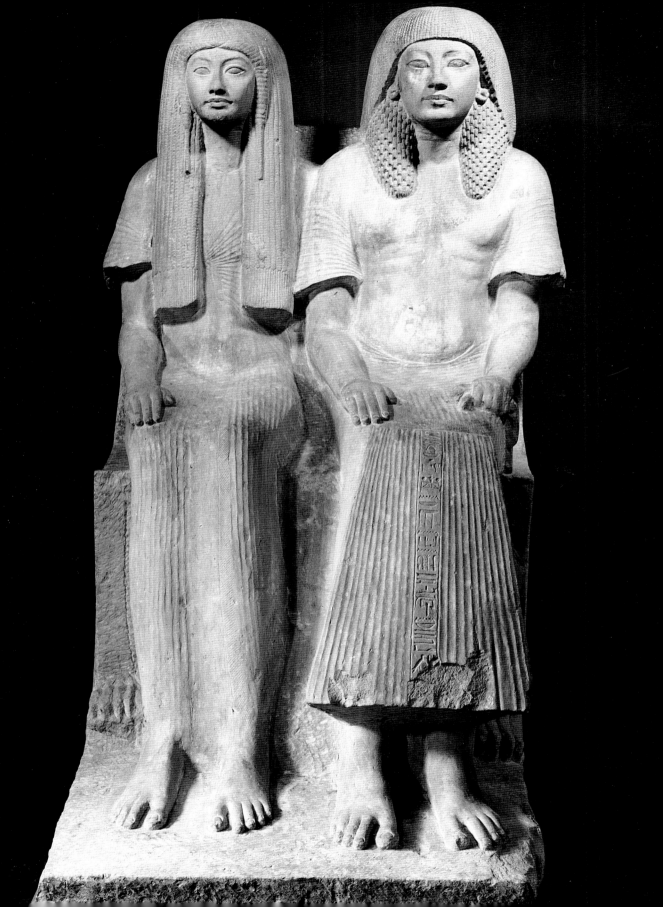

At an uncertain date in the 1820s three statues, virtually complete and undamaged, were acquired by the National Museum of Antiquities in Leiden. These are major masterpieces of Egyptian New Kingdom art, and since they are inscribed for Maya and Meryt they must have come from their tomb at Saqqara. Two of them could have been positioned in the Statue Room recently uncovered, but the original position of all three will have to be worked out once we have measured and studied them in detail. Setting lines in plaster on the emplacements may give the necessary clues. We have found other emplacements for statues, mostly large-scale, during the course of our work in the tomb. Three-dimensional representations of the tomb-owners were very important elements in the decoration of the chapels and courts of New Kingdom funerary monuments in the Memphite necropolis, emphasizing these monuments' resemblance to temples. The statues embodied the spirit of the deceased, and in a practical sense were the recipients of some of the funerary offerings which were placed on the stone altars positioned in front of the plinths on which they were mounted. Maya's tomb presents us with an enigma: the monument itself, though preserving much vital information, was virtually dismantled in antiquity, both mud bricks and reliefs being carted off for re-use. Yet the three Leiden statues are in almost mint condition, and must have survived in or near the tomb until the early nineteenth century. The answer must be that the ancient stone plunderers found no use for cumbersome pieces of masonry, such as life-size statues, and so left them where they were. All told there must have been at least ten statues in the superstructure of the tomb; the missing ones must have been broken up and cast into the lime-kilns.

It is interesting that the series of Maya reliefs in Berlin, recorded by Lepsius and removed from the south wall of the inner court, show a number of statues of Maya being dragged into place in his tomb. One of them is naophorous: Maya is holding a miniature shrine that would have contained the figure of a deity, possibly Osiris, god of the dead, or perhaps Ptah, the ancient Memphite god, in front of him. This statue has not survived, though there is always a possibility that we shall find it in subsequent digging in and around Maya's tomb.

The reliefs on both sides of the short passage linking the inner courtyard with the Statue Room were seen and recorded by Lepsius. We were lucky enough to find parts of them still extant, and they prove to be major works of art. On the south wall Maya is seen facing westwards, grasping two staves in his hand. On the north wall he and his wife are offered incense and libations in the company of his stepmother, Henutiunu.

A small area of painted plaster showing legs and feet, surviving at the level of the dado of the Statue Room, is all that remains of the decoration of the large room. This fragmentary scene, interesting in itself, serves to remind us that until our expedition began work in the Memphite necropolis in 1975 it was always thought that painted plaster was characteristic of the decoration of Theban New Kingdom private tombs. Most, if not all, of the many isolated

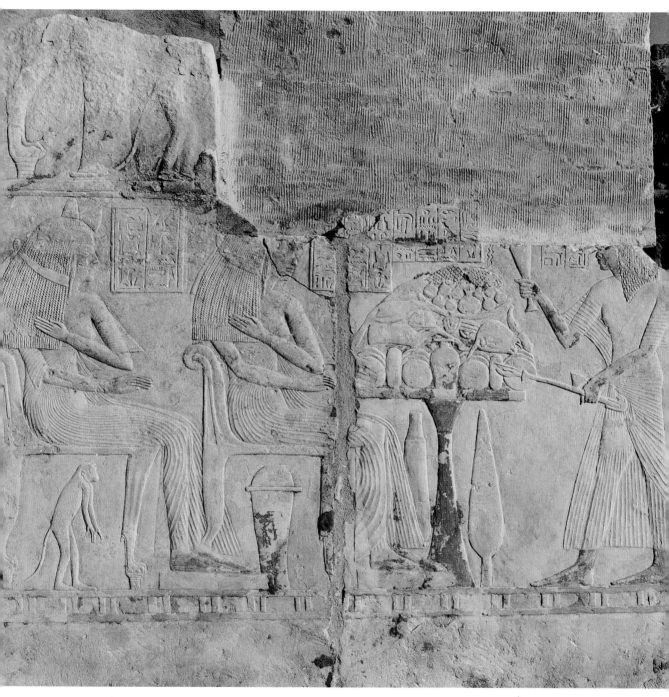

*106 Maya and Meryt before a table heaped with food, being censed and ritualistically cleansed. A monkey stands under the chair of Maya's wife. Far more of this relief was in position on the wall when Lepsius made his drawing of this scene in 1843.*

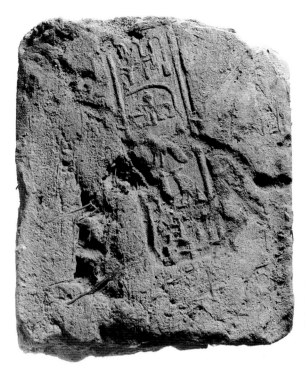

*107 A mud brick stamped with the inscription 'royal scribe, overseer of the treasury Maya, true of voice'. Such bricks were incorporated in the superstructure of the great official's tomb.*

fragments of such plaster decoration in museum collections and in private hands have been unhesitatingly assigned to Thebes. We are finding plenty of evidence (the chapels at the west end of Maya's tomb have already been cited) to prove that the statue rooms and chapels of New Kingdom Saqqara tombs had decoration on a mud-plaster base. The pylons, courtyards and sometimes the principal cult rooms of the great Memphite tombs had limestone relief decoration carved on individual blocks. Such are not found in Theban private tombs, at least in the New Kingdom. So even small and seemingly banal fragments, such as the painted plaster in Maya's Statue Room, may cause us to revise our received and accepted ideas.

It was interesting to find, while we were clearing the Statue Room and adjacent chapels, that some of the mud bricks forming the superstructure were stamped with the name and titles of Maya.

The larger flagstones forming the pavement of the Statue Room are re-used Old Kingdom blocks, split into slices by the New Kingdom architects. They probably derive from the walls of the Unas causeway.

---

IX (Opposite) *A group of people bearing offerings carry food supplies and other produce for Maya and Meryt. Such gifts guaranteed a perpetual source of nourishment for the tomb owners buried below in the substructure of the tomb. One of the bearers is named as 'the scribe of the treasury Sennefer', the other 'the secretary of the overseer of the treasury (Maya) Ptahmose'. Both doubtless worked in the government office of the tomb owner.*

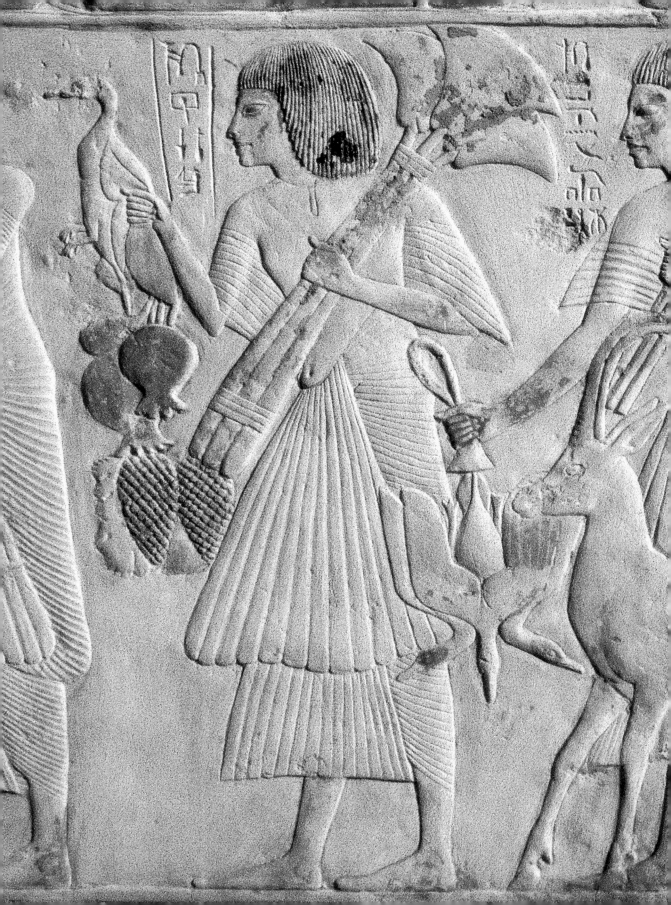

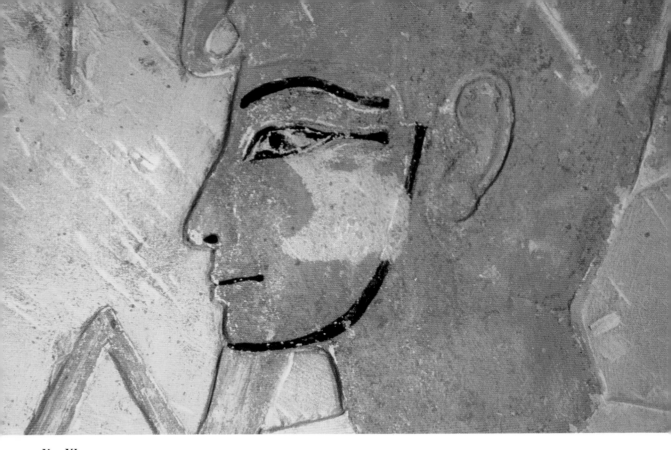

X    XI

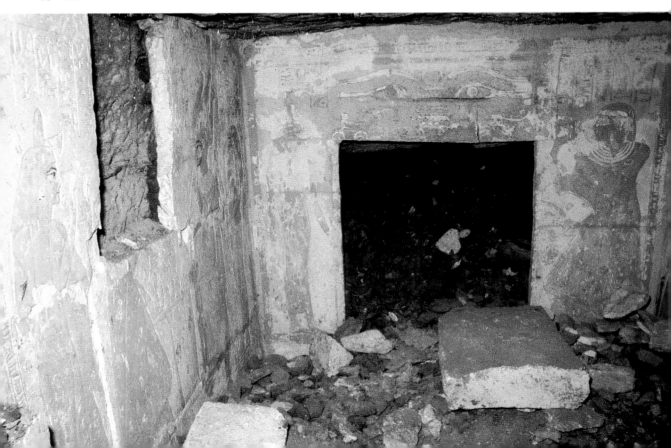

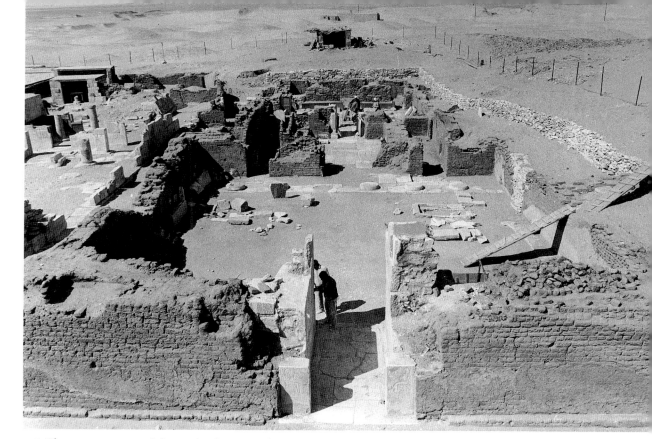

108 *The superstructure of the tomb of Maya and Meryt, looking west towards the pyramid enclosure of Sekhemkhet in the far distance. In the foreground is the great pylon entrance with limestone reliefs on both reveals, now restored by the Expedition. To the left is the tomb of Tia and Tia, with the tomb-chapels of Khay, Pabes and Ramose behind.*

## The outer courtyard

Moving now eastwards we began to excavate, towards the end of our 1987 campaign, the outer court of the tomb of Maya, which ancient visitors to the tomb would have entered through the ceremonial entrance on the east. Up till now the plan of the tomb had been almost a replica of Horemheb's, but in the newly emerging courtyard it was clear that there was a difference: Maya's outer court was colonnaded only on its west side, and the floor of the court was not finished with the expected limestone flagstones but was formed of hard mud. A small and shallow ramp, also in mud, led from the pavement to the centre of the colonnade. Emplacements for two large statues are to be seen in that area, at the entrance to the Statue Room.

Tiny fragments of limestone revetment, and setting lines scratched on the blocks forming its base, show that the inner walls of the great court had been lined with stone blocks, as was to be expected in a tomb of this magnitude. For

---

X *Head of Osiris: detail of a relief in the substructure of the tomb of Maya.*

XI *Overview of decorated chamber H which gave access to the burials of Maya and Meryt, as found by the EES/Leiden Expedition in 1986.*

once the ancient stone plunderers had been very thorough, and took away every block, not even leaving one in the debris of the court. Such a situation is a little unusual; in our excavations over the years we have never failed to find revetment *in situ* or blocks left lying loose for eventual removal. The courtyard, with its mud pavement, gives the impression of being in an unfinished state, and it is perfectly possible that the limestone revetment on the inner side of the walls was never carved and inscribed. If this is the case all the surviving loose blocks from the tomb, including those found by Quibell, must come from the decoration of the inner courtyard and also just possibly from the west wall of the outer court, under the colonnade, though there is no sure evidence that this wall was completely carved; we found one block in sunk relief that could have come from here. It is not particularly unusual to find important funerary monuments of people of rank left unfinished at their death, and a number of reasons can be advanced to account for it. The obvious one is that the tomb-owner died prematurely, though this can hardly be the answer in the case of Maya, who seems to have lived to a 'goodly old age', surviving well into the reign of his erstwhile colleague, Horemheb. A son and heir would have been responsible for finishing the tomb after the father's death; but Maya had only daughters. Perhaps they, or Maya's other surviving relatives, were unable, or unwilling, to put the remaining work in hand.

### The pylon and forecourt

By the end of the 1987 season the excavation of the great court was almost complete, but we still had to reveal the ceremonial entrance or pylon of the tomb and the expected forecourt to the east of it. In some ways this was a satisfactory state of affairs, since we had found more than enough to cope with during that excavating season. In any case we hardly expected any major revelations when we came to excavate the pylon. The most that could be hoped for was the usual massive mud-brick structure, perhaps with the remains of an undecorated casing or revetment of limestone at the lowest level of the walls. At least this had been so in Horemheb's tomb, which was in a much better state of repair than Maya's. But we were in for a great surprise.

Our objective for the 1988 campaign was twofold: to reveal the pylon and forecourt as soon as possible (to have the complete plan of the superstructure of the tomb), and then to concentrate our efforts on the rooms and passages below ground, some of which we had seen in 1986.

When our workmen began to empty the debris between the two 'wings' or towers of the pylon, which were rather badly destroyed, it quickly became clear that both side walls of the entrance passage had been lined with orthostats or slabs of limestone. So had Horemheb's pylon – but the difference here was that the counterpart in Maya's pylon had been carved with reliefs of superlative quality – and on a large scale. Some of the reliefs were still firmly in position (on the north side), others (on the south) had been partly eased out of position in

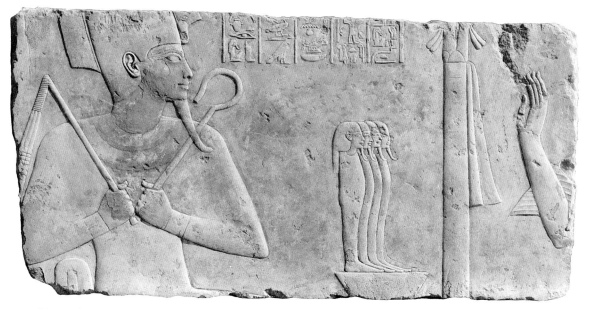

*109 Maya adores Osiris. The presence of this scene at the entrance to the tomb emphasizes its resemblance to a mortuary temple. Before the deity are the four Sons of Horus, represented standing on a lotus bloom.*

antiquity so that they could be taken away for re-use. More blocks clearly belonging to the series were lying higgledy-piggledy in the debris. Before very long we were sure that the stone plunderers had been interrupted in their work or had decided to leave the blocks where they were. Moreover, in the early nineteenth century (when there had been so much activity in the Saqqara necropolis) no-one had had the luck to find them. We are in the happy position of having the more-or-less complete scheme of decoration of the entrance pylon of one of the major tombs of the late Eighteenth Dynasty in the Memphite necropolis. Such a series of reliefs in this position and for this period may well prove to be unique – only future excavations will tell – but it is highly probable that in most great tombs dating to the end of the Eighteenth Dynasty the revetment of the pylons will have been stripped away, since such blocks were so easily accessible.

Our local restoration team had the task of re-assembling the blocks, cleaning, conserving and also mending them where they had been shattered in antiquity. This work was carried out during the months of February and March 1988, and we now know that the original height of the reliefs is almost 3.5 metres. In brief, the resultant decorative scheme is as follows.

### North wall of pylon entrance

Maya and his wife are here represented standing and adoring Osiris, god of the Underworld. The deity is shown seated on his throne under a baldachin. In front of him are the so-called Four Sons of Horus on a lotus flower, and a text consisting of six columns of epithets extracted from hymns to Osiris. By an extraordinary coincidence, while we were clearing the sand and rubble from the forecourt in front of the pylon a master-copy of the same inscription was found, written on the exterior of a pot that had once contained yellow paint.

The presence of Osiris at the very entrance of the tomb is highly unusual, if not unique. It is yet another indicator that the great New Kingdom tombs that we are excavating at Saqqara functioned as mortuary temples and not solely as a safe repository for the mummy. Osiris was pre-eminently the god of the dead.

Below the scene with Osiris there is a beautifully preserved register showing nine offering bearers, some of whom are named (their names also occur on blocks from the inner courtyard which were recorded by Lepsius). They are no doubt minor functionaries in Maya's government office and the personal servants of Maya and Meryt; their presence helps us to build up a picture of the great official's household in Memphis. There are many finely carved details on this scene, including representations of an ibex and a bull-calf, and much of the original colour is preserved. By a miracle of survival we now have for study a major work of art of the time of Tutankhamun.

**South wall of pylon entrance**

Maya is shown on this wall standing and holding his sceptre of office. Round his neck are a quite extraordinary number of heavy gold collars, the traditional rewards bestowed by Pharaoh on his faithful administrators – but only those of the highest rank. Maya's figure is just about life-size. By comparison the figure of his brother Nahuher, seen immediately behind him, is minute. This member of the family is shown elsewhere in the tomb, where he is called a royal scribe and steward. His presence here seems to emphasize that Maya had no sons. The upkeep of the tomb and the maintenance of the vital funerary cult of Maya and Meryt may well have been Nahuher's responsibility. For all we know, the running of Maya's no doubt extensive estates may well have devolved on him, even in his brother's lifetime. In front of Maya, on this scene, are the figures of Meryt and his stepmother Henutiunu, who both raise their hands towards him and welcome him into the tomb. This gesture seems to be an indicator that they predeceased him, and this evidence may be of importance when we try to establish which of the two burial chambers found below ground later in the season was Maya's and which was Meryt's.

In front of the two ladies are inscriptions recording their speech to Maya; Meryt says: 'Welcome, you who are adorned with the favours of Ptah South-of-his-Wall! How well you deserve them, oh praised one who comes forth in front of the praised ones, for you remain leader of the festival of the Lord of the Gods! So says his beloved wife, the lady Meryt, true of voice.' Henutiunu's address was similar, but the text is badly broken.

Above this scene is an inscription which originally consisted of thirty-one columns. Part of it was Maya's address to visitors to his tomb: 'to the people who come and want to divert themselves in the West and to have a walk in the District of Eternity', the latter meaning the Saqqara necropolis; an early reference to 'tourism'. The continuation of the text is in some ways even more interesting since it consists of a laudatory autobiographical account of Maya's career and his relationship with Pharaoh.

... the governance which came into being through me, as something that was ordained for me by my God since my youth, the presence of the King having been granted to me since I was a child. I happily reached the end [of my career], enjoying countless favours of the Lord of the Two Lands.... In the beginning I was good, in the end I was brilliant, one who was revered in peace in the temple of Ptah. I carried out the plans of the King of my time without neglecting anything he had commanded . . . [I made splendid?] the temples, fashioning the images of the gods for whom I was responsible. I entered face to face to the August Image . . .

We have already drawn attention to the fact that during the reign of Tutankhamun's predecessor, Akhenaten, the ancient cult temples had been closed down and their revenues diverted to the new state religion, Atenism. The images of the deities, often of gold or electrum, must have been removed from their shrines, and melted down for re-use, or broken up and dispersed, if they were of stone. Maya's speech seems to refer to the making of new statues of the gods on the accession of Tutankhamun.

We should very much like to know which Pharaoh is referred to in the earlier part of the text. Maya seems rather unwilling to spell out his name, and there is the distinct possibility that it is none other than the heretic ruler Akhenaten. During this later epoch his name was probably anathema (it certainly was in the succeeding Ramesside Period), and it would have been distinctly impolitic to mention him in a tomb inscription. Nevertheless many high-ranking officials in the government of Tutankhamun and his immediate successors must have begun their careers during the ascendancy of Akhenaten and Nefertiti, and may even have been intimately associated with their now proscribed religion, Atenism. It is impossible to know whether, in his heart of hearts, Tutankhamun himself rejected the teachings of Akhenaten, who was very probably his own father, and in any case certainly his father-in-law (Tutankhamun married Akhenaten's third daughter, Ankhesenpaaten, later called Ankhesenamun). Be that as it may, the biographical text in Maya's tomb is a real addition to knowledge.

In the register beneath the scene just described there are yet more offering bearers moving towards the interior of the monument. Among the gifts and equipment they are bringing are sundry pairs of gloves, an article of attire not often seen on Egyptian reliefs. One of the pairs is shown in the form of human hands, with the fingernails rendered.

The reliefs on the side walls of the pylon entrance were originally roofed over with large slabs of limestone, so that a kind of short passageway was formed. We were lucky enough to find parts of these ceiling slabs, the undersides of

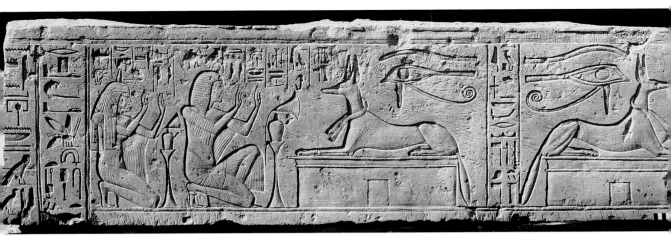

*110 Maya and Meryt adore statues of the jackal god Anubis, seen recumbent on a shrine. The block is part of a massive lintel once positioned over the pylon entrance to the tomb of Maya and Meryt.*

which were painted in a pattern reminiscent of some of the decorated ceilings in the New Kingdom rock tombs at Thebes. On one piece there were traces of a text which name the owner and give some of his titles in the administration. We also found a lintel, practically complete, which would have been positioned over the entrance, or more probably the exit of the passageway. It shows Maya and Meryt kneeling and worshipping Anubis on his shrine. Readers with a penchant for detail will note that the two Eyes of Horus, seen behind each of the two Anubis figures, differ slightly in size. There must be a reason for this: the phenomenon can be seen on other Egyptian reliefs, but no satisfactory answer is yet forthcoming. The ancient craftsmen were perfectly capable of carving both Eyes exactly the same size, if this was what was required.

Parts of the doorjambs of the entrance and exit of the pylon are also extant. Once the work of conserving and restoring the gateway has been completed we shall have an excellent idea about the original appearance of the entrance pylon of a great Memphite tomb of the time of Tutankhamun.

Before quitting the superstructure of the tomb to examine the underground parts, which our workmen were clearing concurrently in 1988, let us look briefly at some of the finds of objects and other things in the various rooms above ground, and also take a glimpse at the outside of the monument.

### The finds

One of the most puzzling discoveries, excavated in the north chapel adjacent to the cult room, was a humerus (or long bone) of a very large animal. There seems no reason to doubt that it is part of the skeleton of an elephant; confirmation of this, together with evidence of date, should be forthcoming once the material is examined scientifically. There is as yet no concrete evidence that it dates from the time of Maya (though it was found just above pavement level in the chapel). More probably it is of the Roman Period, when elephants were used as a powerful arm of the military. There seems every likelihood that one of these gigantic beasts died either in the cultivated area of the Nile Valley or while on manœuvres on the desert plateau. At any rate the disposal of the carcase must have presented a problem. To my knowledge this is the first recorded evidence for the presence of elephants at Saqqara.

We have yet to investigate over twenty tomb shafts, later in date than Maya's tomb, but cut into the walls and courts of his monument. No doubt objects and human remains will be plentiful when we come to investigate these intrusive pits. We did find one complete and undisturbed burial at pavement level in the outer courtyard of the tomb in 1988, positioned against the south wing of the pylon. Under the skeleton were the shawabtis of the deceased, clumsily carved, and with texts that were mumbo-jumbo. The interment dates from the late Ramesside Period or perhaps more probably to the Twenty-first Dynasty, like the burials in Iurudef's shaft that we dealt with in Chapter 5. Like some of the material found there, the newly discovered shawabtis would almost certainly have been condemned as modern fakes had they been presented out of context for examination by experts. This is yet another reminder that it is easy to condemn antiquities that do not quite fall into the well-known categories or are inscribed with 'barbarous' or suspect texts. Such objects however, may well have come from ancient ateliers, the workers in which were mass-producing funerary equipment, and were to all intents illiterate. Such objects are intriguing and well worthy of detailed study and publication since they throw

*111 View showing the small chapel built against the exterior of the south wall of the tomb of Maya. The stela inside names Yamen, the lector-priest who was responsible for the funerary cult of the tomb owner and his wife.*

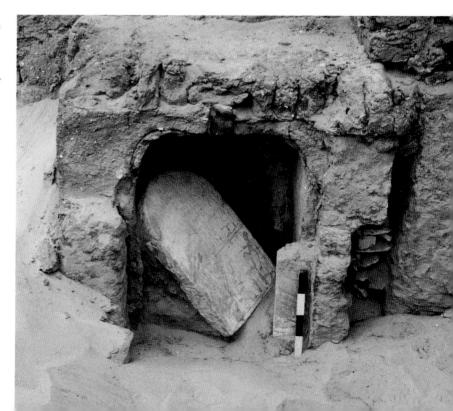

light on the customs of the ancient Egyptians in the later periods of their history, and even to a certain extent give an insight into their mentality.

We have already mentioned the fact that Maya is not particularly forthcoming about his public or his private life, at least in his funerary monument. All the more gratifying was it to find therefore, just as our work in 1988 was drawing to an end, some information on the arrangements he made before his death (in the reign of Horemheb) for the perpetuation of his cult and thus of his memory. This came in the form of a perfectly preserved stela of limestone, found in position in its original niche built on the exterior of the south wall of the tomb. It bears the unusual, if not unique, name of a funerary priest of Maya, an individual who was called Yamen. There are clues to indicate that other niches for stelae (doubtless of mortuary priests) were cut into the walls of Maya's monument, and it may well prove that the presence of such stela-niches is a regular feature of the great Memphite tombs of the Eighteenth Dynasty and even later. Lector priests or funerary officiants were crucial to the survival of the spirits of Maya and Meryt, especially as the latter did not produce a male heir who, had he existed, would have been responsible for his parents' mortuary cult. Associated with Yamen's stela was a slab on which the offerings for Maya and his wife would have been placed, as well as a small wooden statuette and a bunch of plant remains. At present we cannot be certain if this floral offering found its way here by chance (it could have been brought in by desert mice!) at a later period.

## Embalmers' materials

In the narrow passageway between the tombs of Tia and Maya there were found several caches of embalmers' materials. These consisted of bags of natron (sodium carbonate from the Wadi Natrun in the Western Desert) used in the process of drying out corpses, as well as strips of linen, the leftovers from the wrappings of the mummies. We also found the swabs used in wiping the insides of the bodies once they had been purged of their contents. This kind of material is not very inspiring stuff to look at, but again it throws intriguing light on the customs of the ancient Egyptians. Our area of Saqqara is proving to be productive of embalmers' caches; they seem rarely to have been excavated in other parts of Egypt, perhaps because the cemeteries there are so much turned over, or more so than the Memphite necropolis. The Saqqara caches which we have recently unearthed range in date from the New Kingdom through to the Late Period and possibly even down to the Ptolemaic Period. It is clear that everything that had been in contact with the corpse during the mummification ceremonies was in a sense sacrosanct, and had to be buried in a pit or in the sand, not in the tomb but at least adjacent to it. None of the pottery jars, which are always a feature of the caches, bears the name of the deceased, so though it is not improbable that we have the actual embalming materials used in preparing the mummies of Maya and Meryt we cannot prove it.

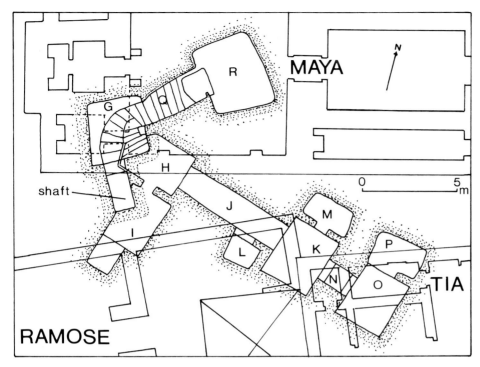

*112 Plan of the lower level of the substructure of the tomb of Maya. Rooms H, K and O are decorated with painted reliefs. The shaft indicated on the plan is situated in the northeast corner of the inner court of the tomb-chapel of Ramose, from which the EES/ Leiden Expedition gained access to Maya's burial chambers in 1986.*

## The substructure of Maya's tomb

The morning of 8 February 1986, will always have a special place in my memory, and no doubt in that of my Dutch colleague, Jacobus van Dijk, when together we stumbled, quite literally, into the first painted chamber of the substructure of the tomb. His memorable cry on that occasion, on catching sight of the inscription naming the tomb-owner ('My God, it's Maya!') reverberated round the world. Without doubt it was a thrilling moment for us both and for the other members of our joint expedition waiting on the surface above. Our exhilaration was tempered by the thought that the task of excavating the enormous amount of spoil below ground, and of restoring and conserving as well as recording the reliefs (and we did not yet know the full extent of the problem) would take us several seasons of hard work. Still, we had had plenty of experience by now, from excavating in the humid conditions underground at Saqqara. At the deepest levels Horemheb's underground chambers were over 28 metres below the desert surface, and the temperature there approached 100 degrees Fahrenheit (38 degrees C). We could expect that the deepest rooms of Maya's complex would be as damp (and as potentially dangerous because of the state of the bedrock) as Horemheb's. But to go back to the beginning . . .

### The discovery of the substructure

In 1986, when we penetrated from Ramose's tomb into the subterranean complex which we identified as Maya's, it was clear that at least two levels were involved. In 1988 we began systematically to empty the main burial shaft in the inner court of the superstructure, and after a day or two found ourselves in a passageway leading southwards into a series of roughly hewn chambers. One of these was the room with an empty shaft descending to a lower level, in which we had stood two years earlier. The upper level of rooms, with some skeletal remains and much pottery, was of interest from the scientific point of view, but need not detain us here. All the burials we saw (and the associated objects) in this level seem to date from a period much later than the time of Maya. I have pointed out more than once that the tombs in the Memphite necropolis, great and small, have been used over and over again. This was why it was such a surprise (anticipating our discoveries in the second level) to find that in that location there was *no* intrusive material of later times. Only a couple of Late Period amulets seem to have fallen down the empty shaft from the intrusive interments in the rooms above. In other words, all the objects and pottery we subsequently found in the debris of the second level are part of the tomb equipment of Maya and Meryt, and just possibly other members of their family.

It is a great puzzle as to why the lower complex of rooms was not used for later burials. Perhaps, as with Horemheb's tomb, the chambers at this depth (approaching 22 metres) were simply too far from the surface. The fact that, in the second level of Maya's tomb, we are dealing only with the primary interments (including the skeletal remains) means that our task of interpretation is vastly simplified: all the objects, pottery, and other material are very closely datable.

## The burial complex of Maya and Meryt

In our 1986 reconnaissance underground we were able only to enter one decorated room in the lower level, which opened from the stairway leading off from the bottom of the empty shaft. Enormous amounts of rubble were evident in side rooms and in the corridor leading off from the first decorated room. Our initial task in excavating the second level in 1988 was to clear the staircase and remove as much rubble as possible to the surface above. Where did all the rubble and chippings come from? As with the subterranean rooms of Horemheb's tomb, this material was the 'spoil' of the original masons, the rock removed as they hewed out the burial chambers, corridors and storerooms underground. The debris thus accumulated was set aside to be used as blocking material, particularly in the approach corridors, once the burials were in position. The entrances to the corridors were then sealed with large stones or slabs. The ancient robbers were faced with the problem of demolishing these and redistributing the loose chippings so that they could penetrate through to the burial chambers.

## The first decorated chamber (H)

The bedrock at this level (some 22 metres below the surface) is extremely bad, and is as soft as putty. With the rise of the water-table in the present century, and more particularly in recent years, conditions are extremely damp in the subterranean rooms. By a miracle the reliefs in the first chamber (and those in two others we subsequently found) have not been affected by the prevailing humidity. It is not easy to explain the reason for this; we have only just finished the excavations and have not yet had the time or opportunity to grapple with this and other problems, especially the question of restoration. The ancient architect, faced with the question of poor rock (and perhaps humidity even in his own day) decided to erect blocks of fine limestone, no more than about 10 centimetres thick, against the walls of the chambers, and the decoration and inscriptions were carved on these. Between the bedrock and the limestone revetment a thick layer of mud was placed. This would have been useful when the blocks were being 'joggled' into position, and it is highly probable that this mud layer has acted as a kind of barrier, preventing salt from efflorescing on the blocks and destroying the reliefs. The result is that, even after the passage of three and a half millennia – and in the damp conditions 22 metres underground – many of the relief blocks we found in 1988 are in an excellent state of preservation (though in some cases smashed by the ancient plunderers), with the paint often in pristine state.

### Reliefs in the first painted chamber (Room H)
It is probable that the ancient robbers did not have to smash their way into this room from the stairway; hence most of the relief blocks are intact. The ancient architect, however, masked with decorated blocks the entrance of the corridor leading to the burial chambers, but the thieves quickly discovered his ruse, removed the slabs, and thus ultimately penetrated to the inner chambers.

The first room (H) served as a kind of antechamber; there is no evidence that there was a burial here. The scenes on the walls in this room (and elsewhere in the substructure) are almost without exception in sunk relief of fine quality. The paintings are monochrome, the favoured pigment being a rich yellow-gold, a colour symbolizing resurrection and rebirth (a concept linked to the splendour of the daily miracle, from the Egyptians' point of view, of the rising sun). Details, such as eyes, are picked out in black and sometimes in blue. The overall effect here, and in the two other chambers nearby, soon to be dealt with, is decidedly regal, and one could almost be describing a small royal tomb in the Valley of the Kings or the Valley of the Queens in Western Thebes.

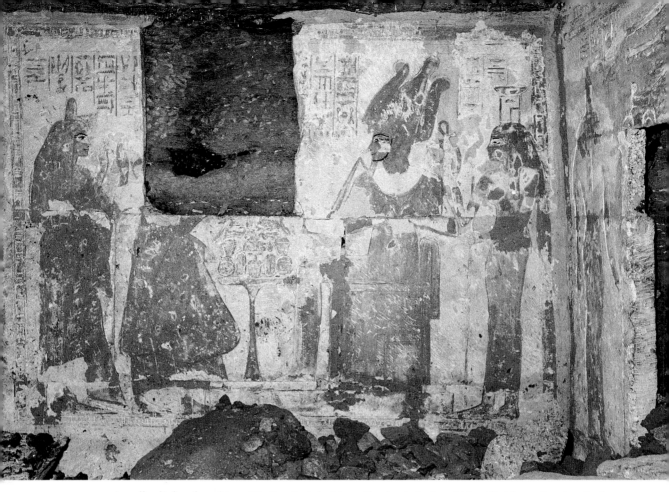

*113 A wall relief as found in 1986. On the left, Maya (head missing) and his wife Meryt, hands raised, worship the god of the underworld Osiris (right), who sits upon a throne. Behind him stands his sister the goddess Nephthys. The eyes of each of the almost totally monochromatic figures are picked out in black to startling effect.*

On the north wall of Room H Maya and Meryt are seen adoring the god Osiris and his sister Nephthys; on the reliefs opposite they again worship Osiris, this time in the company of the sky-goddess Nut. On the blocks which originally disguised the entrance to the corridor (J) the tomb-owners adore the ancient Memphite deity Sokar (who is in a shrine) and the goddess Isis. An unfinished and completely undecorated chamber (I) opens off to the south. No doubt it was intended for the storage of funerary equipment or foodstuffs. The corridor leading from Room H, when we found it in 1986, was full almost to the ceiling with rubble, and all the indications at that time were that the latter was part of the original fill, put there to discourage robbers after Maya and Meryt were buried. As soon as our workmen began to clear away this rubble in our 1988 season it became certain that it had in fact been redistributed in antiquity: fragments of objects and much pottery (part of the funerary equipment) as well as pieces of relief decoration were seen to be mixed in with it. A little way down

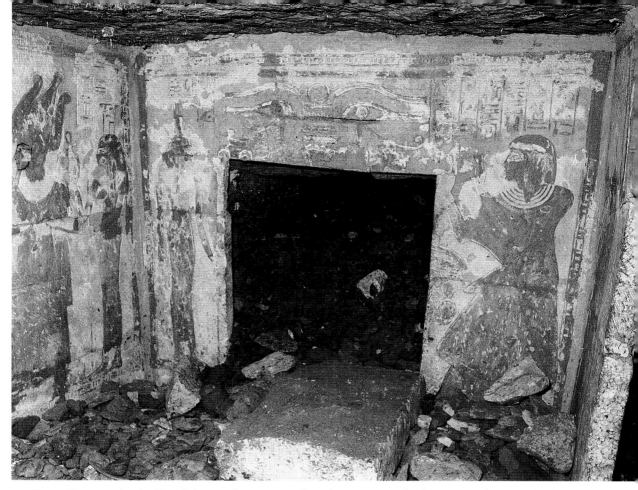

114 *Room H as seen by the Expedition on the morning of 8 February 1986. The doorway in the centre leads to the burial chambers (K and O). On the right Maya is seen in an attitude of worship. The accompanying text over his head identified the tomb and its owner, and was the culmination of many years of archaeological activity in the Saqqara necropolis.*

the corridor (which is itself undecorated) a small room to the south served as a storage area for provisions. We found twelve large pottery jars still stacked there (one for each month of the year?). The ancient plunderers, no doubt hoping they contained valuables, broke off the lids of the vessels, plunged their hands in – and found only flour! We found quantities of this essential commodity still in the bottoms of the jars, as well as fragments that can only be the remains of bread. This is a revealing and interesting find, and emphasizes yet again the overwhelming anxiety which the ancient Egyptians had about the provision of food supplies in the Netherworld.

Shortly after we made the discovery of the flour vessels we found evidence that another side-chamber, further inside the tomb, was intended for oil jars. Though they were smashed to smithereens after the extraction of their valuable contents (we found only sherds) quite a few of them had a note of their contents clearly written in hieratic (the cursive form of hieroglyphic) on the outside. For

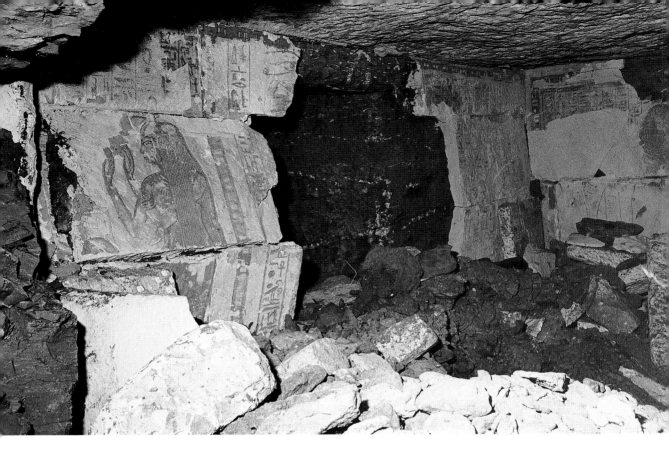

instance we read of 'fresh *neheh*-oil', 'sweet moringa oil', and various kinds of *merhet*-oils. Other commodities named on sherds are 'gum', 'water' (apparently brought from various localities in Egypt), and 'honey for the funeral procession of the Osiris, the royal scribe and overseer of the treasury Maya'. Curiously not many of the texts refer to wine, though we know that this beverage commonly formed part of the tomb provisions in wealthy burials. The comparative lack of wine dockets in Maya's tomb is probably an accident of survival, and does not necessarily mean that the great official was in effect teetotal. One docket even had a date (Year 9). As so often with this kind of written material the scribe was not required, or did not bother, to mention the name of the reigning Pharaoh, since everyone at the time the commodities were bottled knew who this was. It is virtually certain, however, that the king in question is Horemheb. From a text in his Memphite tomb he is known to have reigned for at least thirteen years. Since Horemheb is the Pharaoh of the Maya docket it is possible that Year 9 (1313 BC if referring to that ruler) was the date of the decease either of Maya or of Meryt, when it would have been necessary to prepare (and sometimes label), as part of the funerary offerings, foodstuffs, oil, and other comestibles. It is highly unlikely that perishable items such as food would have been prepared for funerary use years in advance. They would surely have been placed in the tomb at the time of burial in peak condition.

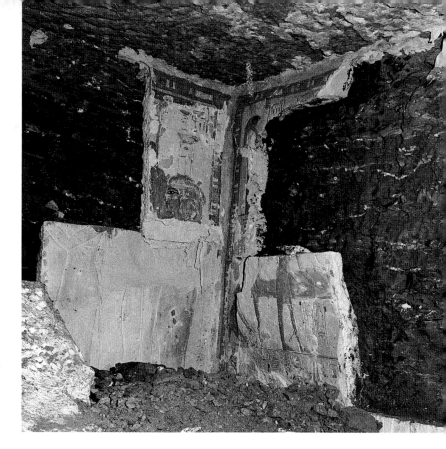

115 *(Left) Two walls of burial chamber O, as seen by the Expedition. To the left are blocks showing Meryt adoring.*

116 *(Right) Burial chamber K in the lower level of the substructure of the tomb of Maya and Meryt, as found in 1988. The ancient plunderers smashed the reliefs and prised them from the walls in their search for hidden chambers.*

## Second painted chamber (Room K)

A scene of utter chaos met our eyes when we eventually penetrated to the second decorated room. The ancient robbers had been here before us, of course; the hope of finding anything *intact* in such circumstances is remote. The plunderers had pulled down some of the reliefs from the walls (doubtless in the hope of finding entrances to hidden chambers). This activity loosened other blocks, which eventually tumbled to the ground. We are therefore faced, in the immediate future, with the need to piece together all the reliefs (and others in Chamber O, soon to be described) and to replace them on the walls so that they can be studied and recorded in detail: a gigantic ancient jigsaw puzzle – but for once with all the pieces present.

Room K is certainly a burial chamber, but at this stage we cannot be sure if it is Maya's or Meryt's. The artist who planned the decoration of this room was here more adventurous with his repertoire. The sequence of scenes, beginning to the right of the entrance of the room, shows a mummy on a bier, with the jackal god Anubis (or a priest masquerading as him) presiding over the last rites. This is a well-known vignette from the Book of the Dead (Chapter 151A). Isis and Nephthys kneel at either end of the funerary bed. We also note a jackal on a shrine and a depiction of the Four Sons of Horus, whom we saw on a relief in the pylon entrance on the surface above. On the south wall Maya and his wife worship Osiris, Nut (the sky goddess), Isis and Nephthys. The next wall, adjacent to the doorway leading to the innermost burial chamber, furnishes us with a hymn, inscribed in 13 columns. It is a very valuable addition to knowledge since it seems to be without parallel. Among other things it mentions the rarely cited divinity, Horus-imy-shenut, ('Horus-who-is-in-the-town of (?) Shenut'). An extract from the hymn will serve to give an impression of the content:

Hail to you, Osiris Onnophris, son of Geb . . . you have appeared wearing your *wereret*-crown, you have seized the great *atef*-crown, [lord of a]we, mighty of majesty, august god who dwells in the Thinite nome [an administrative district], perfect of forms in Busiris and Mendes, your Ennead which follows you has prevailed over your enemy, they drive him away, they ward off the Evil One, his gang is overthrown under your feet (and put) upon the brazier of Horus-imy-shenut.

Curiously, the text here, and the inscriptions elsewhere in the substructure of the tomb, teem with scribal errors and misspellings, which makes it more difficult than usual to grasp the meaning.

Continuing the sequence of scenes (on the other side of the doorway) we observe Maya and Meryt adoring the Earth-god Geb, who is often named in religious texts and in epithets, but is hardly ever depicted, as he is here. Lastly we see Sokar, the god of the Saqqara necropolis, from whom perhaps the cemetery took its name, and the ancient god of Abydos, Wepwawet, 'the Opener of the Ways'.

A short corridor, with part of the original blocking of stone still in position, leads to Room O, which again is a burial chamber. The decoration is not unlike that of the first burial room.

### The third decorated room (O)

Beginning as before with the wall to the right of the entrance we see that the scene is virtually identical to the corresponding scene in K, as is the south wall. On the east wall Maya and Meryt adore Osiris, Nut, Isis and Nephthys. The north wall shows Maya worshipping Osiris, and Meryt adores Anubis, the scene continuing on an adjacent wall. Above is inscribed a hymn in eight columns of hieroglyphs. A doorway on the north gives access to a large undecorated storage chamber.

As one stands in these subterranean chambers, decorated with figures of some of the most ancient deities of Egypt, one gets a real impression of being in the Netherworld. There are no other burial chambers like these in the Saqqara necropolis, since this kind of iconography was, until the Ramesside Period, usually reserved for Pharaoh and members of his family. That Maya was able to commission such work gives an inkling of his status in the realm.

He and Meryt were buried in wooden coffins; we found absolutely no trace of stone sarcophagi. The tomb-owners were surrounded and protected in death by the most potent of gods. The underground rooms in the tomb of the great military commander Horemheb, who outranked Maya, had only rather crude linear decoration. Even this was exceptional for the period; most tomb chambers, even of important officials, were without texts or decoration. How can we account for the fact that Maya's subterranean chambers were so lavishly decorated? We can only speculate, but it must be supposed that Maya was especially influential at court. Indeed we learn from the newly discovered biographical text on his pylon, that he was brought up in the royal entourage, and it is there that he would have made all the vital contacts that would have smoothed his path in later stages of his career. Can he even have been a minor member of the royal family? This seems a little unlikely; at least, there is no evidence that he was a claimant to the throne after the unexpected death of Tutankhamun, when the kingship passed in succession to three military men of non-royal origin: Ay, Horemheb, and Paramessu.

## Burial goods (ills. 117–119)

The burial equipment of Maya and Meryt must have been sumptuous, as befitted their exalted rank. The robbers who were the first to break into the tomb at an undetermined date in the remote past must have known this. We can judge of it from the shattered remnants they left behind. There were doubtless repeated robberies over the years. Almost all the fragments we found were mixed in with the rubble from the approach corridor (J). This fill had been pushed aside by the plunderers and gradually distributed throughout the underground complex. From the remnants of the funerary objects, which are being studied in detail, we can build up a picture of what was in place in the burial chambers when the funerary priests and officials made their final retreat after the last interment, some time during the reign of Horemheb.

As has been mentioned, the coffins of Maya and Meryt were of wood. The great official and his wife could have had 'nests' of coffins, one inside the other, like their illustrious contemporary, Tutankhamun. Wooden sarcophagi seem to have been in favour in the Memphite necropolis for persons of rank in the late Eighteenth Dynasty; examples in granite and other stones were introduced into the funerary repertoire for the most part in the succeeding Ramesside Period. The coffins of Maya and Meryt, though of timber, were surely fine examples of the carpenters' and inlayers' art, but sadly they have been broken up and the fragments have decayed to shapeless lumps of wood, as have other objects in the same material, in the very moist conditions underground at Saqqara.

In the debris we found many pieces of gold leaf that no doubt covered the sarcophagi and perhaps also the wooden funerary figurines and statuettes that would have formed part of the equipment. From the point of view of tomb-robbers gold leaf, if present in sufficient quantity, was worthwhile adzing off the surface of funerary objects. This is apparent from a number of royal examples, now exhibited in the galleries of the Cairo Museum, found in the Valley of the Kings and elsewhere at Thebes. Plunderers rarely overlook objects of solid gold, but in their haste to snatch what they could and make their way up the shafts and out of the tomb, they sometimes broke precious objects, and fragments fell to the ground, to be trampled in the debris by succeeding robbers. This must have happened in Maya's tomb, because we were lucky enough to recover pieces of a very fine gold chain. This very probably was round the neck of Maya (or Meryt), and would have supported a pectoral or heart scarab, which, doubtless gold-mounted, we were not lucky enough to find.

In the subterranean chambers were hundreds of pieces of inlay in glass, stones of various kinds, and faience. These too are a veritable jigsaw puzzle, and whether we shall be able to arrange them in their original patterns is problematical. Alabaster vessels, containing mainly precious oils, also featured among the tomb offerings. One large fragment of fine alabaster is all that remains of the shawabti figures of Maya and his wife. Exquisite ivory fragments (some bearing the name of Horemheb as Pharaoh) were also present. They probably came from boxes or pieces of furniture. We have already mentioned above the enormous amounts of pottery for the storage of food and drink, found in the substructure. Some of the vessels bear dockets written in hieratic on the exterior, specifying the contents.

## Human remains

None of us expected to find the mummies of the tomb-owners. These would have been bedecked with jewels and amulets in precious materials, and would have been the primary target of the tomb-robbers once they had broken into the burial chambers. What we did have the good fortune to excavate were many fragments of bone, scattered throughout the several rooms of the substructure. Every tiny fragment was carefully collected. Though it is too early to give precise details, it is virtually certain that these bone fragments are the remains of Maya and Meryt, since we are sure that no intrusive burials were positioned in the lower level of the substructure of Maya's tomb, where the owner and his wife were interred. It is rare indeed that one has the chance of examining the skeletal remains of any famous person who lived in the past. We can only speculate at this stage what the physical anthropologists will tell us about the pitiful remains of Maya and Meryt – but I am positive that it will be revealing, from many points of view. We should like to know, for example, about their medical history, and how old they were when they died.

Before we leave the underground parts of Maya's tomb there are two curious and puzzling features there which remain to be mentioned.

I have discussed in outline the relief decoration of the two burial chambers. This was carried out on slabs of limestone, as was the decoration of the buildings above ground. It is certain, from fragments we found in the debris of

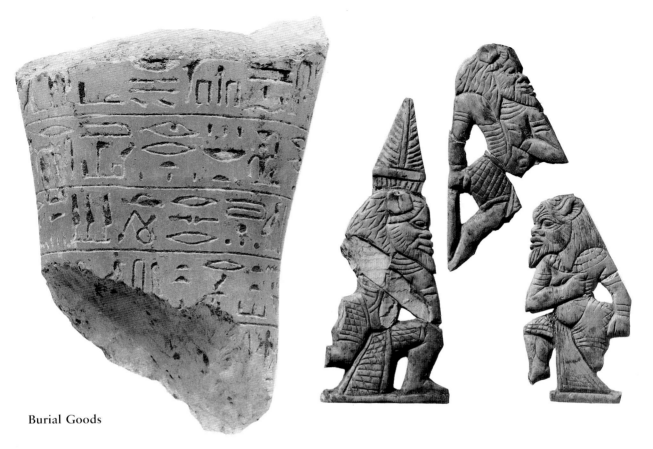

## Burial Goods

*117 (Above) Part of the torso of a calcite shawabti figure of 'the overseer of the treasury of the Lord of the Two Lands [Tutankhamun] Maya'. The text is the standard formula extracted from Chapter VI of the Book of the Dead.*

*118 (Above, right) Inlays of ivory depicting the god Bes, a genial deity associated with women, domestic bliss and the bedchamber. The fragments doubtless were once fixed to items of furniture forming part of the funerary equipment of Maya and Meryt.*

*119 (Right) Fragments of ivory inlays inscribed with the names of King Horemheb as well as Maya and Meryt. Originally they formed part of the decoration of boxes and other pieces of funerary equipment provided for Maya and his wife. There are traces of paint in the hieroglyphs.*

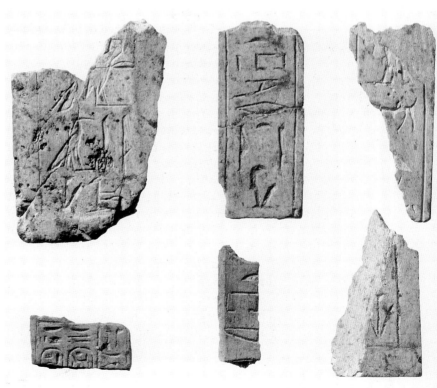

the rooms, that the blockings of the doors leading to the two burial chambers (K and O) were themselves formed of slabs of limestone. This was to be expected, but the extraordinary and unique fact is that these blocks were also carved and decorated on the side facing inwards towards the burial. This means that each wall of the two burial apartments was complete in itself. It would have been easy to fill up the doorways with undecorated blocks; this was the usual system. In the case of Maya's tomb the ancient architect and his craftsmen went to the extraordinary expedient of carving and decorating the stones which were to form the blocking of the two doorways. In each instance they must have been set aside until the interments were in place. The lower courses could conceivably have been plastered into place in advance, leaving a space for the coffined mummy to be lifted over and placed in the centre of the burial room. The remaining blocks to fill the door aperture were then mortared into position, making sure that the iconographical detail (which could no longer be seen, because the mason was doing his work from behind, in the passageway leading to the chamber) was in its true position. The resultant sealed burial chamber has then to be visualized as a kind of closed and decorated box.

The second fact is that we were expecting that the burial chambers of Maya and Meryt would be positioned under the western part of the superstructure of their funerary monument. This seems to have been the usual procedure in the Memphite New Kingdom tombs. In the case of Maya and his wife it would have meant that their bodies would have lain directly under the offering room where their mortuary priest had been commissioned to carry out the requisite services. The burial complex we have just described lies, however, not in the western part of the tomb but towards the east, even though it would theoretically have been possible for the architect to have descended to a third level and then to have 'doubled back' in a westerly direction in order to hew the burial chambers. Careful probing underground at the existing second level has failed to yield any evidence of a shaft or stairway descending to a hypothetical third level. The ancient Egyptian architects were adept, in planning funerary monuments, at confusing and deluding the potential robbers, though it must be confessed that their efforts have almost always been in vain. Nevertheless it is just possible that the substructure of Maya's tomb has not yet revealed all its secrets.

# PART III Epilogue

## CHAPTER SEVEN

---

# COURT, GOVERNMENT, AND DAILY LIFE IN THE NEW KINGDOM

---

In this chapter I shall draw together some of the threads by summarizing the achievements of our joint expedition since work began at Saqqara in 1975. The tombs we have uncovered have given us new glimpses into the daily life, religious activities, and arts and crafts of the people who lived in Memphis. Details, too, of the state functions of citizens in the higher echelons of the administration, who thronged the royal court, have also been revealed. I shall also sketch in some details about the administration of Egypt, the key to the country's prosperity in the New Kingdom as well as in the other high points of its long history. The New Kingdom was the time when Egypt rose to the peak of her fame and influence among the countries of the Near East, only to sink, as the Twentieth Dynasty advanced, into apathy, administrative chaos, and economic decline. No tombs dating from the later part of the New Kingdom have ever been found at Saqqara, but there is evidence, from recently published papyri, that funerary monuments of the Twentieth Dynasty did exist in the Memphite necropolis.

## Aspects of religion and arts and crafts in the New Kingdom

In this book I have tried to show how the tombs we have revealed in Saqqara have given us new details and insights into the lives of government employees, the military, and members of the priesthood. In the case of the generalissimo Horemheb we learnt how crucial his role was in reasserting Egyptian domination over Western Asia and Nubia in the aftermath of Akhenaten's lackadaisical foreign policy. In scenes unprecedented in Egyptian art we saw him acting almost as a pharaoh, well before his own accession to that office. The vivid depiction of foreigners in his Memphite tomb makes one feel that as a result of his campaigns he was very familiar with the peoples of Syria–Palestine, as well as with the tribesmen of Libya and Nubia.

One of the tombs we have cleared can justifiably be called a royal tomb, in that it was prepared for one of Ramesses II's sisters, Tia, and her husband.

Only very rarely do we get intimate glimpses into the private lives and activities of the royal family in their funerary monuments. One example, and the most celebrated, is the tomb of the pharaoh Akhenaten in the hills behind Amarna. In scenes unique in Egyptian iconography Akhenaten and Nefertiti are shown weeping over the death of one of their daughters: for once Pharaoh is shown as a frail human being rather than as a potent god. In the tomb of Ay in the western branch of the Valley of the Kings at Thebes that Pharaoh is shown with his wife, Queen Teye, spearing a hippopotamus and bird-fowling in a canoe, activities normally depicted only in the tombs of private individuals.

The tomb of Tia and Tia at Saqqara is not one of the exceptions to the rule for royal monuments. I must confess that it would have been interesting to see the royal pair deviating, if only by a little, from the norm. At least there was an attempt at a personal touch on the part of the artists who decorated their tomb: in one of their chapels we saw that the Tias made arrangements to have their favourite horses on board with them when they made their ritualistic voyage to Abydos to worship at the temple of Osiris. By contrast the other scenes in the tomb show the royal pair conscientiously carrying out their sacred duty of adoring and offering to the gods, but some of the reliefs, particularly those in the chapel just mentioned, are works of art in their own right.

The smaller tomb-chapels too are packed with information. Paser gave us very useful details of his family, a prominent one connected with the cult of deceased royal ancestors, and his tomb gives us a clue to the location of the long-lost tomb of his more important brother, Tjuneroy. In Raia's little chapel we are transported momentarily into the great temple of Ptah during the reign of Ramesses II to eavesdrop, as it were, on a musical 'recital', and are offered a unique glimpse of the choir that performed daily in front of the deity. In Khay's tomb-chapel we see him supervising work in his gold-refiner's atelier, an unusual, if not unique, scene in Egyptian art. In the chapel of his son, Pabes, we noted a scene in the dockyards of Memphis, which must have been a hive of activity at all times during the long history of the city. One wonders how many sunken ships with their cargoes lie buried deep in the silt of the great river that used to flow so close to the eastern boundary of Memphis. We must not neglect to mention Ramose's tomb; though any decoration it might have had was stripped away in antiquity one of his shafts gave us entry into the long-sought tomb of Maya and Meryt. Iurudef's tomb-shafts too were informative, giving us new insights into burial customs in the Memphite necropolis, a wealth of contexted and datable objects, and not least a great mass of skeletal material, the physical remains of a group of citizens of Memphis who lived at the beginning of the first millennium BC. It is hardly too much to say that we are almost overwhelmed with new information. Some of it has been highlighted in this book; much more will be revealed in the future.

## Aspects of religion in the New Kingdom

We have seen how their tombs have given valuable details about the lives of military men, government employees, and the various grades of the priesthood: the people who were responsible for the administration of Egypt in the New Kingdom. But we can also point to new clues and facts about religion and art in this important period. As regards religious activities the reign of Tutankhamun was crucial. During his administration the old religion, with its multiplicity of gods, almost all of which had been repudiated by his predecessor Akhenaten, was reinstated in all its glory. Once again the pantheon was firmly entrenched, not to be overthrown for another seventeen centuries when Christianity triumphed in the Nile Valley. In the pages of this volume we have seen how the great officials, such as Horemheb and Maya, make no mention of the royal 'heretic' Akhenaten, even though they without doubt lived in his reign and very probably also served in his government. His innovations, his beliefs and aspirations, pass unremarked in their tomb inscriptions and reliefs. Maya, though, seems to hint that he was brought up in the entourage of the Amarna royal family – no doubt therefore at Akhetaten itself – though he pointedly does not mention Akhenaten by name. A tomb at Amarna inscribed for an official named May was very probably his at an earlier stage of his career while the seat of government was in Akhetaten. After the abandonment of Amarna and the return to Memphis the officials quickly set about building their 'houses of eternity' in the Saqqara necropolis. From the presence of lengthy and adulatory hymns to the ancient deities in such funerary monuments – especially in those of Horemheb and Maya – and from the iconography of the scenes represented, one would never suspect that Egypt had been convulsed, from the religious standpoint, only a short time previously. Officials like Horemheb and Maya were probably involved in Akhenaten's 'revolution' and in the Aten cult when it was the court religion. It would be unjust to call such great officials 'trimmers' or time-servers. We do not have any firm evidence about the events which surrounded the final overthrow of the Aten religion, which ongoing excavation and research show was not in any case sudden, so it would be harsh to judge or condemn their 'apostasy'.

Once the old faith was reinstated one of the great religious centres that must speedily have swung into action was the temple of Ptah at Memphis, and the 'temple-university' at Heliopolis, the seat of the cult of the sun-god Re. Though we have lists of the high-priests who controlled these important centres in the New Kingdom much research still needs to be done on the various ranks of the priesthood and auxiliary staffs who serviced the shrines. Much of the evidence is available (in the form of tomb reliefs stemming from Memphite tombs) about monuments still waiting to be uncovered in the Saqqara necropolis, and from tombs we have discovered there. When we consider how informative just one small tomb-chapel – that of Raia – has been, one's mind reels at the prospect of the information that might be forthcoming from just *one* high-priest's tomb;

for example, that of Ptahemhat called Ty, a block from whose Saqqara tomb shows members of the Egyptian government, including Horemheb, in the reign of Tutankhamun or Ay. Ptahemhat was high-priest of Ptah, and it is easy to believe that at least some of the walls of his tomb would record or depict aspects of the cult of one of the most important of the Egyptian deities.

## Arts and crafts

It is not too much to say that a whole new area of research into Egyptian art has been opened up by the work of our joint expedition at Saqqara. Many of the reliefs we have found, particularly in the tombs of Horemheb and Maya, are by any standard, masterpieces. All the material is closely datable and much of it is in a fine state of preservation with much original colour still present. Before our discoveries not a great deal was known about Memphite, as opposed to Theban, art of the New Kingdom. The reason was straightforward: the Theban reliefs and paintings, studied in great detail since the pioneer days of Egyptology early in the last century, were well known. As we have seen, so much contemporary Memphite material is still lying buried under the sands of the Saqqara desert, the Memphite temple reliefs have all but vanished for ever, and the tomb blocks, now for the most part in museum collections, are scattered far and wide and until recently no attempt had been made to study them in detail as an entity.

Many questions now need to be asked: for instance, is there a distinct and peculiar Memphite style of art in the New Kingdom? Does Memphite iconographical detail differ markedly from Theban and provincial work? Are there echoes of the art of the Amarna Period in the reliefs executed at Memphis during and immediately after the reign of Tutankhamun? (There is hardly any Memphite New Kingdom material pre-dating this reign.) Who were the artists and craftsmen, and where were they trained? To what extent did Memphite funerary architecture affect their work and indeed their style? In this regard the abandonment of rock tombs, in which the decoration was carved directly into the living rock, in favour of temple-like funerary monuments, is no doubt significant. The masons who built the latter type of tomb could choose their materials with care, if they and their patrons were so minded. In fact, in the case of tombs and blocks dating from the late Eighteenth Dynasty it is clear that limestone of high quality was selected from the quarries east of Memphis. Stone of this type was ideal for delicate and detailed carving. Tombs dating from the Ramesside Period show a marked deterioration: inferior stone was used, at least from the time of Ramesses II, the carving was often slovenly, and paint was applied in a very carefree manner. Mass production of monuments was now common, there was feverish building activity throughout the land, and highly skilled craftsmen were at a premium.

To touch on only one of the questions outlined above: the possibility of influence from Akhenaten's capital at Amarna on late Eighteenth Dynasty and

Ramesside art in Memphis. Some of the reliefs in Horemheb's tomb could well have been carved by artists trained in the ateliers at Akhetaten, who were dispersed, some no doubt to Thebes, others to Memphis, when Amarna ceased to be the capital and seat of influence after the death of Akhenaten. If some of the blocks we found dating from the time of Tutankhamun had instead been in museum collections and out of context it is not at all unlikely that they would have been dated to the Amarna Period or even to the Ramesside Era.

## Administration

We now touch on the problem of the administration of Egypt, particularly as seen from the standpoint of the chief city of the New Kingdom, Memphis.

The configuration of Egypt is remarkable: an extremely long and narrow valley hemmed in by deserts, opening out in the north into the lotus-shaped Delta. The geography of the country had an effect on the administrative system which, as surviving records show, was carefully articulated and complex even from early dynastic times. A degree of local autonomy was always necessary, however, since it was hardly possible to oversee and administer effectively the entire country from Memphis.

As yet the finer detail of the administrative system operating in Egypt in the New Kingdom eludes us. The overall picture is fairly clear, however, and quite a lot is known about some of the individual government 'departments', such as the vizierate or the treasury, as well as the cadres of military officers and army personnel. But more needs to be done, especially in connection with material emanating from the northern part of the country, such as the evidence we have been unearthing at Saqqara which is largely concerned with the metropolitan area of Memphis.

It is important to observe that from the Eighteenth Dynasty the Egyptian government had territorial ambitions in Western Asia (Syria–Palestine). This was in the aftermath of the expulsion of the Hyksos invaders and the fear that there might be a repetition of such a calamity if effective steps were not taken to strengthen the frontiers of Egypt and to set up a 'buffer zone' of dependent or semi-autonomous city states between Egypt and its increasingly powerful neighbours. Whether the personal ambition or prowess of individual pharaohs entered into the question is a matter for argument. Certainly the reliefs showing the ruler as the all-powerful warrior, and adulatory texts in the New Kingdom temples up and down the land, and even in far-off Nubia, are suggestive in this respect.

The fact that Egypt was very much involved in wars, and in punitive expeditions to put down actual or potential rebellions, was bound to have profound repercussions on administrative affairs, social life, and economic activities, not to mention the impact of foreign religious cults introduced into Egypt at this period. Memphis was at the very heart of all these things, since it was from here that the armies and navies were organized and despatched. The

Memphite dockyards were no doubt piled high with the spoils of war, later to be distributed to the royal exchequer and the temples. Thus one of the consequences of Egypt's involvement in Asia was the increase in the importance of the army, and in the power and prestige of individual military officers, such as Horemheb, at this time. Horemheb's tomb exemplifies this increased importance, and there are still, as we have seen, many tombs of army officers of the New Kingdom to be located in the Saqqara cemeteries.

The second fact to note is that in the Eighteenth and Nineteenth Dynasties, but particularly under Tuthmosis III and Ramesses II, the temples became immensely enriched, mainly as the result of munificent gifts of bullion, booty, land, slaves, and cattle on the part of the reigning Pharaoh to the gods, especially for victories in Western Asia and to a certain extent in Nubia. The principal beneficiary was the Theban Amun, but other important cult centres, not least Memphis and Heliopolis, came in for a share of the spoils. The direct result of this was an enormous increase in the wealth, patronage, and influence of the priesthood. Temple staffs were greatly enlarged to cope with the volume of administrative work involved in running the temple estates. Temples were rebuilt, sometimes by commandeering land occupied by private houses, or existing shrines were added to or embellished. All this is in dramatic contrast to the situation that obtained in the temples of the Old Kingdom and the Middle Kingdom, which were very modest in size and wealth.

I mentioned previously the high-priests of Memphis and Heliopolis, holders of two of the most powerful sacerdotal posts in the New Kingdom. So far not one of their tombs has been unearthed in the Saqqara necropolis. Though the Heliopolitan high-priests may well have been interred elsewhere for the most part, there is plenty of evidence to show that their Memphite counterparts, so important in the Egyptian religious hierarchy, are somewhere awaiting discovery in Saqqara, probably within a stone's throw of our present work in the desert: an exciting prospect.

Since Memphis was the seat of government throughout the Eighteenth Dynasty, apart from the Amarna interlude, and also probably for part of the Nineteenth (Thebes being the religious capital), all the chief administrators and a host of lesser functionaries worked in the great metropolitan centre, and ultimately were laid to rest in Saqqara. Only a few of their tombs have been disinterred; some have come to light as a result of our work and that of Egyptian colleagues working some distance to the east of our site. Hundreds of monuments, with certainty, await discovery.

### The various branches of the administration

The life of every Egyptian was controlled by the bureaucrats of the Pharaoh, and the entire economy was organized throughout Egypt by these ubiquitous officials in the name of the ruler, who was in theory the supreme landlord. Very little is known in detail about the actual land-holdings of the Pharaoh, the state, the temples, and private individuals. In the earlier periods it is possible that all land belonged to the king, but as time went on an important distinction must have arisen between the various kinds and owners of land.

From surviving textual sources it is clear that the civil service was very large, certainly from the Old Kingdom onwards, and had a graded hierarchy of officials in charge of the various government departments. One of the chief offices was the treasury, involved in the receipt of taxes in kind for later distribution as salaries to civil servants and other government employees, as well as to the court. The royal court and the palace in a sense was at the top of the hierarchical pyramid. The administration of fields and the irrigation system was of course crucial, as was the control of herds, flocks, granaries, lakes and swamps. The forced labour or corvée department was doubtless not very popular, at least with the people at large, but it had a crucial role to play, not only in organizing the repair, cleaning, and cutting of canals, but also in the construction and decorating of royal tombs, temples, and other public monuments. The enormous hidden wealth in the many cemeteries was the responsibility of the necropolis officials. When their vigilance was relaxed the royal and private tombs were plundered, as the ancient Egyptians knew to their cost. Justice, prisons, police-forces, expeditions to the mines and quarries, control of the frontiers and desert fringes, all employed great numbers of officials. The temples, as we have seen, had their own elaborate administrative system, as did the army, and to some extent the navy. These are just some of the branches of the central government, in the New Kingdom and at other times in the course of Egyptian history.

The administration was usually centralized – at Memphis – but inevitably much of the day-to-day running of affairs was controlled locally in the nomes. Local administrations were to a certain extent the central administration in miniature. These were the men who saw to the tilling of the soil, the gathering of crops and taxes, the local corvée and militia, the staffing of country shrines and temples. Such local administrations, in which the ancient landed nobility played a crucial role until the late Twelfth Dynasty, were usually effectively controlled from Memphis, but there were times when they were in opposition to the Crown.

Such a vast and intricate bureaucracy must have produced masses of documents from the pens of armies of scribes, who are so often represented on the monuments. They were responsible for cadastral surveys, indicating the names and status of land-owners for tax purposes, taxation lists, fiscal returns, letters on every conceivable subject in which the government was concerned; these were just some of their main tasks. Other pies in which they had at least one finger were matters relating to the payment or salaries of officials and others, reports on government projects such as the amounts of stone delivered from the quarries for use in state enterprises, complaints from government officials and private citizens, reproofs from superiors for dereliction of duty, wills, transfers of property, title deeds, and a host of others.

The tragedy is that comparatively few written documents from the pens of these ubiquitous officials have survived the ravages of time. Papyrus is a fragile writing material, vulnerable to damp and to the appetite of the white ant and other hazards. Ideally one would base a detailed study of the administration on such written documents. For the New Kingdom we are better off than for earlier periods of Egyptian history. To mention only two precious records, the two largest administrative documents to have come down to us: the Great Harris Papyrus in the British Museum, which lists royal donations to the cult temples, and dates from the time of Ramesses III, and the Wilbour Papyrus in the Brooklyn Museum. This latter dates from the somewhat obscure reign of Ramesses V, and gives precious documentation on land-holdings, parcels of property in different localities in Egypt.

For lack of actual documents the student of administration has to turn to other sources.

## The evidence of prosopography

The scarcity of administrative papyri has forced scholars to depend for a great deal of their information about the way Egypt was governed, in the New Kingdom and at other times, on the titles and epithets of innumerable officials. In this regard their tombs, not least at Saqqara, are of great value, especially when, in addition to their titularies, the administrators furnish information on their lives in government service and even illustrate, in the form of carved reliefs, certain high points in their careers in the civil service, the army, and the temples. We have seen how valuable Horemheb's tomb is in this respect.

In Egypt there was scarcely any office or job which was not graded either in the royal court, central or local government, or temple administration. No official, great or small, wrote his name without giving his titles which, in the absence of surnames, doubtless was a valuable means of identification and differentiation, especially in connection with common names such as Amenhotep, Ramose, and Ptahmose. Sometimes, especially in tomb biographies, officials would list every title they ever held (the Old Kingdom tomb of Mereruka at Saqqara is an excellent example). As well as titles, whether actual or honorific, the great officials in their monuments and on their stelae describe or hint at the special missions upon which they were sent by Pharaoh, or mention the plenipotentiary powers conferred on them for certain tasks. We have seen an instance of this in connection with Horemheb, and no doubt other tombs in the Saqqara necropolis, especially of military men, would furnish similar examples.

The Pharaoh, in investing his prime minister or vizier, exhorted him to 'take the office . . . watch over everything which has to do with it, for the existence of the entire country depends on it'. From the time of Tuthmosis III Egypt was governed under the king by two viziers, one based in Thebes, the other operating from Memphis and administering the Memphite area and Lower

Egypt. I suspect that the Lower Egyptian vizier, having daily access to the sovereign, had the greater influence. Yet not very much is known about the prime ministers of Lower Egypt in the New Kingdom. Egyptian colleagues have recently found the tomb of one of Ramesses II's viziers named Neferronpet, but there must be many monuments of New Kingdom chief ministers awaiting discovery under the sands of the Saqqara desert. However, it is not only the tomb reliefs that have new facts to yield up. In the museum collections there is much information, some of it dormant, in the form of inscribed objects, including stelae, and papyri. Scholars on the whole have concentrated hitherto on the mass of Theban material, and it has often been assumed that the results apply to Egypt as a whole. The evidence now being collected on New Kingdom Memphite officials – some of whom undoubtedly had links with the southern part of the country – and the large amounts of new documentation forthcoming from the Saqqara cemeteries, is bound to alter the accepted position, perhaps quite radically. Indeed, the evidence begins, even at this early stage, to suggest that the great officials of state, as well as the military men of rank, were based in Memphis in the New Kingdom, that they lived out their lives, and most of them died, in that great and vast city.

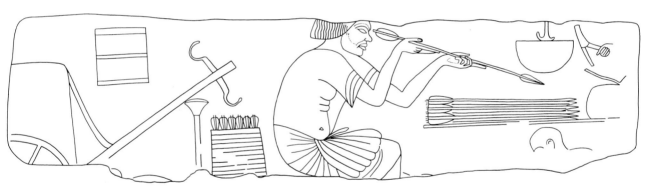

120 *A scene in a military atelier, doubtless in Memphis. A craftsman checks the straightness of an arrow. Two other workers and other items of army equipment are also shown on this relief, which stems from a now lost tomb beneath the sand at Saqqara.*

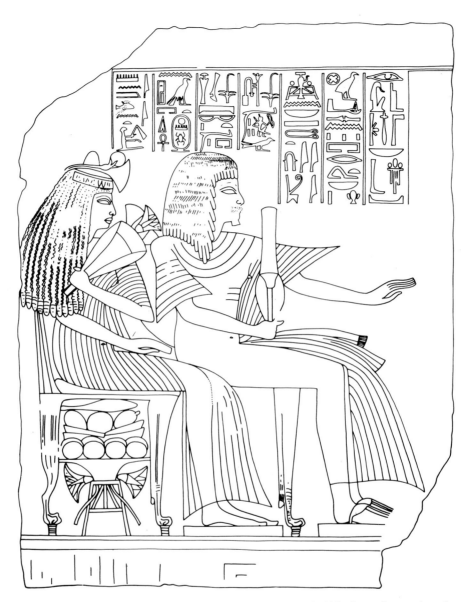

121 A retired general and his wife. He is named on this relief block as 'the royal scribe, generalissimo, first royal herald, chief of bowmen, steward of the temple of Tuthmosis III Amenemone'. The last-named title was doubtless the one that he was given after he ceased to be active in the field.

CHAPTER EIGHT

# THE LOST TOMBS OF MEMPHIS

We have outlined the results of the discoveries we have made over the last decade and more, and the information they give us on the New Kingdom in the Memphite area and beyond. What of the future?

## Treasure under the desert sands

Even before our work began in 1975 scholars were aware that there was a vast quantity of facts on the northern part of Egypt in New Kingdom times locked away, in a sense, in our museum collections. This material consists of stelae (tombstones), statues, inscribed and decorated blocks (all these from tombs or temples), papyri, and innumerable objects, mainly funerary. Such things came to light in Saqqara, and to a certain extent in Memphis, as the result of official excavations and illicit or chance finds extending over a century and a half down to the 1970s. All this material, if exhaustively analyzed, would provide information on the personalities of the times – careers, family relationships, religious beliefs, to name only some. From our point of view, though, one of the most useful surviving sources is the large number of inscribed and decorated blocks from tomb walls, such as we have discussed above in connection with the newly excavated monuments in the Memphite necropolis. There must be as many as 500 of these reliefs scattered in museum collections throughout the world. Until recently they had not been studied in detail. Since most of them stem from Saqqara they give us very valuable clues about the status of tomb-owners whose funerary chapels still lie hidden beneath the sands of the desert.

Aside from the tombs which *must* be at Saqqara, to judge from the loose blocks deriving from them, there surely are very many others, the names of whose owners are still unknown to us. We do not, of course, know exactly where individual tomb-chapels are, but the indications on the surface of the desert, showing rough outlines of courtyards buried deep beneath the sand, are suggestive. In fact, we have to conjure up a picture of a veritable city of tombs, with funerary monuments laid out on interconnecting streets and alleyways. A modern parallel, that will be familiar to many visitors to Egypt, is the vast Moslem cemetery known as the City of the Dead, in Old Cairo.

From an analysis of the names and titles inscribed on the blocks in the museum collections we can be reasonably sure, and in some cases completely certain, that the tombs of those officials mentioned in the accompanying list (I give only a selection) are waiting to be discovered. Those marked with an asterisk (*) were even seen in 1843 by Karl Richard Lepsius, though over the past century and a half they have completely disappeared again under the sand. They have never been fully excavated in any case; only small areas of them were exposed when Lepsius and his assistants were busy there. From their titles and functions, not all of which are listed, the reader will see that a wealth of new information on administration, daily and family life, religion, and art would accrue if these important monuments were located, cleared, and fully published. As it is, we have at our disposal only loose pieces, completely out of context, but waiting to take their proper place in the history of Memphis and its populace.

### The missing tombs

Amenhotep called Huy, high steward in Memphis, etc. Time of Amenhotep III

Merymery, custodian of the treasury of Memphis. Probably time of Amenhotep III

Meryre, overseer of nurses of the good god [Pharaoh], etc. Probably time of Amenhotep III

Ptahmose, high-priest of Ptah, etc. Time of Amenhotep III

Wesy, standard-bearer of the ship, 'Front-of-the-beauty-of-Amun', chief of bowmen of the Lord of the Two Lands, etc. Time of Amenhotep III

Merytyneith (altered to Merytyaten), steward of the temple of the Aten. Time of Akhenaten

Iny, overseer of goldworkers of the Lord of the Two Lands, one who knows the secrets in the house of gold, etc. Late Eighteenth Dynasty

Amenemone, first chief in Memphis, general of the Lord of the Two Lands, steward in the temple of Tuthmosis III, etc. Late Eighteenth Dynasty.

Ipy, high steward, fanbearer on the right of the King, etc. Late Eighteenth Dynasty

Meryptah, high-priest of Ptah. Late Eighteenth Dynasty

Nia, high steward, overseer of the cattle of Amun, etc. Late Eighteenth Dynasty

Ptahemhet called Ty, high-priest of Ptah. Late Eighteenth Dynasty

Roy, chief of bowmen, overseer of horses, etc. Late Eighteenth Dynasty

*Hormin, overseer of the royal apartments of the harim at Memphis, true royal scribe, etc. Early Nineteenth Dynasty

Parahotep (or Rahotep), governor of the town [the capital city], vizier. Time of Ramesses II

Tjuneroy, overseer of works on all monuments of the King, royal scribe, etc. Time of Ramesses II

Horemheb, royal scribe, fanbearer on the right of the King, steward. Time of Ramesses II

Iryiry, high-priest of Ptah. Time of Ramesses II

Khaemwese, son of Ramesses II, high-priest of Ptah. Time of Ramesses II

Pahemnetjer, high-priest of Ptah. Time of Ramesses II

*Raia, overseer of the royal apartments of the harim at Memphis, etc. Nineteenth Dynasty

Pay, overseer of the royal apartments of the King's wife. Nineteenth Dynasty

Ptahmose, royal scribe of the treasury, overseer of the cattle of Amun, etc. Nineteenth Dynasty

Sety, sword-bearer [in front of] the Lord of the Two Lands, armour-bearer of the company, 'Ruler-in-the-Two-Lands'. Nineteenth Dynasty.

Kairy, chief of chariot-makers, overseer of a workshop in the armoury, etc. Nineteenth Dynasty

Harmose, steward of the Lord of the Two Lands. Nineteenth Dynasty

Ptahemhab and Amenemhab, chiefs of goldworkers. Nineteenth Dynasty

Ramose, scribe of recruits of the Lord of the Two Lands, deputy of the temple. Nineteenth Dynasty

Niay, royal scribe, priest of Sekhmet in the temple of Sekhmet. Nineteenth Dynasty

Pagerger, chief of chisellers. Nineteenth Dynasty

*Iurokhy, true royal scribe, general. Ramesside

Iry, scribe of Usermaatre-setepenre [Ramesses II] in the domain of Amun. Ramesside

Penrennut, chief of police. Ramesside

Hori, high-priest of Ptah. Ramesside

Ptahmose, high steward of the temple of Ramesses II in the domain of Ptah, etc. Ramesside

Ramessesemperre, fanbearer on the right of the King, royal butler, etc. Ramesside

Sayempeteref, chief of goldworkers of the estate of Sety I. Ramesside

Serbykhen, priest of Amun, Astarte, and Baal, etc. Ramesside

## Lost tombs of the Teti pyramid cemetery

There is a chance that a number of the 'missing' tombs were located somewhere in the cemetery surrounding the Old Kingdom pyramid of Teti in the north part of Saqqara. All the evidence at present available suggests that the New Kingdom necropolis here was not very extensive. It has been excavated, at least in part, notably by the French archaeologist Victor Loret, and by the English Egyptologists, J.E. Quibell and C.M. Firth. Quite a few New Kingdom officials and others are known to have had funerary monuments in the Teti area; the remains of their tombs were excavated and published by the scholars just mentioned. Sad to say, all trace of these monuments has gone; the blocks have been transported to the Cairo Museum and the foundations have been quarried away in recent work on the site. Somewhere in the area there remain to be found the tomb-chapels of Thay, overseer of horses of the Lord of the Two Lands, Huy, scribe of troops of the Lord of the Two Lands, and of Merya, a merchant. These all date to the end of the Eighteenth Dynasty. One day someone may be lucky enough to find, also in the area of the Teti pyramid, the

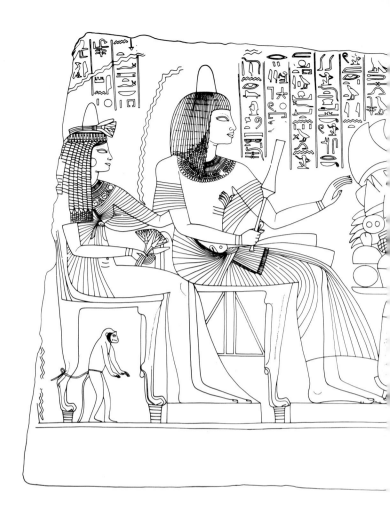

122 A military officer and his wife receive incense, a libation of water and funerary gifts. This high-ranking official is called 'the chief of bowmen and overseer of horses Roy', and his wife 'the chantress of Amun-Re Maia'. Some of the offering-bearers are named, enabling a picture to be built up of a great official's entourage.

123 (Below) A block from the lost tomb of Ramessesemperre, 'fanbearer on the right of the King, chief royal butler of the Lord of the Two Lands' (the pharaoh). The tomb-owner salutes the cow-headed goddess Hathor, lady of the Southern Sycamore, a temple in the city of Memphis. In front of her is a simple offering table with a water jar, two loaves of bread, and a lotus blossom.

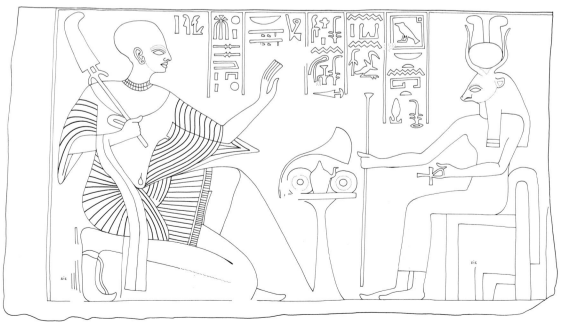

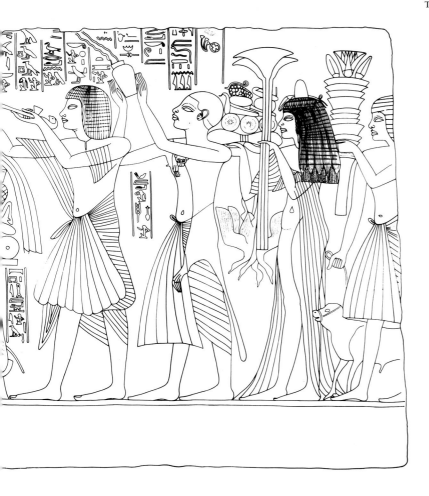

Ramesside tombs of Meryre, chief of custodians, Nakhtamun, chief of servants of the royal butler Hori, and Wenefdjedsen, first royal butler of His Majesty.

Individual blocks from many of the tombs listed above are to be found in the museum collections. A few were excavated and have a known provenance, others come from the Monastery of Apa Jeremias and are now in the Cairo Museum. Most were removed from the Saqqara cemeteries early in the last century, passed on to antiquities dealers, and eventually found their way abroad, mainly to Europe and America. Quite a few have been published as photographic illustrations in books dealing with Egyptian art, of which many are prime examples.

The present writer's interest in them lies mainly in the clues they give to the existence under the desert sands of funerary monuments. The names and titles on the blocks we already have, some of which are itemized above, have helped to build up our prosopography or index of officials and others who lived and worked in Memphis and its environs during and after the reign of Tutankhamun, down to the end of the Nineteenth Dynasty. At the moment

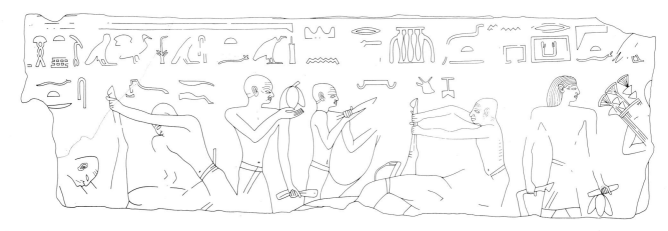

124 *Butchers at work dismembering cattle for the funerary rites. The worker on the left has a marked turricephalic skull. Khaemwese, high-priest of Ptah in Memphis, built his tomb in Saqqara, from which this block derives. The tomb owner was one of the many sons of Ramesses II.*

hardly anything is known about the citizens of Memphis in the later Ramesside Period. We can only hazard a guess as to how many officials will ultimately figure in our index. But it is not just a question of *lists*. We are sure we shall be able to demonstrate family relationships, different functions in the state, some of them perhaps peculiar to Memphis, religious affiliations, and many more facts that will throw light on the lives, work, and beliefs of the people.

Since relief blocks from Memphite tombs have a major part to play in the overall strategy of our work in Saqqara my duty – or perhaps I should say agreeable task – has been to study them and to bring them together in the form of a corpus of drawings with appropriate commentary. The first volume has already been published. The illustrations which figure in the present chapter have been taken from that work.

The Saqqara cemeteries will not give up all their secrets in my lifetime. With excavation and recording techniques improving all the time it is desirable in any case that we should leave a reasonable amount of material undisturbed for later generations of archaeologists. We have enormous amounts of fascinating new evidence from the Memphite cemeteries to publish and assimilate, and there is even more to find and make known in the future.

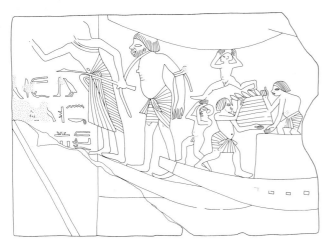

125 *Disembarking a prisoner and unloading produce, probably at the dockyard in Memphis. A block from a hitherto unlocated tomb in the Memphite necropolis.*

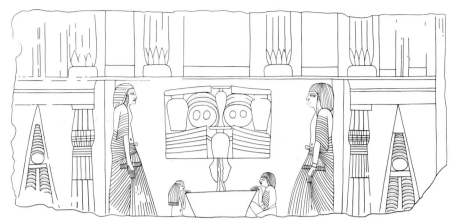

126 The interior of a Memphite tomb-chapel, seen through the eyes of a sculptor working at the end of the Eighteenth Dynasty. In the background there is a stela and perhaps relief blocks. In the centre is an offering table heaped with food and drink, flanked by two large statues of the anonymous tomb owner. The latter and his wife are quenching their thirst from a basin which is catching liquid poured by funerary priests on the offering table. The table would in actuality probably have been positioned in the main cult room at the west end of the tomb. In side rooms conical stands contain plentiful supplies of circular loaves.

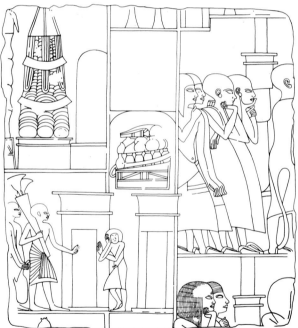

127 At the funeral of a person of rank. The interior of a Memphite New Kingdom tomb-chapel is the setting for this scene, carved on a block deriving from Saqqara. The high status of the anonymous tomb owner is indicated by the fact that at his funeral the chief mourners, depicted above to the right, are the two prime ministers or viziers of Upper and Lower Egypt.

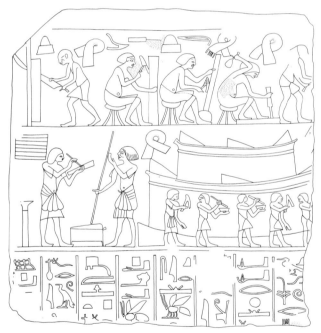

128 Men at work in a carpenters' workshop. probably in Memphis. In the upper register workmen are sawing and adzing planks, while another labourer is wielding a chisel. Below, a supervisor gives instructions to a clerk, while craftsmen put the finishing touches to a catafalque or funerary shrine. This block originally formed part of the decoration of the tomb of a high-ranking official, whose titles included those of 'hereditary prince' and 'count'.

# Visiting Memphis and Saqqara

Those who have the opportunity of visiting Egypt will find that Memphis and Saqqara, sited only a few miles south of Cairo, are easy of access, though there is no direct service to either place using public transport. Individual travellers can use taxis or join coach tours. Taxis are not expensive, especially when hired by a small group of people, but it is best to negotiate a fare before setting out. Arrangements for tourists visiting Memphis and Saqqara can also be made by hoteliers and tourist agencies in Cairo. At least half a day should be set aside; a full day will give the visitor the chance of seeing all the major monuments open to the public.

**Memphis** was the administrative capital of ancient Egypt throughout most of its history. Today much of the site is under modern settlements and cultivation; the rest is a large ruinfield undergoing archaeological excavation. A number of the finds from the site have been gathered together in one place and this is well worth a visit. Among the many fine objects to be seen are:

A colossal limestone statue of Ramesses II, housed in its own building. This statue is one of the largest of Ramesses in Egypt; although most of its legs are missing, the remains measure over ten metres.

The open-air museum in the adjacent garden. Here a sphinx, possibly of Hatshepsut, and other statues and monuments from the temples of ancient Memphis are displayed.

The embalming place of the Apis bulls, including huge alabaster tables on which the animals were placed during the embalming process.

**Saqqara** the necropolis of the ancient city, is a vast site sprawling over the sands. Not every part of Saqqara is accessible to the visitor, but a number of ancient tombs may be seen, among them:

The Step Pyramid complex of Zoser, including the entrance colonnade, great courtyard, mortuary temple, and *heb-sed* court. The substructure of the pyramid and Zoser's 'Southern Tomb' are not accessible.

The pyramid of Unas (including the substructure), its mortuary temple, and causeway. A small portion of the covering of the causeway, with its walls carved in relief, is still present.

The Serapeum, the burial place of the Apis bulls. (There is a large hospitality tent at this site where the visitor will find welcome refreshment in the form of tea, cold drinks and light snacks.)

The mastaba tomb of Akhethotep and Ptahhotep. This late Fifth Dynasty double tomb of father and son has many fine reliefs of ancient life, including hunting and children's games.

All these monuments are in the south and west parts of Saqqara. Moving to the north, the visitor can see the pyramids of Userkaf and Teti (the substructure of the latter is usually open), as well as the important Sixth Dynasty mastaba tombs of Mereruka, Kagemni and Ankhmahor.

*Please note that since the area is still under excavation, the tombs described in the present volume have not yet been opened to visitors by the Egyptian Antiquities Organization.*

# Chronology

**Archaic Period** (*c.*3150–2686 BC)

**Old Kingdom** (*c.*2686–2181 BC)

**First Intermediate Period** (*c.*2181–2040 BC)

**Middle Kingdom** (*c.*2040–1782 BC)

**Second Intermediate Period** (*c.*1782–1570 BC)

**New Kingdom** (*c.*1570–1070 BC)

**Dynasty XVIII**
Ahmose I (*c.*1570–1546 BC)
Amenhotep I (*c.*1551–1524 BC)
Tuthmosis I (*c.*1524–1518 BC)
Tuthmosis II (*c.*1518–1504 BC)
Tuthmosis III (*c.*1504–1450 BC)
Hatshepsut (*c.*1498–1483 BC)
Amenhotep II (*c.*1453–1419 BC)
Tuthmosis IV (*c.*1419–1386 BC)
Amenhotep III (*c.*1386–1349 BC)
Amenhotep IV-Akhenaten (*c.*1350–1334 BC)
Smenkhkare (*c.*1336–1334 BC)
Tutankhaten-Tutankhamun (*c.*1334–1325 BC)
Ay (*c.*1325–1321 BC)
Horemheb (*c.*1321–1293 BC)

**Dynasty XIX**
Ramesses I (formerly Paramessu) (*c.*1293–1291 BC)
Sety I (*c.*1293–1278 BC)
Ramesses II (*c.*1279–1212 BC)
Merenptah (*c.*1212–1202 BC)
Amenmesse (*c.*1202–1199 BC)
Sety II (*c.*1199–1193 BC)
Siptah (*c.*1193–1187 BC)
Twosret (*c.*1187–1185 BC)

**Dynasty XX**
Sethnakht (*c.*1185–1182 BC)
Ramesses III (*c.*1182–1151 BC)
Ramesses IV (*c.*1151–1145 BC)
Ramesses V (*c.*1145–1141 BC)
Ramesses VI (*c.*1141–1133 BC)
(Ramesses VII)
(Ramesses VIII)
Ramesses IX (*c.*1126–1108 BC)
(Ramesses X)
Ramesses XI (*c.*1098–1070 BC)
Herihor (*c.*1080–1072 BC)

**Third Intermediate Period** (*c.*1069–525 BC)

**Late Period** (*c.*525–332 BC)

**Graeco-Roman Period** (*c.*332 BC – AD 323)

# Select Bibliography

## General

For the history of Egypt and its neighbours in the New Kingdom the most easily accessible sources are the *Cambridge Ancient History*, 3rd ed., vol. II in 2 parts (Cambridge, 1973, 1975), with excellent bibliography; Gardiner, Sir A., *Egypt of the Pharaohs* (Oxford, 1961; reprinted with corrections 1962); Aldred, C., *Akhenaten, King of Egypt* (London, 1988), and Kitchen, K.A., *Pharaoh triumphant: the life and times of Ramesses II* (Warminster, 1982).

## Memphis, Saqqara and their Environs

The tomb-chapels of Paser and Raia have been published, and the volume can be consulted by readers who desire more information on those two small but fascinating tombs. The great tomb of Horemheb will shortly be published. The tomb of Tia and Tia, as well as the other tomb-chapels described above, have been recorded in full, but are still being studied by members of the Expedition with a view to publication.

ANTHES, R. *Mit Rahineh 1955*, Philadelphia, 1959.
—— *Mit Rahineh 1956*. Philadelphia, 1965.
BADAWI, A. *Memphis als zweite Landeshaupstadt im Neuen Reich*, Cairo, 1948.
BAINES, J. and MÁLEK, J. *Atlas of Ancient Egypt*, Oxford, 1980, pp. 134–65.
BERLANDINI, J. 'Les tombes amarniennes et d'époque Toutânkhamon à Sakkara: critères stylistiques'. In *L'Égyptologie en 1979: axes prioritaires de recherches*, II, Paris, 1982, pp. 195–212.
CAPART, J. and WERBROUCK, M. *Memphis à l'ombre des pyramides*, Brussels, 1930.
DIJK, J. VAN. 'The symbolism of the Memphite djed-pillar'. *Oudheidkundige Mededelingen van het Rijksmuseum van Oudheden te Leiden*, 66, 1986, pp. 7–17.
—— 'Zerbrechen der roten Töpfe'. In Helck, W., and Westendorf, W. eds. *Lexikon der Ägyptologie*, VI, Wiesbaden, 1986, cols. 1389–96.
DIMICK, M.T. *Memphis, the city of the White Wall*, Philadelphia, 1956.
JEFFREYS, D.G. *The Survey of Memphis*, I, London, 1985.
KAMIL, J. *Sakkara: a guide to the necropolis and the site of Memphis*, London and New York, 1978.
KEES, H. *Ancient Egypt: a cultural topography*, London, 1961, pp. 147–82.

KITCHEN, K.A. 'Memphite tomb-chapels in the New Kingdom and later'. In *Festschrift für E. Edel*, Hamburg, 1979, pp. 272–84.
LAUER, J.-P. *Saqqara, the royal cemetery of Memphis: excavations and discoveries since 1850*, London, 1976.
MÁLEK, J. 'Saqqara, Nekropolen, NR'. In Helck, W., and Westendorf, W. eds. *Lexikon der Ägyptologie*, V, Wiesbaden, 1984, cols. 410–12.
—— 'Two problems connected with New Kingdom tombs in the Memphite area'. *Journal of Egyptian Archaeology*, 67, 1981, pp. 156–65.
MARTIN, G.T. *Corpus of reliefs of the New Kingdom from the Memphite Necropolis and Lower Egypt*, I, London, 1987.
—— 'The New Kingdom necropolis at Saqqâra'. In Reinecke, W.F. ed. *Acts of the First International Congress of Egyptology, Cairo, 1976*, Berlin, 1979, pp. 457–63.
MORGAN, J. DE. *Carte de la nécropole memphite*, Cairo, 1897.
MURNANE, W.J. *The Penguin guide to Ancient Egypt*, London, 1983, pp. 145–79.
PORTER, B. and MOSS, R.L.B. *Topographical bibliography of Ancient Egyptian hieroglyphic texts, reliefs, and paintings*, 2nd ed. revised and augmented by J. Málek, III, part 1. Abû Rawâsh to Abûsîr, Oxford, 1974; part 2. Saqqâra to Dahshûr Oxford, 1978–81.
ZIVIE, A.-P., ed. *Memphis et ses nécropoles au Nouvel Empire: nouvelles données, nouvelles questions*, Paris, 1988.
ZIVIE, C.M. *Giza au deuxième millénaire*, Cairo, 1976.
—— 'Memphis'. In Helck, W., and Westendorf, W. eds. *Lexikon der Ägyptologie*, IV, Wiesbaden, 1982, cols, 24–41.

Preliminary reports on the survey and excavation of Memphis, by H.S. Smith, D.G. Jeffreys, and J. Málek may be consulted in *Journal of Egyptian Archaeology*, 69, 1983, pp. 30–42; 70, 1984, pp. 23–32; 71, 1985, pp. 5–11; 72, 1986, 1–14; 73, 1987, pp. 11–20; 74, 1988, pp. 15–29. See also Smith, H.S., and Jeffreys, D.G. 'A survey of Memphis, Egypt'. *Antiquity*, 60, 1986, pp. 88–95.

Preliminary reports on the excavations of the Egypt Exploration Society – Leiden Museum mission in the New Kingdom necropolis, Saqqara, by G.T. Martin, M.J. Raven, D.A. Aston, B.G. Aston, and J. van Dijk, are published in *Journal of Egyptian Archaeology*, 62, 1976, pp. 5–13; 63, 1977, pp. 13–19; 64, 1978, pp. 5–10;

65, 1979, pp. 13–16; 69, 1983, pp. 25–9; 70, 1984, pp. 5–12; 72, 1986, pp. 15–22; 73, 1987, pp. 1–9; 74, 1988, pp. 1–14.

## Memphite personalities of the New Kingdom and their Saqqara tombs

BERLANDINI, J, 'Découverte à Sakkara'. *Connaissance des Arts*, 413–14, 1986, pp. 62–9.
—— 'Varia Memphitica, I–V'. *Bulletin de l'Institut français d'Archéologie orientale*, 76, 1976, pp. 301–16; 77, 1977, pp. 29–44; 81, 1981, pp. 9–20; 82, 1982, pp. 85–103.
DIJK, J. VAN. 'A Ramesside naophorous statue from the Teti pyramid cemetery'. *Oudheidkundige Mededelingen van het Rijksmuseum van Oudheden te Leiden*, 64, 1983, pp. 49–58.
GABALLA, G.A. *The Memphite tomb-chapel of Mose*, Warminster, 1977.
GOMÀA, F. *Chaemwese, Sohn Ramses' II. und Hoherpriester von Memphis*, Wiesbaden, 1973.
GRAEFE, E. 'Das Grab des Schatzhausvorstehers und Bauleiters Maya in Saqqara'. *Mitteilungen des Deutschen Archäologischen Instituts. Abteilung Kairo*, 31, 1975, 187–220.
HANDOUSSA, T. 'A newly found tomb-stela from the Ramesside Period in Saqqara'. In *Hommages à François Daumas*, Montpellier, 1986, pp. 409–19.
HAYES, W.C. 'A writing-palette of the chief steward Amenḥotpe and some notes on its owner'. *Journal of Egyptian Archaeology*, 24, 1938, pp. 9–24.
LÖHR, B. 'Ein memphitisches Grab vom Ende der 18. Dynastie (um 1320 v. Chr.)'. *Pantheon*, 28, 1970, pp. 467–74.
MÁLEK, J. 'The Saqqara statue of Ptahmose, mayor of the Memphite suburbs'. *Revue d'Égyptologie*, 38, 1987, pp. 117–37.
—— 'The tomb-chapel of Hekamaetre-neheh at North-ern Saqqara'. *Studien zur Altägyptischen Kultur*, 12, 1985, 43–60.
—— 'Two monuments of the Tias'. *Journal of Egyptian Archaeology*, 60, 1974, pp. 161–7.
MARTIN, G.T.. *The Memphite tomb of Ḥoremḥeb, commander-in-chief of Tutʻankhamūn*, I, London, 1989.
MARTIN, G.T., and others. *The tomb-chapels of Paser and Raʻia at Saqqâra*, London, 1985.
PETERSON, B.J. 'Some reliefs from the Memphite necropolis'. *Medelhavsmuseet Bulletin*, 5, 1969, pp. 3–15.
SCHNEIDER, H.D. 'Maya l'amateur de statues'. *Bulletin de la Société française d'Égyptologie*, 69, 1974, pp. 20–48.
ZIVIE, A.-P. 'La tombe d'un officier de la XVIII<sup>e</sup> dynastie à Saqqara'. *Revue d'Égyptologie*, 31, 1979, pp. 135–51.
—— 'Tombes rupestres de la falaise du Bubasteion à Saqqarah – campagne 1980–1981'. *Annales du Service des Antiquités de l'Égypte*, 68, 1982, pp. 63–9.
—— 'Tombes rupestres de la falaise du Bubasteion à Saqqarah. II<sup>e</sup> et III<sup>e</sup> campagnes 1982–1983'. *Annales du Service des Antiquités de l'Égypte*, 70, 1984–5, pp. 219–32.
ZIVIE, C.M. 'A propos de quelques reliefs du nouvel empire au Musée du Caire, I, I–II'. *Bulletin de l'Institut français d'Archéologie orientale*, 75, 1975, 285–310; 76, 1976, pp. 17–36.

For the skeletal remains attributed to Queen Mutnodjmet see Strouhal, E. 'Queen Mutnodjmet at Memphis: anthropological and paleopathological evidence'. *In L'Égyptologie en 1979: axes prioritaires de recherches*, II Paris, 1982, pp. 317–22.

On the possibility of Twentieth Dynasty tombs in the Memphite necropolis see Posener-Kriéger, P. 'Construire une tombe à l'ouest de Mn-nfr (PCaire 52002)'. *Revue d'Égyptologie*, 33, 1981, 47–58.

# Acknowledgments

My first and very pleasant duty is to acknowledge the help and cooperation I have received from friends and colleagues who have worked with me at Saqqara since 1975. No expedition can be a one-man band, even though the field director sometimes seems to get all or most of the credit for what was in fact a collaborative effort. My colleagues in the Organization of Egyptian Antiquities, archaeologists as well as administrators, have always been encouraging, and have gone out of their way to be helpful on my behalf. After more than a quarter of a century in *Ta-mery* ['the Beloved Land'] I am greatly attached to them and to Egypt.

The Committee of the Egypt Exploration Society and the authorities of the Rijksmuseum van Oudheden at Leiden, have kindly given me permission to reproduce photographic and other material from the excavations of our joint expedition. My own Alma Mater, University College London, has given me leave of absence every year since I joined the staff, in order to carry out field excavation and epigraphy, continuing the tradition started by the revered founder of the Department of Egyptology in the College, Sir Flinders Petrie, and his enlightened sponsor, Amelia B. Edwards. Part of this book was drafted in 1987 in Saronis, the charming resort in Attica, while staying at the house of Liana and Manos Souvaltjis. Their friendship on this occasion is acknowledged with gratitude. I would also like to thank Dr. Yvonne Harpur for her assistance with the maps.

I owe a great deal also to the inspiration and encouragement of some of my first teachers and mentors of long ago: Winifred M. Collins, Wilhelmina K. Saunders, the Rev. E.C.L. Ovenden, the Rev. D.P. McNeice (Aveley), the Rev. Frank Hughes, John R. Hayston (Palmer's School, Grays Thurrock). They provided the initial spark which ultimately ignited my interest in antiquity, the medieval and early modern world, and other aspects of learning. I recall them, and several more, with gratitude and affection. Thames and Hudson has been a model of patience and restraint, despite the fact that more than one 'deadline' has passed since I was asked to write the present volume. The task has been congenial, if only because it is my firm belief that the fruits of fieldwork should not be confined to the pages of ponderous and expensive monographs, or even more to 'microfiches' or other modern methods of information storage, but should be made widely accessible to a cultivated public, whose interest in the ancient peoples of the Nile Valley seems inexhaustible. Fortunate indeed is the archaeologist who is privileged to excavate in the Land of Egypt and to extend the frontiers of knowledge about its wondrous civilization.

GEOFFREY T. MARTIN

# List of Illustrations

Photographs of the work of the EES/Leiden Expedition are published by courtesy of the Egypt Exploration Society and the Rijksmuseum van Oudheden, Leiden. Photographers: C.J. Eyre, M. Vinkesteijn, P.J. Bomhof. Line drawings are by the author, plans and sections by K.J. Frazer, adapted by the author for this publication. All reliefs are of limestone.

## Colour plates

## Monochrome illustrations

# Index

Numerals in *italics* refer to illustration numbers

d = deity; k = king; loc = location; pr = prince; prs = princess; q = queen